ISBN 978-1-332-99966-8
PIBN 10448330

COLLECTION

OF

ENGLISH

OR

CONTAINING

TEN DRAMAS FROM THE CHESTER, COVENTRY, AND TOWNELEY SERIES, WITH TWO OF LATTER DATE.

TO WHICH IS PREFIXED,

AN HISTORICAL VIEW OF THIS DESCRIPTION OF PLAYS.

BY

WILLIAM MARRIOTT, Ph. Dr

BASEL:

SCHWEIGHAUSER & CO.,

AND BROCKHAUS & AVENARIUS, PARIS.

1838.

CONTENTS.

PREFACE.

The Editor of the following pages has been induced to publish the present Collection of English Miracle-plays or Mysteries, from its appearing to him to be a desideratum. This will no doubt be apparent, if it be considered, that, although much has been done to illustrate the history of the English theatre, especially of the sixteenth century, not one of the various publications on this subject, contains a single play of the Chester, Coventry, or Townely series. That these dramas are particularly deserving of attention, can scarcely be denied, as they are the oldest pieces of the kind in existence, and present us moreover with the only connected view, that is to be had, of the manner in which the whole Bible was theatrically represented. It is also a little singular, that the publications of Dodsley, Hawkins and others, afford but little information on this subject; that of Collier on the contrary much more, though his remarks are unfortunately too much scattered in his excellent work. That so little has been done as yet to give a correct view of the ancient history of the English stage, is much to be regretted, although it cannot surprise us, if we weigh the assertion of Malone, that «a minute investigation of the origin and progress of the drama in England, will scarcely repay the labour of inquiry.» Other writers appear to have held the same opinion, and not to have reflected, that the early Miracle-plays afford one of the best illustrations of the manners and customs of our forefathers. Moreover we learn from them the opinions of our ancestors on various subjects, their manner of thinking, and are perhaps better enabled to judge of the state of civilisation in which they were, than from other sources. Such must be the light in which unprejudiced minds will regard the ancient English theatre, whatever they may think of the later and present state of the drama. It must, however, be observed, that the following pages contain, with few exceptions, only facts and not remarks on these plays, as this volume is intended to be used as a lecture book. In conclusion, the Editor must remark, that, although he is fully aware of the imperfections of his attempt to give a concise view of the history of English Miracle-plays, yet he believes he has not omitted any notice of importance recorded by any writer on the theatre, or that is to be found in any work that was likely to illustrate the subject.

Basel, June 30th, 1838.

AN HISTORICAL VIEW

OF

ENGLISH MIRACLE-PLAYS OR MYSTERIES.

Religion, which has in all countries first excited dramatic representation, was the subject of the English Miracle-plays or Mysteries. These productions were either founded on the various histories of the Old and New Testament, or on the legends of the lives of the saints, which latter appear, however, to have afforded fewer subjects for exhibition. The English religious dramas were, during the period of their represèntation and for a long time afterwards, termed Miracle-plays; most probably from the first or chief pieces being a representation of the miracles of our Lord, or from their containing a narration of the wonders of the christian faith. In latter times they have been usually called Mysteries, under which appellation they are at present best known. This term, although at a very early date applied to them in France, was most probably first given to them in England by Dodsley, in the preface to the Collection of Old

Plays, which he published in 1744. They are also in some MSS. termed Pageants, by which name they were generally called, although not in all instances, when performed by members of trading companies.

Not a few writers have speculated on the origin of English Miracle-plays, but it must unfortunately be confessed that their theories afford no very satisfactory explanation of the subject. Although such is the case, it may not be uninteresting to quote what Warton says on this point, as he is generally considered the first authority on all subjects connected with English literature. He remarks: « About the eighth century trade was principally carried on by means of fairs, which lasted several days. Charlemagne established many great marts of this sort in France; as did William the Conqueror, and his Norman successors, in England. The merchants, who frequented these fairs in numerous caravans or companies, employed every art to draw the people together. They were therefore accompanied by juglers, minstrels, and buffons; who were no less interested in giving their attendance, and exerting all their skill, on these occasions. As now but few large towns existed, no public spectacles or popular amusements were established; and as the sedentary pleasures of domestic life and private society were yet unknown, the fair-time was the season for diversion. In proportion as these shews were attended and encouraged, they began to be set off with new decorations and improvements; and the arts of buffoonery being rendered still more attractive by extending their circle of exhibition, acquired an importance in the eyes of the people. By degrees the clergy, observing that the entertainments of dancing, music, mimicry, exhibited at these annual celebrities, made the people less religious, by promoting idleness and a love of festivity, proscribed these sports, and excommunicated the performers. But finding that no regard was paid to their censures, they changed their plan, and determined to take these recreations into their own hands. They turned actors; and instead of profane mummeries, presented, stories taken from legends or the Bible. This was the origin of sacred comedy*. » That Warton has formed an erroneous opinion on this subject, seems not improbable, if we reflect that religious dramas are of a much earlier origin than is generally considered; for we have an account of a religious play, performed perhaps before the final destruction of Jerusalem, but certainly not later than the second century, portions of which have come down to our day†. Moreover mention is made of religous dramas by writers in the first centuries of the christian æra, and although it is difficult to prove that such were performed in every age since the time of Christ; which is not to be wondered at, if we consider the state of literature during the dark ages, and how much has been lost in such a period of time, yet enough authorities are still existing to show that such performances

* History of English Poetry, vol. ii. pp. 366, 367, edit. 4to.

† Ezechielis Tragici Judaicarum historiarum poetæ, eductio seu liberatio Hebræorum Tragoedia sacra, exodo respondens: ex libro IX Eusebii de Præp. Evang. selecta, et plerisque in locis castigata. Paris 1590. 8vo.

have been from the earliest times*. The origin of religious dramas, should this view of the subject be considered correct, must be ascribed to the influence that the ancient theatre exercised on the first christians. It may, perhaps, from the foregoing observations, not be deemed improbable, that, as religious plays can be proved to have been written in the first centuries, and acted as late as the year 990†, they were not improbably performed during the following century, although we have no account of it. If this may be assumed, and it appears to be no far fetched hypothesis, especially as it will hereafter be shown, that the firs Miracle-play performed in England, was written by a Frenchman about the year 1100; and as there are, moreover, very good grounds for believing, that the earliest English religious plays are, at least in part, translations from the French; it follows, that what are termed Miracle-plays are nothing more than a continuation of the sacred dramas, that were written since the first centuries. Should this view of the subject not be deemed correct, the opinion of Percy may, perhaps, be considered more satisfactory. He remarks, that «they were probably a kind of dumb shews, intermingled, it may be, with a few short

* As it does not lie within the limits of these pages to enter on this subject more at large, the following notices of works, which contain remarks on this point, must suffice. Socrates, Eccles. Hist. p. 305, edit. 1663. Lardner, vol. ii. p. 463. 4to. Hone, Ancient Mysteries Described, pp. 148—156. Cabinet Cyclopædia, Literary and Scientific Men, vol. i. pp. 174—179.

† Cedren. Compend. Hist. p. 639. B. 1647. Comment. ad Canon. lxii. Synod. vi. in Trullo. Apud Beverigium Synodic. tom. i. pp. 230, 231. fol. Oxon. 1672.

speeches; at length they grew into a regular series of connected dialogues, formally divided into acts and scenes *." This observation, although by him only applied to English Miracle-plays, appears to be at least quite as applicable to the religious exhibitions in the first ages of Christianity.

The first mention of theatrical representations in England, is recorded by Matthew Paris, who wrote as early as 1240. He relates in his *Vitæ Abbatum, etc.*, that while Geoffrey, afterwards Abbot of St. Albans, was yet a secular person, he was invited from Normandy by Richard, the then Abbot of St. Albans, to teach the school established there; that, in consequence of some delay, when Geoffrey arrived the vacant office had been filled, and that he, therefore, took up his residence at Dunstaple, and brought out the Miracle-play of St. Catherine: — *Legit igitur apud Dunestapliam, expectans scholam S. Albani sibi repromissam; ubi quendam ludum de S. Katerina, (quem Miracula vulgariter appellamus) fecit; ad quæ decoranda petiït a Sacrista S. Albani, ut sibi capæ chorales accommodarentur, et obtinuit* †. We learn from the testimony of Bulæus, in his *Historia Universitatis Parisiensis*, that Geoffrey was a member of the University of Paris, and that he died in 1146, having been raised to the dignity of Abbot of St. Albans in 1119 §. From the before mentioned quotation, it is quite clear, that Geoffrey brought out the play of St. Catherine long before he assumed

* Reliques of Ancient English Poetry, vol. i. p. 128, edit. 1794.

† Vit. Abb. ad calc. Histor. Major. tom. i. p. 56, edit. 1640

§ Vol. ii. p. 225. Paris 1665.

the religious habit, and considering that he could not attain the dignity of Abbot, which he obtained in 1119, till after a number of years, the opinion of Percy, that it was «probably written within the eleventh century,» is likely not to be far from the truth*. Bulæus informs us also, that this play of St. Catherine was not then by any means a novely: *non novo quidem instituto, sed de consuetudine magistrorum et scholarum.*

William Fitzstephen who wrote about 1182 his *Vita Sancti Thomæ Archiepiscopi et Martyris*, to which is appended a description of London, says: — *Lundonia pro spectaculis theatralibus, pro ludis scenicis, ludos habet sanctiores, repræsentationes miraculorum quæ sancti confessores operati sunt, seu repræsentationes passionum quibus claruit constantia martyrum.* This early notice of English Miracle-plays was first published by Stow in his Survey of London, 1599. He translates the passage as follows: — «London, for the shews upon theatres, and comical pastimes, hath holy plays, representations of miracles, which holy confessors have wrought; or representations of tormentes, wherein the constancie of martirs appeared†.»

It has been supposed, that the pilgrims who returned from the Holy Land, and who composed songs on their travels, mixing with them a recital of the life and death of Christ, contributed greatly

* Reliques, vol. i. p. 134.

† P. 68. It is necessary to remark, in order to understand correctly this quotation, that Fitzstephen had previously referred to the state of the theatres in Rome, and seems to be drawing a comparison between the public amusements there and in London.

to increase the taste for these religious representations; but whatever influence they may have exercised in France*, and in other countries, on such performances, there is no certainty of there having in any way promoted these exhibitions in England †.

That plays were frequently performed about the middle of the thirteenth century, may be inferred from a regulation under the date of A. D. 1228 in the *Annales Burtonenses*, which prohibits strolling players from performing in presence of the inmates of the monastery; yet which allows their wants to be relieved, not because they were players, but because they were poor: — *Histrionibus potest dari cibus, quia pauperes sunt, non quia histriones; et eorum ludi non videantur, vel audiantur, vel permittantur fieri coram Abbate vel monachis* §.

About the year 1268 Miracle-plays were performed in Chester, and continued to be acted there for many successive centuries; but as the religious dramas brought out in that city, form one of the three series of Miracle-plays now in existence, they will be referred to more at large hereafter.

Towards the end of the thirteenth century, the religious ceremony of the Corpus Christi Play was instituted at York, and was celebrated each year on the Thursday after Trinity Sunday. Drake,

* Some information respecting the influence that French pilgrims exercised on the Mysteries of their own country, may be gathered from Bayle's Dict. art. Chocquet, which contains some observations by Menestrier on this subject.

† The characters, however, in the play of St. George, seem to afford proof of an eastern origin.

§ Gale, Rerum Anglic. Script. Vet. tom. i. p. 437.

the historian of this city, says, « this ceremony must have been in its time one of the most extaordinary entertainments that could be exhibited. Évery trade in the city, from the highest to the lowest, was obliged to furnish out a pageant at its own expense on this occasion. » Many orders and ordinances, existing in the registers of the city, regulate the performance of this religious ceremony. One of these recites, that « Whereas for a long course of time the artificers and tradesmen of the city of York have, at their own expense, acted plays; and particularly a certain sumptuous play, exhibited in several pageants, wherein the history of the Old and New Testament in divers places of the said city, in the feast of Corpus Christi, by a solemn procession is represented, in reverence to the sacrament of the Body of Christ; beginning first at the great gates of the Priory of the Holy Trinity in York, and so going in procession to and into the Cathedral Church of the same; and afterwards to the Hospital of St. Leonard, in York, leaving the aforesaid sacrament in that place; preceded by a vast number of lighted torches, and a great multitude of priests in their proper habits, and followed by the mayor and citizens, with a prodigious crowd of the populace attending. And whereas, upon this, a certain very religious father, William Melton, of the order of friars minors, professor of holy pageantry, and a most famous preacher of the word of God, coming to this city, in several sermons recommended the aforesaid play to the people; affirming that it was good in itself and very commendable so to do; yet also said, that the citizens of the said city, and other foreigners coming to the said feast, had greatly disgraced the play by revellings, drunkenness, shouts, songs and other insolencies, little regarding the divine offices of the said day, and what was to be lamented, they loose, for that reason, the indulgences by the holy father pope Urban IV. in this part graciously conceded; those, viz. faithful in Christ, who attended at morning service at the said feast in the church where it was celebrated, a hundred days; those at the mass, the same; those also, who came to the first vespers of the said feast, the like a hundred days; the same in the second; to those also, who were at the first, third, sixth, and ninth completory offices, for every hour of those forty days; to those also, who attended service on the octaves of the said feast, at mattins or vespers, mass or the aforesaid hours; a hundred days for every day of the said octaves, as in the holy canons, for this end made, is more fully contained: and therefore, as it seemed most wholesome to the said father William, the people of the city were inclined that the play should be played on one day, and the procession on another, so that the people might attend divine service at the churches, on the said feast, for the indulgences aforesaid. Wherefore Peter Buckey, mayor of this city of York, [10 Aldermen, 2 Sheriffs, and 21 others whose names are mentioned] were met in the council chamber of the said city the 6th day of June, in the year of grace 1426, and of the reign of king Henry VI. after the conquest of England, the fourth, and by the said wholesome exhortations and admonitions of the said father William being incited, that it is no crime, nor can it offend God, if good be converted into better. Therefore, having diligently considered of the premises, they gave their express and unanimous consent, that the cause aforesaid should be published to the whole city in the common hall of the same, and having their consent that the premises should be better reformed. Upon which the aforesaid mayor convened the citizens together in the said hall the tenth day of the month aforesaid and the same year, and made proclamation in a solemn manner, where it was ordained, by the common assent, that this solemn play of Corpus Christi should be played every year on the vigil of the said feast, and that the procession should be made constantly on the day of the said feast, so that all people being in the said city might have leisure to attend devoutly the mattins, vespers and the other hours of the said feast, and be made partakers of the indulgences, in that part by the said Roman pope Urban the fourth most graciously granted and confirmed.»

A solemn proclamation for the play of Corpus Christi, made on the aforesaid vigil, commands on behalf of the king, the mayor, and the sheriffs, that the players «play at the places that is assigned therefore, and no where else on the pain of the forfeiture that is ordained therefore; that is to say xls.; and that men of crafts, and all other men that find torches, that they come forth in array, and in the manner as it has been used and customed before his time.» The following is an extract of an order for the regulation of the play of Corpus Christi, dated the 7th of June, 1417; and signed by William Bowes, mayor. «It is ordained for the convenience of the citizens, and of all strangers coming to the said feast, that all the pageants of the play called Corpus Christi play, should begin to play first at the gates of the Priory of the Holy Trinity in Mikel-gate, next at the door of Robert Harpham, next at the door of the late John Gyseburn, next at Skelder-gate-hend and North-strete towards Castel-gate, next at the end of Jubir-gate, next at the door of Henry Wyman deceased, in Conyng-strete, then at the common hall at the end of Conyng-strete, then at the door of Adam del Brygs deceased, in Stayne-gate, then at the end of Stayne-gate at the Minster-gates, then at the end of Girdler-gate, and lastly upon the Pavement, etc. And father William Melton, willing to destroy sin, and a great lover of virtue, having, by preaching, exhorted the populace that they would cause to be removed all public concubines in fornication or adultery; wherefore the mayor, by consent of the community, ordained that they should depart the city within eight days, on pain of imprisonment, unless any of them should find good security that she would not exercise her illegal vocation for the future.» The following list of the trading companies with the parts they played, will, perhaps, be found not entirely void of interest*.

«The order of the Pageants of the Play of Corpus Christi, in the time of the mayoralty of William Alne, in the third year of the reign of King Henry V. anno 1415, compiled by Roger Burton, town clerk: —

* Drake, History of York, pp. 223–246.

Tanners.	God the Father Almighty creating and forming the heavens, angels and archangels; Lucifer and the angels that fell with him into hell.
Plasterers.	God the Father, in his own substance, creating the earth, and all which is therein, in the space of five days.
Carde-makers.	God the Father creating Adam of the slime of the earth, and making Eve of the rib, and inspiring them with the spirit of life.
Fullers.	God prohibiting Adam and Eve from eating of the tree of life.
Coupers.	Adam and Eve with a tree betwixt them; the serpent deceiving them with apples; God speaking to them and cursing the serpent, and an angel with a sword driving them out of paradise.
Armourers.	Adam and Eve, an angel with a spade and a distaff assigning them labour.
Gaunters.	Abel and Cain killing sacrifices.
Shipwrights.	God foretelling Noah to make an ark of light wood.
Fyshmongers, Pessyners, Mariners.	Noah in the ark with his wife and three children, and divers animals.
Perchemyners, Bukbynders.	Abraham sacrificing his son Isaac; a ram, bush, and angel.
Hosyers.	Moses exalting the serpent in the wilderness: king Pharaoh; eight Jews admiring and expecting.
Spicers.	Mary and a docter declaring the sayings of the prophets about the future birth of Christ: an angel saluting her. Mary saluting Elizabeth.

Mary, Joseph willing to put her away, an angel speaking to them that they should go to Bethlehem.

Mary, Joseph, a midwife, the child born lying in a manger betwixt an ox and an ass, and the angel speaking to the shepherds.

The shepherds speaking by turns; the star in the east; an angel giving joy to the shepherds that a child was born.

The three kings coming from the east, Herod asking them about the child Christ; with the son of Herod, two counsellors and a messenger.

Mary with the child and the star above, and the three kings offering gifts.

Mary with the child; Joseph, Anna, and a nurse with young pigeons; Simeon receiving the child in his arms, and two sons of Simeon.

Mary with the child, and Joseph flying into Egypt, by an angel's telling them.

Herod commanding the children to be slain, four soldiers with lances, two counsellors of the king, and four women lamenting the slaughter of them.

The doctors, the child Jesus sitting in the temple in the midst of them, hearing them and asking them questions. Four Jews, Mary and Joseph seeking him and finding him in the temple.

Jesus, John the baptist baptizing him, and two angels helping them.

Jesus, Mary, bridegroom and bride, master of the household with his family with six water-pots, where water is turned into wine.

Smythes, *Fevers.*	Jesus upon the pinnacle of the temple; Satan tempting with stones; two angels administering, etc.
C[orvisors.]	Peter, James and John; Jesus ascending into the mountain and transfiguring himself before them. Moses and Elias appearing, and a voice speaking from a cloud.
Elennagers.	Simon the leper asking Jesus if he would eat with him. Two disciples; Mary Magdalene washing the feet of Jesus, and wiping them with her hair.
Plummers, *Patten-makers.*	Jesus, two apostles, the woman taken in adultery, four Jews accusing her.
Pouch-makers, *Botillers,* *Cap-makers.*	Lazarus in the sepulchre; Mary Magdalene, Martha, and two Jews admiring.
Vestment-makers, *Skynners.*	Jesus upon an ass with its foal; twelve apostles following Jesus; six rich and six poor men, with eight boys with branches of palm trees, constantly saying blessed, etc., and Zaccheus ascending into a sycamore tree.
Cuttelers, *Blade-smythes,* *Shethers,* *Scalers,* *Bukle-makers,* *Horners.*	Pilate, Caiaphas, two soldiers, three Jews, Judas selling Jesus.
Bakers, *Waterleders.*	The supper of the Lord and paschal Lamb, twelve apostles; Jesus, tied about with a linen towel, washing their feet. The institution of the sacrament of the body of Christ in the new law, and communion of the Apostles.
Cordwaners.	Pilate, Caiaphas, Annas, forty armed soldiers, Malchas, Peter, James, John,

Jesus, and Judas kissing and betraying him.

Jesus, Annas, Caiaphas, and four Jews striking and bastinadoing Christ. Peter, the woman accusing him, and Malchas.

Jesus, Pilate, Annas, Caiaphas; two counsellors and four Jews accusing Christ.

Herod, two counsellors, four soldiers, Jesus, and three Jews.

Pilate, Annas, Caiaphas, two Jews, and Judas carrying from them thirty pieces of silver.

Judas hanging himself.

Jesus, Pilate, Caiaphas, Annas, six soldiers carrying spears and ensigns, and other four leading Jesus from Herod desiring Barabbas to be released and Jesus to be crucified, and then binding and scourging him, putting a crown of thorns upon his head; three soldiers casting lots for the vesture of Jesus.

Jesus covered with blood bearing his cross towards mount Calvary, Simon Sereneus, etc.

The cross, Jesus extended upon it on the earth; four Jews scourging him with whips, and afterwards erecting the cross, with Jesus upon it, on Mount Calvary.

The cross, two thieves crucified and Jesus suspended betwixt them; Mary the mother of Jesus, John, Mary, James and Salome; a soldier with a lance, and a servant with a sponge. Pilate, Annas, Caiaphas, a centurion, Joseph of Arimathea, and Nichodemus taking him down and laying him in the sepulchre.

Satellers, Sellers, Glasiers. Jesus destroying hell; twelve good and twelve evil spirits.

Carpenters, Joyners. The Centurion declaring to Pilate, Caiaphas and Annas, with other Jews, the signs appearing on the death of Jesus.

Cartwrights, Carvers, Sawyers. Jesus rising from the sepulchre, four soldiers armed, and three Marias lamenting; Pilate, Caiaphas, and Annas; a young man clothed in white sitting in the sepulchre and talking to the women.

Wyedrawers. Jesus, Mary, Mary Magdalene with spices.

Broggers, Wool-pakkers, Wadsmen. Jesus, Luke and Cleophas in the form of travellers.

Escriviners, Lumners, Questors, Dubbors. Jesus, Peter, John, James, Philip and other Apostles; Thomas feeling the wounds of Jesus.

Taillyoures. Mary, John the Evangelist, two angels, and eleven Apostles; Jesus ascending before them, and four angels bearing a cloud.

Potters. Mary, two angels, eleven Apostles, the Holy Ghost descending upon them, and four Jews admiring.

Drapers. Jesus, Mary, Gabriel with two angels, two virgins and three Jews of the kindred of Mary, eight Apostles, and two devils.

Lynwevers. Four Apostles bearing the shrine of Mary, Fergus hanging upon it with two other Jews, and one angel.

Wevers of wollen. Mary ascending with a multitude of angels; eight Apostles, with Thomas preaching in the desert.

Hostilers. Mary, and Jesus crowning her with a great number of angels.

Mercers. Jesus, Mary, twelve Apostles; four angels with trumpets, and four with a lance with two scourges; four good and four bad spirits, and six devils.

Robert Mannyng, or as he is more commonly called Robert de Brunne, a Gilbertine canon in the monastery of Brunne, near Depyng, in Lincolnshire, translated in the year 1303 an Anglo-French poem, entitled the *Manuel de Peché*†, written about the middle of the thirteenth century, and which contains a notice of Miracle-plays.

Hyt ys forbode hym yn the deere
Myracles for to make or se;
For myracles, zyf you bygynne,
Hyt ys a gaderynt, a syght of synne.
He may yn the cherche, thurgh thys resun,
Pley the resurreccyun;
That is to seye, how god rose,
God and man yn myght and los,
To make men be yn beleve gode,
That he ros with flesshe and blode;
And he may pleye wythoutyn plyght
Howe god was bore yn thole nyght,
To make men to beleve stedfastly
That he lyght yn the vyrgyne Mary.
Zyf thou do hyt in weyys or grenys,
A syght of synne truly hyt semys.

Robert Baston, a Carmelite friar of Scarborough, who lived in the reign of Edward II.,

† Robert Grosthead, Bishop of Lincoln, who died in 1253, is supposed to be the author of this work. Warton, Hist. of Eng. Poet. vol. i. pp. 59, 78, 88.

and accompanied that king in his expedition to besiege Stirling Castle, in Scotland, is mentioned by Bale as a writer of *Tragœdiæ et Comœdiæ vulgares**. None of these pieces are now extant, but no reasonable doubt can be entertained that they were Miracle-plays, for Bale calls his own productions of a similar kind, «tragedies and comedies;» and it is not at all improbable, that some of these religious dramas might be in existence at the time when Bale wrote, which was towards the middle of the sixteenth century.

Robert Longlande, a secular priest, and a fellow of Oriel College, Oxford, who wrote about the middle of the fourteenth century, in his *Piers Ploughman's Crede*, puts two lines into the mouth of a friar, which refer to the performance of Miracle-plays in market towns: —

> We haunten no tauernes, ne hobelen abouten,
> At marketes and miracles we medely vs neuer †.

Chaucer has many allusions to these religious dramas, and he represents his Wife of Bath amusing herself with these fashionable diversions, while her husband is absent in London, during the holy season of Lent: —

> Therefore made I my visitations
> To vigilies and to processions,
> To prechings eke, and to thise pilgrimages,
> To playes of myracles and to mariages,
> And werid upon my gay skarlet gites §.

* Scriptor. Illust. M. Brit. p. 369. Basil 1557.

† Signat. A. iii. b. edit. 1561.

§ The Wif of Bathes Prologue. v. 6137. Tyrwhitt's edit.

In 1355, the guild of Corpus Christi at Cambridge, on that festival, represented *Ludus filiorum Israelis**.

It cannot but be considered a little singular, that we have no account of Miracle-plays being performed in London from the time of Henry II., till nearly two hundred years afterwards. That there were such exhibitions during this period in the metropolis, can scarcely be doubted, if we consider that other places of much less importance were honored with them. In 1378, the scholars or choristers of St. Paul's Cathedral in London, presented a petition to Richard II., praying him «to prohibit some unexpert people from presenting the History of the Old Testament, to the great prejudice of the said clergy, who have been at great expense to represent it publicly at Christmas †.» This restraint, if it were imposed, appears not to have applied to the parish clerks of London, who had been incorporated into a guild by Henry III. about the year 1240, under the patronage of St. Nicholas. Stow acquaints us, that in 1391 they performed a play at Skinner's Well, near Smithfield, in the presence of the king, queen, and the nobles of the realm, which lasted for three days. The same authority informs us, that «this yeere (1409) was a great play at the Skinners Well, neere unto Clearkenwell, besides London, which lasted eight daies, and was of matter from the creation of the world §.»

* Master, History of Corpus Christi College, Cambridge, vol. i. p. 5.

† Warton, Hist. of Eng. Poet. vol. ii. p. 391.

§ Stow, Chronicle, p. 349, edit. 1615. The ancient perform-

In 1416, the Emperor Sigismund was in England, having come for the purpose of endeavouring to make peace between this kingdom and France. He was magnificently received and entertained at Windsor; and a chronicle in the Cottonian Collection gives a description of a performance before him and Henry V., on the incidents of the life of St. George of Cappadocia. The representation seems to have been divided into three parts, and to have been accomplished by certain artificial contrivances, exhibiting, first, «the armyng of Seint George, and an Angel doyng on his spores;» secondly, «Seint George ridyng and fightyng with the dragon, with his spere in his hand;» and thirdly, «a castel, and Seint George and the Kynges daughter ledyng the lambe in at the castel gates*.»

The English fathers at the Council of Constance caused, on the 24th January, 1417, a sacred drama to be represented before the government of that city, the subjects of which were, the Nativity of our Saviour; the arrival of the Magi; and the massacre by Herod. This play appears to have given such satisfaction, that it was acted again on the 31st of the same month before the members of the Council †.

ances of the parish clerks are memorialized in raised letters of iron, upon a pump on the east side of Rag Street, now called Ray Street, beyond the Sessions-house, Clerkenwell; from which exhibitions, as well as from the well, the parish takes its name.

* Cotton MS., Calig. B. II. Apud Collier, Annals of the Stage, vol. i. p. 20.

† Dacher, an eye-witness, quoted by Herman, gives the following account.: — «Am 24ten tag des Monats Januarii, das war auff Timotheus tag, da luden die Bischöff aus Engeland, der Bischoff Salis-

John Lydgate, a monk of the Benedictine abbey of Bury in Suffolk, who lived in the first half of the fifteenth century, and was a most voluminous writer, being the author of upwards of two hundred and fifty poetical pieces, is said to have written Miracle-plays*.

Corpus Christi day, at Newcastle upon Tyne, was celebrated with the exhibition of religious dramas. The earliest mention of such performances there, is in the ordinary of the coopers, dated January 20th, 1426. They are mentioned also in those of the smiths and glovers, 1436; barbers, 1442; slaters, 1451; sadlers, 1459; and of the fullers and dyers, 1477. By the ordinary of the goldsmiths, plumbers, glaziers, pewterers and painters, dated 1536, they were commanded to play at their feast « the three Kynges of Coleyn. » In 1552, mention occurs of the merchant-adventurers as being concerned in the exhibition of five plays, one

burgensis, der Bischof von London, und demnach fünff Bischoff von England, alle Raht zu Costnitz und sonst viel ehrbar Bürger daselbst, in Burchart Walters Haus, das man vorzeiten nennt zu dem Burgthor, itzt zu dem gulden Schwert, allernächst bei S. Laurenz. Und gab ihnen fast ein köstlich mahl, je 3. Gericht nach einander, jedes Gericht besonder mit 8. Essen: Die trug man allweg eins mal dar, deren alweg waren 4. verguld oder versilbert. In dem mahl, zwischen dem Essen, so machten sie solch bild und geberd als unser Frau ihr Kind unsern Herrn und auch Gott gebahr, mit fast kostlichen Tuchern und Gewand. Und Joseph stellten sie zu ihr. Und die heiligen 3. Könige, als die unser Frauen die Opffer brachten. Und hatten gemacht einen lautern guldnen Stern, der ging vor ihnen, an einen kleinen eisern Drat. Und machten Konig Herodem, wie er den drey Konigen nachsandt, und wie er die Kindlein ertodtet. Das machten sie alles mit gar kostlichen Gewand, und mit grossen guldenen und silbernen Gurteln, und machten das mit groster Gezierd, und mit grosser Demuht. Corp. Act. et Decret. N. Constant. Conc. tom. IV. p. 1009.

* Ritson, Bibl. Poet. p. 79.

of which is assigned to the ostmen, and charged to the account of the corporation. The drapers, mercers and boothmen had probably each one, and the last might belong to the spicers, who appear anciently to have been a branch of the merchant-adventurers. A law was made by the merchants of this city, March 23rd, 20 Edw. IV. for settling the order of their procession on Corpus Christi day. By the ordinary of the millers, dated 1578, we may infer that the Corpus Christi plays were at that time on the decline, and never acted but by special command of the magistrates of Newcastle. «Whensoever,» says that authority, «the generall plaies of the towne shall be commanded by the mayor, etc.» they are to act «the antient playe of their fellowship, the Deliverance of the Children of Isrell out of the Thraldome, Bondage, and Servitude of King Pharo.» Thus also in that of the house-carpenters, dated July 3rd, 1579, it is ordered, that «whensoever the general plaies of the towne shall be plaied,» they shall perform «the Buriall of Christ,» pertaining anciently to the said fellowship. To the same effect it was ordered by that of the masons, 1581; whose play was «the Buriall of our Lady, Saint Mary the Virgin:» and lastly, by the joiners' ordinary, in 1589. Of the ancient sacred dramas performed by the trading companies of Newcastle, only one has come down to our times, entitled, «Noah's Ark, or the shipwrights ancient play or dirge,» which may be seen in *Brand's History of Newcastle**, from which the foregoing account is taken.

* Vol II. pp 369 – 379.

The Guild of the Holy Trinity of St. Botolph without Aldgate, appears, from the expenses recorded in their registers, to have been engaged between the years 1443 and 1448, in the performance of Miracle-plays; and to have possessed at this time «a rolle of velom,» containing what is called «the Pagent of the Holy Trinity*.»

In the year 1487, while Henry VII. resided at his castle of Winchester, on occasion of the birth of prince Arthur, on a Sunday, during the time of dinner, he was entertained with a religious drama called *Christi descensus ad inferos* †.

It is stated in *Dives and Pauper*, a book printed in 1496, that «to represente in playnge at Crystmasse, herodes, and the thre kynges, and other processes of the gospelle, both than, and at Ester, and other tymes also, it is lefull and commendable §.»

The accounts of the churchwardens of Bassingborne, in Cambridgeshire, for 1511, contain an account of the expenses and receipts for performing the Miracle-play of St. George. Among other circumstances that are mentioned, it is stated that twenty-seven neighbouring parishes contributed money towards furnishing the play, which was acted on a stage in an open field in the before mentioned parish ||.

* Hone, Anc. Myst. Desc. pp. 84, 85.

† Registr. Priorat. S. Swithin. Winton. Apud Warton, Hist. Eng. Poet. vol. ii. p. 206.

§ Sandys, Christmas Carols, Introduction, p. xxii.

|| Warton, Hist. Eng. Poet. vol. iii. p. 326.

It appears from the *Earl of Northumberland's Household Book*, 1512, that the children of his chapel performed Miracle-plays during the twelve days of Christmas, and at Easter, under the direction of his Master of the Revels *.

A MS. written in the seventh year of the reign of Henry VIII., enumerates certain articles which were most probably used in the representation of some Miracle-play before this monarch. Among others are mentioned, «A long garment of cloth of golde and tynsell, for the Prophete upon Palme Sonday.» «Item a littill gowne for a woman, the virgin, of cloth of silver.» «Item a littill coote for a childe of cloth of silver †.

In the Chapter-house, Westminster, is preserved a MS. containing an account of payments of money in the year 1527, for the entertainment of Henry VIII. Among other sums, is to be found one for «dyvers necessaries bought for the trymmyng of the Father of Heaven §.»

Ralph Radcliffe, educated at Oxford, opened in the year 1538 a school at Hitchin, in Hertfordshire; and, obtaining a grant of the dissolved friery of the Carmelites in that town, converted the refectory into a theatre. He was the author of several Miracle-plays, the names of which only have come down to our times ||.

At Christmas 1546, the Miracle-play of *Jephtha*, taken from the eleventh chapter of the book

* Percy, Reliques. vol. i. p. 133.

† Collier, Annals of the Stage, vol. i. p. 80, 81.

§ Ibid. p. 99.

|| Bale, Scriptor. Illust. M. Brit. p. 700.

of Judges, and written both in Latin and Greek, was acted in the University of Cambridge. It was composed by John Christopherson, one of the first Fellows of Trinity, afterwards Master, Dean of Norwich, and Bishop of Chichester *.

John Bale, Bishop of Ossory, in Ireland, and a most voluminous writer, was the author of at least eleven sacred dramas †, of which only four are now extant: — *1. The three Laws of Nature, Moses, and Christ. 2. God's Promises* §. *3. John the Baptist's preaching in the Wilderness. 4. The Temptation of Christ.* Bale's plays are deserving of attention as containing the first attempt, by means of the stage, to promote the Reformation. The following is a short extract from the epilogue of *The Temptation of Christ*, in which he attacks the Roman Catholics, who would keep the people in ignorance and from the use of the Scriptures, and which passage will afford a sufficient specimen of the manner in which he treats his antagonists.

What enemyes are they, that from the people wyll have
The scriptures of God, whych are the myghty weapon
That Christ left them here their sowles from hell to save,
And throw them headlondes into the devyls domynon.
If they be no devyls, I saye they are devyls non.
They bryngc in fastynge, but they leave out *Scriptum est.*
Chalke they geve for gold, soch fryndes are they of the Beest.

Eduard VI. is stated by Bale to have written a Miracle-play called *De meretrice Babylonica* ||.

* Retrospective Review, vol. xii. p. 9.

† Bale, Scriptor. Illust. M. Brit. pp. 702—705.

§ Reprinted in this Collection, p. 221.

|| Bale, Scriptor. Illust. M. Brit. pp. 673, 674.

Such attacks as the before mentioned induced Mary to issue a proclamation on the 16th August, 1553, the object of which was, among other things, to prevent the performance of plays calculated to advance the principles and doctrines of the Reformation. On the 30th of April, 1556, the Privy Council addressed a letter to the Earl of Shrewsbury, President of the North, complaining that «certain lewd persons, to the number of six or seven in a company, naming themselves to be servants unto Sir Francis Leek, and wearing his livery and badge on their sleeves, had wandered about those north parts, and represented certain plays and interludes, containing very naughty and seditious matter touching the King's and Queen's Majesties, and the state of the realm, and to the slander of Christ's true and catholic religion *.»

In the year 1556, the *Passion of Christ* was represented at Grey Friers in London, on Corpus Christi day, before the lord mayor, the privy council, and many great persons of the realm †. Strype mentions, under the year 1557, a play with a similar name, that was acted at the same place, on the day that war was proclaimed against France, and in honour of that occasion §. On St. Olave's day in the same year, the holiday of the church in Silver Street which is dedicated to that saint, was kept with much solemnity. «At eight o'clock at night, began a play of goodly matter, being the

* Lodge, Illustrations of British History, vol. I. p. 212.

† Strype, Life of Sir Thomas Pope, pref. p. vii.

§ Ecclesiastical Memorials, vol. iii. c. xlix.

miraculous history of the life of that saint, which lasted four hours*.

Queen Elizabeth, during her progress in the summer of 1564, visited the University of Cambridge, and was entertained at King's College with a play called *Ezechias*†.

At Tewkesbury, in the years 1578 and 1585, Miracle-plays were performed, which fact is recorded in the accounts of the churchwardens§.

Carew, who wrote in Queen Elizabeth's time, observes, that «the Guary Miracle, in English a Miracle-play, is a kind of interlude compiled in Cornish, out of some Scripture-History. For representing it they raise an amphitheatre in some open field, having the diameter of his inclosed plain, some 40 or 50 foot. The country people flock from all sides many miles off, to see and hear it; for they have therein devils and devices to delight the eye as the ear||.»

Weever relates, that he had «seen Corpus Christi plays acted at Preston, Lancaster, and at Kendall, in the beginning of the reign of James I., the subjects of which were the sacred Scriptures from the creation of the world**.»

It is generally considered that the last Miracle-play represented in England, was that of *Christ's Passion*, in the reign of James I., which Prynne

* Strype, Ecclesiastical Memorials, vol. iii. p. 379.

† Nichols, Progresses of Queen Elizabeth, vol. i. p. 186. edit. 1815.

§ Collier, Annals of the Stage, vol. ii. p. 140.

|| Survey of Cornwall, p. 71. edit. 1602.

** Funeral Monuments. p. 405.

informs us was «performed at Elie House in Holborn, when Gundomar lay there, on Good-friday at night, at which there were thousands present*.»

Although this historical view of Miracle-plays terminates properly at this period, yet we find traces of their existence even in the present century.

The author of the *Lives of Literary and Scientific Men* states, that in 1809 he «witnessed, on the borders of Lancashire and Yorkshire, on Good Friday, Saracens and Christians, Saladin, Richard, and other notable persons, represented by some young men; whose uncouth, fantastic garbs were not the least remarkable feature of the scene. The dialogue was in verse, and though somewhat modernised, bore marks of considerable antiquity†.

Collier mentions, that a kind of Miracle-play is still exhibited in Gloucestershire at Christmas, with the characters of Herod, Belzebub, and others§.

Sandys remarks, that «the Christmas-play of St. George and the Dragon is still preserved in the western and northern parts of the kingdom||.» It may not, perhaps, be uninteresting to give here this play as performed at the present time in the county of Cornwall; particularly as the old Miracle-play of St. George, from which this is undoubtedly derived, has not come down to our days.

* Histriomastix, p. 117. edit. 1633.

† Vol. i. p. 183.

§ Annals of the Stage, vol. i. p. 17. edit. 1831.

|| Christmas Carols, p. 17. edit. 1833.

CHARACTERS.

SAINT GEORGE.
THE DRAGON.
FATHER CHRISTMAS.
THE DOCTOR.
KING OF EGYPT.
TURKISH KNIGHT.
THE GIANT TURPIN.

Enter the Turkish Knight.

Open your doors, and let me in,
I hope your favors I shall win;
Whether I rise or whether I fall,
I'll do my best to please you all.
St. George is here, and swears he will come in,
And, if he does, I know he'll pierce my skin.
If you will not believe what I do say,
Let Father Christmas come in — clear the way.

[*Retires.*]

Enter Father Christmas.

Here come I, old Father Christmas,
Welcome, or welcome not,
I hope old Father Christmas
Will never be forgot.

I am not come here to laugh or to *jeer*,
But for a pocketfull of money, and a skinfull of beer,
If you will not believe what I do say,
Come in the King of Egypt — clear the way.

Enter the King of Egypt.

Here I, the King of Egypt, boldly do appear,
St. George, St. George, walk in, my only son and heir.
Walk in, my son St. George, and boldly act thy part,
That all the people here may see thy wond'rous art.

Enter Saint George.

Here come I, St. George, from Britain did I spring,
I'll fight the Dragon bold, my wonders to begin.
I'll clip his wings, he shall not fly;
I'll cut him down, or else I die.

Enter the Dragon.

Who's he that seeks the Dragon's blood,
And calls so angry, and so loud?
That English dog, will he before me stand?
I'll cut him down with my courageous hand.
With my long teeth, and scurvy jaw,
Of such I'd break up half a score,
And stay my stomach, till I'd more.

[*St. George and the* Dragon *fight, the latter is killed.*]

Father Christmas.

Is there a doctor to be found
All ready, near at hand,
To cure a deep and deadly wound,
And make the champion stand.

Enter Doctor.

Oh! yes, there is a doctor to be found
All ready, near at hand,
To cure a deep and deadly wound,
And make the champion stand.

Father Christmas.

What can you cure?

Doctor.

All sorts of diseases,
Whatever you pleases,
The phthisic, the palsy, and the gout;
If the devil's in, I'll blow him out.

Father Christmas.

What is your fee?

Doctor.

Fifteen pound, it is my fee,
The money to lay down.
But, as 'tis such a rogue as thee,
I cure for ten pound.

I carry a little bottle of alicumpane;
Here Jack, take a little of my flip flop,
Pour it down thy tip top;
Rise up and fight again.

[*The Doctor performs his cure, the fight is renewed, and the Dragon again killed.*]

Saint George.

Here am I, St. George,
That worthy champion bold,
And with my sword and spear
I won three crowns of gold.
I fought the fiery dragon,
And brought him to the slaughter;
By that I won fair Sabra,
The King of Egypt's daughter.
Where is the man, that now will me defy?
I'll cut his giblets full of holes, and make his buttons fly.

The Turkish Knight advances.

Here come I, the Turkish Knight,
Come from the Turkish land to fight.
I'll fight St. George, who is my foe,
I'll make him yield before I go;
He brags to such a high degree,
He thinks there's none can do the like of he.

Saint George.

Where is the Turk, that will before me stand?
I'll cut him down with my courageous hand.

[*They fight, the Knight is overcome, and falls on one knee.*]

Turkish Knight.

Oh! pardon me, St. George, pardon of thee I crave,
Oh! pardon me this night, and I will be thy slave.

Saint George.

No pardon shalt thou have, while I have foot to stand,
So rise thee up again, and fight out sword in hand.

[*They fight again, and thn Knight is killed. Father Christmas calls for the Doctor, with whom the same dialogue occurs as before, and the cure is performed.*]

Enter the Giant Turpin.

Here come I, the Giant, bold Turpin is my name,
And all the nations round do tremble at my fame.
Wheree'r I go, they tremble at my sight,
No lord or champion long with me would fight.

Saint George.

Here's one that dares to look thee in the face,
And soon will send thee to another place.

[*They fight, and the Giant is killed; medical aid is called in as before, and the cure performed by the Doctor, to whom then is given a basin of girdy grout and a kick, and driven out.*]

Father Christmas.

Now, ladies and gentlemen, your sport is most ended,
So prepare for the hat, which is highly commended.
The hat it would speak, if it had but a tongue;
Come throw in your money, and think it no wrong.

There are, besides several single Miracle-plays, three distinct series, — the Chester, the Coventry, and the Towneley or Widkirk.

It is supposed, on pretty good grounds, that the Chester series is the most ancient, though if internal evidence were to decide the question, it would be in favour of the Towneley. All have undoubtedly been frequently transcribed, so that no correct opinion can be formed concerning the age in which they were compiled from the style in which they are written. «The Banes,» a prologue to the Chester Plays, which was always read previous to the representation, supplies us with some data enabling us to assign a period approximating at least to the true one.

Reverende lordes and ladyes all,
That at this time here assembled bee,
By this messenge understand you shall,
That some times there was mayor of this citie,
Sir John Arnway, knyghte, who most worthilie
Contented himself to sett out in playe,
The devise of one Dom Randall, monke of Chester abbey.

This prologue, modernised as it evidently is, appears to have been written at a period subsequent to the dramas themselves. From the testimony of ancient, almost of contemporary documents, it is certain that John Arnway was the chief magistrate of Chester between 1268 and 1276*. An attempt, however, has been made to invalidate the antiquity of this period by two assertions; first, that the Dom Randall here mentioned was no other than the celebrated Runulf, or Randal Higden, compiler of the *Polychronicon;* and secondly, that the period in which he lived will not agree with the time when John Arnway was mayor. Randal Higden, according to Bale, died in 1363†, and even supposing he had attained an unusual great age, could not have written these plays between 1268 and 1276. It deserves to be remarked, that the name of Randal is one of frequent recurrence in the old archives, whether public or private, of Chester. It is not, perhaps, to be disputed, that Higden was in some way, and at some period, concerned in the performance of the Chester Miracle-plays; though in what way is not so clear. He may have made several additions, though it is,

* Cabinet Cyclopædia. Literary and Scientific Men. vol. i. p. 193.

† Script Illust M. Brit. p. 462.

perhaps, more probable that he only translated them. A note to one of the MSS. of these productions, informs us*, that Higden «was thrice at Rome before he could obtain leave of the Pope to have them in the English tongue;» and a remark appended to another one states, that these plays were written by him in 1328†. The only way, however, of explaining in any satisfactory manner the mention of John Arnway and Randall in «the Banes,» is to consider the latter as the translator, and that they were previously performed in the mayoralty of the former. The Chester-plays began on Whit-monday, and continued until Wednesday. They consist of twenty-four dramas§, and were annually performed, with some interruptions, until 1577.

* Harl. No. 2124. Apud Collier, vol. ii. p. 129.

† Harl. No. 2013. Apud Warton, vol. ii. p. 179.

§ *I. The Fall of Lucifer*, by the Tanners. *II. The Creation*, by the Drapers. *III. The Deluge*, by the Dyers. *IV. Abraham, Melchisedech, and Lot*, by the Barbers and Wax-chandlers. *V. Moses, Balak, and Balaam*, by the Hatters and Linen-drapers. *VI. The Salutation and Nativity*, by the Wrights. *VII. The Shepherds feeding their flocks by night*, by the Painters and Glaziers. *VIII. The three Kings*, by the Vintners. *IX. The Oblation of the three Kings*, by the Mercers. *X. The Killing of the Innocents*, by the Goldsmiths. *XI. The Purification*, by the Blacksmiths. *XII. The Temptation*, by the Butchers. *XIII. The Blindmen and Lazarus*, by the Glovers. *XIV. Jesus and the Lepers*, by the Corvisors. *XV. The last Supper*, by the Bakers. *XVI. The Passion and Crucifixion of Christ*, by the Fletchers, Coopers, and Ironmongers. *XVII. The Descent into Hell*, by the Cooks. *XVIII. The Resurrection*, by the Skinners. *XIX. The Appearing of Christ to the two Disciples*, by the Saddlers. *XX. The Ascension*, by the Tailors. *XXI. The Election of St. Mathias, sending of the Holy Ghost*, by the Fishmongers. *XXII. Ezekiel*, by the Clothiers. *XXIII. Antichrist*, by the Dyers. *XXIV. The*

The sacred dramas anciently exhibited at Coventry drew immense multitudes to that city, which was as much owing to its central situation, as to these exhibitions being sometimes frequented by royalty. In 1416, Henry V. and his nobles took great delight in seeing the Pageants; and in 1456, «on Corpus Christi yeven at nyght came the quene [Margaret] from Kelyngworth to Coventre, at which tyme she wold not be met, but came prively to se the play there on the morowe, and she sygh the pagentes pleyde save domes day, which might not be pleyde for lack of day, and she was loged at Richard Wodes the grocer, where Richard Sharp sometyme dwelled, and there all the pleys were furst pleyde, and there were with her then lordes and ladyes.» Richard III. in 1484, came to see the Corpus Christi Plays. In 1486, Henry VII. was present at the performance of the Pageants on St. Peter's day, and much commended them; and in 1492 again visited the city, to see the plays acted by the Grey Friers*. Before the suppression of the Monasteries, the Grey Friers of Coventry were greatly celebrated for their exhibitions on Corpus Christi day; their Pageants, says Dugdale, «being acted with mighty State and Reverence by the Friers of this House, had Theaters for the several Scenes, very large and high, placed upon Wheels, and drawn to all the eminent Parts of the City,

Day of Judgment, by the Websters. Of this series, there are two copies among the Harleian MSS. in the British Museum, one at the Bodleian, and one in the possession of the Duke of Devonshire. They bear the dates of 1600, 1607, 1604, and 1591 respectively. It is from that of 1600 the pieces in this Collection are printed.

* Sharpe, Dissertation on the Coventry Mysteries, pp. 4, 5. 4to.

for the better Advantage of Spectators: And contained the Story of the Old and New Testament, composed in the old English Rithme, as appeareth by an antient MS. intituled *Ludus Corporis Christi*, or *Ludus Coventriæ*. I have been told by some old people, who in their younger years were eye-witnesses of these Pageants so acted, that the yearly confluence of people to see that shew was extraordinary great, and yielded no small advantage to this City*.» These plays certainly formed no part of the entertainments exhibited by the trading companies of Coventry. The subjects are for the most part identical with those of the two other series, but more numerous, consisting of forty-two plays †.

The Towneley Miracle-plays, (so named from being in the possession of this family,) called also

* Dugdale, History of Warwickshire, p. 116, edit. 1656.

† I. The Creation. II. The Fall of Man. III. The Death of Abel. IV. Noah's Flood. V. Abraham's Sacrifice. VI. Moses and the Two Tables. VII. The Genealogy of Christ. VIII. Anna's Pregnancy. IX. Mary in the Temple. X. Her Betrothment. XI. The Salutation and Conception. XII. Joseph's Return. XIII. The Visit to Elizabeth. XIV. The Trial of Joseph and Mary. XV. The Birth of Christ. XVI. The Shepherds' Offering. XVII. Caret in MS. XVIII. Adoration of the Magi. XIX. The Purification. XX. Slaughter of the Innocents. XXI. Christ disputing in the Temple. XXII. The Baptism of Christ. XXIII. The Temptation. XXIV. The Woman taken in Adultery. XXV. Lazarus. XXVI. Council of the Jews. XXVII. Mary Magdalen. XXVIII. Christ betrayed. XXIX. Herod. XXX. The Trial of Christ. XXXI. The Dream of Pilate's Wife. XXXII. The Crucifixion. XXXIII. The Descent into Hell. XXXIV. Sealing of the Tomb. XXXV. The Resurrection. XXXVI. The Three Marias. XXXVII. Christ appearing to Mary Magdalen. XXXVIII. The Pilgrim of Emaus. XXXIX. The Ascension. XL. Descent of the Holy Ghost. XLI. The Assumption of the Virgin. XLII. Doomsday. This MS. was written at least as early as the reign of Henry VII., and is in the British Museum in the Bibl. Cotton, Vesp. D. VIII.

the Widkirk, are written in a style that may be referred to the reign of Henry VI. or Edward IV. Where the plays constituting this series were originally performed, is a matter of some doubt. These dramas are frequently called the Widkirk, from a tradition, that, prior to the dissolution of the monasteries, they belonged to the Abbey of Widkirk, near Wakefield, in the County of York. This tradition has marks of a genuine character. There is, however, no place called Widkirk in the neighbourhood of Wakefield, and neither there nor in any part of England was there an Abbey of Widkirk. But there is a place called Woodkirk in that neighbourhood, and at Woodkirk there was a cell of Augustinian friars. Whatever weight there may be attached to the tradition respecting the original possession, must, therefore, be given to the claim of this Cell of Monks at Woodkirk. This place is about four miles to the north of Wakefield. A small religious Community was established there in the first half century after the Conquest by the Earls Warren, to whom the great Lordship of Wakefield belonged, and they were placed in subjection to the house of Nostel. Henry I. granted to the friars of Nostel, a charter, for two fairs to be held at Woodkirk, — one at the Feast of the Assumption, the other on the Feast of the Nativity of the Blessed Mary. This grant was confirmed by King Stephen. Now it was at such places and on such occasions, that sacred dramas were usually exhibited. Moreover internal evidence confirms the tradition. Words and phrases that are peculiar to this part of Yorkshire, at least more frequently to be heard there than in any other part, and are still existing in the vernacular language of that district, in the sense in which they are used in these plays, are often to be met with in this series. Though the original possession of this MS. must be attributed to the Friars of Woodkirk, yet it seems very probable that some of these dramas were performed at Wakefield. Thus at the beginning of the first is written in a large hand «WAKEFELDE» and «BERKERS,» the meaning of which seems to be, that this Miracle-play was represented at the town of Wakefield by the company or fellowship of the Barkers or Tanners. To the second is prefixed «GLOVER PAG...,» without the word Wakefield. The imperfect word seems to have been «Pagina.» At the head of the third, we find «WAKEFELD,» without the name of any trade. There are also two more allusions of the same kind. In the language as well as the style of this series, a diversity may be perceived, arising, perhaps, from their not having proceeded from one hand, and from the collection having been made up partly of compositions strictly original, and partly of compositions from other similar collections *. The Miracle-play entitled *Secunda Pastorum*, reprinted in this Collection, is, perhaps, the most singular religious drama, if such a term may be applied to it, now in existence. This series consists of thirty-two plays †.

* Perface to the «Towneley Mysteries," 8vo. 1836.

† I. Creatio. II. Mactatio Abel. III. Processus Noe cum filiis. IV. Abraham. V. Isaac. VI. Jacob. VII. Processus Prophetarum. VIII. Pharao. IX. Cæsar Augustus. X. Annunciatio. XI. Salutatio

In what language the early English Miracle-plays were written, is a subject of some uncertainty, and which is undoubtedly owing, in a great measure, to the destruction at the time of the Reformation of numbers of MSS. that savoured of Roman Catholicism *. If we consider, that the first piece of this kind we have an account of was written by a Frenchman, that William the Conqueror as well as his successors endeavoured to bring the French language into general use in England, and that till the reign of Edward III. this tongue was the prevailing one in England †, we shall have some reason for concluding that this was the language in which these performances were first written §. Several verses are to be found in these

Elizabeth. XII. Prima Pagina Pastorum. XIII. Secunda Pagina Pastorum. XIV. Oblatio Magorum. XV. Fugatio Joseph et Mariæ in Egyptum. XVI. Magnus Herodes. XVII. Purificatio Mariæ. XVIII. Pagina Doctorum. XIX. Johannes Baptista. XX. Conspiratio et Captio. XXI. Coliphizatio. XXII. Flagellatio. XXIII. Processas Crucis. XXIV. Processus Talentorum. XXV. Extractio Animarum ab Inferno. XXVI. Resurrectio Domini. XXVII. Peregrini. XXVIII. Thomas Indiæ. XXIX. Ascensio Domini. XXX. Juditium. XXXI. Lazarus. XXXII. Suspensio Judæ.

* Leland, the antiquary and one of the most enlightened men of his age, who was appointed by Henry VIII. to search for and preserve such works as might rescue remarkable English events and occurrences from oblivion, was nevertheless a destroyer of MSS. that contained any reference to the peculiar doctrines of the Roman Catholic religion. He remarks, in a report, that one of his purposes in the examination of the different libraries, was to expel »the crafty coloured doctrine of a rowt of Romayne bysshopps.'

† Ellis, Early English Poets, vol. i. pp. 124—126. ed. 1811.

§ The Abbé de la Rue and Monsieur Chateaubriand are of opinion, that the first Miracle-play performed in England was composed in French. *Études sur les Mystères, par Onésime le Roy, p. 9. ed.* 1837. There has recently been discovered in the Royal Library at

plays in Latin, but it is no proof of their having been composed in that tongue; for it was a custom of the early English poets to interweave their pieces with lines in that language. It must, nevertheless, be remarked, that though the general opinion of English writers favours a French original in preference to a Latin, yet many reasons might be assigned to make it extremely doubtful; but as this is a subject on which authors are not agreed, it is useless, on the present occasion, to enter on a review of suppositions and theories, while engaged in the consideration of matters of fact*.

It has been already remarked, that Higden, supposed to be the author of the Chester series, was three times at Rome before he could obtain leave to have these plays in English, and not long afterwards a law was passed requiring «all pleas in the Courts of the King, or of any other lord, shall be pleaded in the English tongue†.» Many of the

Paris a fragment of a play of the Resurrection in Anglo-Norman, and which is supposed to have been composed about the middle of the twelfth century. It was published in 1834 by Monsieur A. Jubinal.

* The opinions of French writers on this point may be best gathered from *Études sur les Mystères*, *par Onésime le Roy*, *Introduction*, pp. IX, XVI—XIX, edit. 1836. and *Mystères inédits du quinzième siècle par Achille Jubinal, Préface*, pp. X—XVII. edit. 1837.

† 36th of Edward III. It appears probable, that previous to this period these dramas were written in Anglo-Norman, if not still earlier in Latin. Besides the Miracle-play in Anglo-Norman mentioned in a former note (see p. XLV note §), two others written in the same language have been lately discovered; one of them is by Hermann, an Anglo-Norman poet, who lived 1127—1170; the other by Archbishop Langton. M. Raynouard has printed in his *Choix de poésies des Troubadours* a Miracle-play — *the wise and foolish Virgins*, a drama of the eleventh century written in Latin, French, and the language of Provence.

plays strengthen the supposition that they were originally written in French, at least show pretty plainly that some of them were translations from that language. In *Le Mistère du viel Testament par personnages, joué à Paris*, printed by Antoine Verard about 1490, but acted at a much earlier date, we find the following exclamation of Isaac: —

> Mais vueillez moy les yeulx cachier,
> Affin que le glaive ne voye;
> Quant de moy vendres approchier,
> Peult étre que je fouyroye.

In the fourth play of the Chester series, we find these lines: —

> Also, father, I pray you, hyde my eyen,
> That I see not your sworde so keene;
> Your stroke, father, I would not see,
> Least I against it grill.

The fifth play of the same collection affords still further evidence to the same point: it relates to King Balak, and Balaam the prophet. In the French *Mistère*, the Ass, sorely beaten, thus addresses his rider: —

> Baalam, suis je pas ta beste,
> Sur qui tu a toujours este,
> Tant en yver comme en este?
> Te feiz jamais tell chose?

In the Chester play the passage occupies one line more: —

> Ame not I, master, thyne owne asse,
> To beare thee whether thou wilte passe,

11 Henry VIII., «Lusoribus cum adjutorio Conventus, 2s.:» — 12 Henry VIII., «Jocatoribus cum adjutorio Conventus, 2s.* »

Although we have shown that the clergy assisted in these performances, yet it does not appear that they had, at least in latter times, the chief hand in them. Such appears to have been the case at Chester, York, and Newcastle, where Miracle-plays were performed by trading-companies, each guild undertaking a portion of the performance, and sustaining a share of the expense. The authentic information regarding the exhibition of the Corpus Christi plays at Coventry, extends from 1416 to 1591, and during the whole of that period there is not the slightest indication that the clergy in any way co-operated.

Miracle-plays were most probably at first exhibited in churches. Some MSS. contain the direction, *cum cantu et organis*, — a proof that they were acted in holy places. In the register of William of Wykehan, Bishop of Winchester, under the year 1384, an episcopal injunction is recited against the exhibition of *Spectacula* in the cemetery of his cathedral †. Burnet informs us, that Bonner, Bishop of London, issued a proclamation to the clergy of his diocese, dated 1542, prohibiting «all manner of common plays, games, or interludes to be played, set forth, or declared, within their churches, chapels, etc. §.»

* Apud Collier, vol. ii. p. 142.

† Apud Warton, vol. i. p. 240.

§ History of the Reformation, i Coll. Rec. p. 225, edit. fol.

It is not very easy to give a clear and correct account of the mechanical contrivances used in the representation of Miracle-plays, owing to the different changes which must from time to time have taken place in the manner of exhibiting them in the earlier times, from the way in which they were acted in the sixteenth century. Sacred dramas, as we have already seen, were frequently represented in churches, but with what assistance, except that of the choir and organ, we are ignorant. They were sometimes exhibited in a field, as was the case in 1511, in the parish of Bassingborne, in Cambridgeshire; and we find in the play *Mactatio Abel* of the Towneley series, Cain at plough with a team of horses, which could not have been shown on a scaffold. In latter times they appear to have been frequently represented on moveable stages. Archdeacon Rogers, who died in 1595, and saw the Miracle-plays acted in Chester, gives the following account of the way in which they were exhibited: — « The maner of these playes weare, every company had his pagiant, wch pagiants weare a high scafolde with 2 rowmes, a higher and a lower, upon 4 wheeles. In the lower they apparelled themselves, and in the higher rowme they played, beinge all open on the tope, that all behoulders might heare and see them. The places where they played them was in every streete. They begane first at the Abay gates, and when the first pagiante was played, it was wheeled to the highe crosse before the Mayor, and so to every streete, and soe every streete had a pagiant playinge before them at one time, till all the pagiantes for the daye appoynted weare played, and when one pagiant was neere ended, worde was broughte from streete to streete, that soe they mighte come in place thereof, exceedinge orderlye, and all the streetes have their pagiantes afore them all at one time playeinge togeather; to se which playes was great resorte, and also scafoldes and stages made in the streetes in those places where they determined to playe theire pagiantes *.»

Strutt gives the following description of the manner of performing these plays: — «In the early dawn of literature, and when the sacred Mysteries were the only theatrical performances, what is now called the stage did then consist of three several platforms or stages, raised one above another; on the uppermost sat the *Pater Cœlestis*, surrounded with his angels; on the second appeared the holy saints and glorified men; and the last and lowest was occupied by mere men, who had not yet passed from this transitory life to the regions of eternity. On one side of this lowest platform was the resemblance of a dark pitchy cavern, from whence issued appearance of fire and flames; and when it was necessary the audience were treated with hideous yellings and noises, as imitative of the howlings and cries of the wretched souls tormented by the relentless dæmons. From this yawning cave the devils themselves constantly ascended, to delight and to instruct the spectators; to delight, because they were usually the greatest jesters and buffoons that then appeared; and to instruct, for that they treated

* Sharpe, Dissertation on the Coventry Mysteries, p. 17. 4to.

Anno 1182.

of a record in Winchester

work done

Soldeyringe & repairynge

St. Joseph ——

ynge & ornamentynge

the Holy Ghost —— —

yinge ye Virgin Mary

& behynde & makynge } 4.

new Chylde ——

inge a nose on the D—l

a horne on his hede } 5.

a bytt on his tayle

[illegible]. 4

the wretched mortals, who were delivered to them, with the utmost cruelty, warning thereby all men carefully to avoid the falling into the clutches of such hardened and remorseless spirits*.»

The Pageants exhibited in Coventry by the different guilds, were performed on moveable scaffolds, as is plainly proved by numerous entries from 1450 to 1591, which are still to be read in the accounts of their expenses, and which may be seen in the work of Sharp†. The Cappers' Company had twelve, and the Drapers' ten men, to draw their scaffolds. Only one instance occurs of horses having been employed, and that is in the records of the Drapers' Company for 1591, the last year in which they performed.

The accounts of the various guilds contain entries of sums paid for machinery, dresses, etc., which tend to throw some light on the way in which these Pageants were represented. The subject of the Smith's Pageant was the Trial, Condemnation, and Crucifixion of Christ, as will appear from the following list of Characters, Machinery, etc. collected from various entries of charges in the records of this company between 1449 and 1585, the last year of their exhibiting: —

CHARACTERS.

God, sometimes Jesus.	Peter and Malchus.
Cayphas.	Anna.
Heroude.	Pilate.
Pilate's Wife.	Pilate's Son.

* Manners and Customs, vol iii. p. 150.

† Dissertation on the Coventry Mysteries, p. 20. 4to.

The Beadle.	2 Knights.
The Devil.	4 Tormentors.
Judas.	2 Princes, A. D. 1490 only.

MACHINERY, etc.

The Cross with a Rope to draw it up, and a Curtain hanging before it.
Gilding the Pillar and the Cross.
2 Pair of Gallows.
4 Scourges and a Pillar.
Scaffold.
Fanes to the Pageant.
Mending of Imagery occurs 1469.
A Standard of red Buckram.
Two red Pensiles of Cloth painted, and silk Fringe.
Iron to hold up the Streamer.

DRESSES, etc.

4 Gowns and 4 Hoods for the Tormentors. — (These are afterwards described as Jackets of black buckram with nails and dice upon them.) Other 4 gowns with damask flowers; also 2 Jackets party red and black.
2 Mitres (for Cayphas and Annas).
A Rochet for one of the Bishops.
God's Coat of white leather, 6 skins.
A Staff for the Demon.
2 Spears.
Gloves (12 pair at once).
Herod's Crest of Iron.
Scarlet Hoods and a Tabard.
Hats and Caps.
Cheverel [Peruke] for God.
3 Cheverels and a Beard.
2 Cheverels gilt for Jesus and Peter.
Faulchion for Herod.
Scarlet Gown.
Maces.

Girdle for God.
A new Sudere [the *veronica*] for God.
A Seldall [seat] for God.
Sceptres for Herod and his Son.
Poleaxe for Pilate's Son.

THE EXPENSES FOR 1490, VERBATIM.

This is the expens of the furste reherse of our players in ester weke.

Inprimis in Brede . . . . iiij^{d}
Itm in Ale. . . . . viij^{d}
Itm in kechyn . . . . xiij^{d}
Itm in Vynegre . . . . j^{d}
Itm payd at the Second Reherse in Whyttson-weke in brede, Ale and kechyn. . . . ij^{s} iiij^{d}
Itm for drynkynge at the pagent in having forthe in Wyne and ale . . . . . vij^{d}
Itm in the mornynge at diner and at Sopper in Costs in Brede . . . . . . vij^{d}
Itm for ix galons of Ale . . . . . . xviij^{d}
Itm for a Rybbe of befe and j gose. . . . vj^{d}
Itm for kechyn to dener and sopp . . . . ij^{s} ij^{d}
Itm for a Rybbe of befe . . . . . . iij^{d}
Itm for a quarte of wyne . . . . . . ij^{d}
Itm for an other quarte for heyrynge of procula is gowne . . . . ij^{d}
Itm for gloves . . . . ij^{s} vj^{d}
Itm spend at the repellynge of the pagantte and the expences of havinge it in and furthe xiiij^{d}
Itm in paper . . . . ob.

Md payd to the players for corpus xisti daye.

Inprimis to God . . . . ij^{s}
Itm to Cayphas . . . . iij^{s} iiij^{d}
Itm to Heroude . . . . iij^{s} iiij^{d}
Itm to Pilatt is wyffe . . . . ii^{s}
Itm to the Bedull . . . . iiij^{d}
Itm to one of the Knights . . . . . ij^{s}
Itm to the devyll and to Judas . . . . xviij^{d}

Itm to Petur and malchus . . . . xvj^{d}
Itm to Anna . . . . ij^{s} ij^{d}
Itm to Pilatte . . . . iiij^{s}
Itm to Pilatte is sonne . . . . iiij^{d}
Itm to an other knighte . . . . ij^{s}
Itm to the Mynstrell . . . . xiiij^{d}*

Minstrels appear to have taken no inconsiderable part in these performances, for we find them very frequently assisting in their execution. It is, however, impossible to discover at what time they first performed in these exhibitions, as the earliest MS. we have of these sacred dramas is not much older than the middle of the fifteenth century; though if we may judge from the popularity of minstrels in England, even as early as the Conquest, it is not at all improbable that they assisted at a very early period. In the second play of the Chester series, « mynstrells playinge » is noted in the margin not less than four times; and in the eighth play of the same series they also take part in the execution of the piece. The accounts of the Trading Companies of Coventry contain many entries of sums of money paid to minstrels between the years 1450 and 1590. It seems not improbable that they, besides performing in their peculiar quality, acted such parts as required to be sung, which certainly would be very appropriate for them, and could not have been well performed without their assistance.

We meet often with the character of *God* in these dramas, and this, according to our ideas, appears to be highly improper and even irreverent.

* Sharpe, pp. 14—16.

It must, however, be considered, that as one of the designs of Miracle-plays was to instruct the people in the Scriptures, this character was partly necessary; at least our forefathers could have seen no great impropriety in it, or they would not have admitted it in these performances to the extent they did. It is worthy of remark, that in the accounts of the Cappers' Company of Coventry for 1565, the following entry is found: — «Itm payd to God..... xij[d]," which is the more singular as it occurs some years after the Reformation was effected in England. This does not, however, at all prove, that even at that time when there was a greater sense of propriety prevalent, it was considered by any irreligious; for we must recollect that these plays were generally performed every year, so that persons accustomed to behold them from their earliest infancy, did not perceive those improprieties, which would have occurred to others differently circumstanced.

A character even more irreverent than the foregoing was the *Holy Ghost*, who, though sometimes represented as a dove, was occasionally as a human figure. The eleventh play of the Chester series has this personage. The following entries, which are to be found in the books of the Cappers' Company, prove that the Holy Ghost was represented by a real person: —

Itm payd to the sprytt of god	xvj[d]
Itm payd for the spret of gods cote . . .	ij[s]
Itm payd for the making of the same cote .	viij[d]
Itm payd for ij yardes and halfe of bockram to make the spyrits cote	ij[s] j[d]

Of all the various characters that played in these religious dramas, no one appears to have acted so prominent a part as the *Devil*. This can be easily accounted for, as he seems clearly to have been the harlequin in Miracle-plays, and therefore a great favorite with the spectators. It is not unlikely, from the extracts given by Sharpe*, that he was usually represented with horns, a very wide mouth (by means of a mask), staring eyes, a large nose, a red beard, cloven feet, a tail; and was furnished with a good thick club.

Several of the pieces of the Chester and Coventry series have characters named *Expositor*, *Doctor*, and *Contemplation*, whose office appears to have been to deliver a prologue, epilogue, or, as is the case in the thirteenth play of the last mentioned series, to make remarks on what passes. The following is the epilogue to this drama, which is spoken by *Contemplation*, and is curious on account of the introduction of a number of persons with English names, who are summoned to appear before the *Bishop*; as well as that it informs us, in the seventh verse, that money was collected for the performances. It is necessary to remark, in order to understand correctly the first and last verses, that the following play is *The Trial of Mary and Joseph*.

Avoyd, sers, and lete my lorde the buschop come,
  And syt in the courte the lawes for to doo;
And I schall gon in this place them for to somowne,
  The that ben in my book, the court ye must com too.

* Dissertation on the Coventry Mysteries, pp. 57, 58.

I warne you here all a bowte,
That I somown you, all the rowte,
Loke ye fayl for no dowte
At the court to pere:

Both John Jurdon, and Geffrey Gyle,
Malkyn Mylkedoke, and fayr Mabyle,
Stevyn Sturdy, and Jak at the style,
And Sawdyr sadelere.

Thom Tynker, and Betrys belle,
Peyrs Potter, and Whatt at the welle,
Symme Smalfeyth, and Kate Kelle,
And Bertylmew the bocher.

Kytt cakeler, and Colett crane,
Gylle fetyse, and fayr Jane,
Powle pewter, and Pinel prane,
And Phelypp the good fleccher.

Cok crane, and Davy drydust,
Luce Lyer, and Letyce lytyl trust,
Miles the miller, and colle crake crust,
Both bette the baker, and Robyn Rede.

And loke ye rynge wele in yowr purs,
For ellys yowr cawse may spede the wurs,
Thow that ye slynge goddys curs,
Evyn at myn hede.

Bothe Bontyng the browster, and Sybyly Slynge,
Megge Mery wedyr, and Sabyn Sprynge,
Tyffany Twynkeler, fayle for no thynge;
Fast com a way
The courte schal be this day.

Several of the Miracle-plays are founded on the New Testament Apocrypha. This is more especially the case with those of the Coventry series, of which eight owe their origin to this source. In the eighth play of this series, *Anna's Pregnancy*, *Joachim* says,

> So shulde every curat, in this werde wyde,
> Geve a part to his channcel, I wys;
> A part to his parocheners, that to povert slyde;
> The thyrd part to kepe for hym and his.

In the New Testament Apocrypha we find in the book of *Mary*, Chap. I. v. 3. Their lives were plain and right in the sight of the Lord, pious and faultless before men. For they divided all their substance into three parts: 4. One of which they devoted to the temple and officers of the temple; another they distributed among strangers, and persons in poor circumstances; and the third they reserved for themselves and the uses of their own family.

In the ninth play, *Mary in the Temple*, the *Bishop* says,

> A gracyous lord! this is a mervelyous thynge
> That we se here all in syght,
> A babe of thre yer age so zynge,
> To come vp these greeys so vp right;
> It is an hey meracle.

The parallel passage is in the book of *Mary*, Chap. IV. v. 4. The parents of the blessed Virgin and infant Mary put her upon one of these stairs; 5. But while they were putting off their clothes, in which they had travelled, and according to custom putting on some that were neat and clean. 6. In the mean time the Virgin of the Lord in such a manner went up all the stairs one after another, without the help of any to lead her or lift her, that any one would have judged from hence, that she was of perfect age.

In the fourteenth play, *the Trial of Joseph and Mary,* the *Bishop* says,

Her is the botel of Goddys vengeauns;
This drnyk shall be now thi purgacion.

We find in the book of *Protevan*, Chap. XI. v. 17. But he wept bitterly, and the priest added, I will cause you both to drink the water of the Lord, which is for trial, and so your iniquity shall be laid open before you.

The New Testament Apocrypha has been used not only in the compilation of the Coventry series, but also in the Chester and Townely. The *Descent of Christ into Hell*, founded upon the apocryphal gospel of Nicodemus, forms part of each of these three collections. There can be litttle doubt, that the Apocrypha was chosen by the writers of these plays as best suited to the barbarous ages in which they appeared, from its containing more improbabilities and absurdities.

The feeling of propriety that our ancestors entertained was certainly rather of a lax kind, which is seen from the contents of many of these plays, but especially from the stage directions to the second play of the Chester series. This drama comprised the creation, temptation and fall: after this event the direction in the margin is, that Adam and Eve shall cover *genitalia sua cum foliis*, whereas until then *stabunt nudi, et non verecundabuntur* *. Perhaps our forefathers thought it no indecency to give such representations, considering they had the authority of scripture for such exhibitions; but it must nevertheless strike us as not a little extraordinary, that at least as late as the close of the sixteenth century such scenes were to be found in England. We learn this fact from a play entitled *The Travailes of the three English Brothers*, 1607. 4to., of which the following is an extract.

Seruant.

Sir, heres an Englishman desires accesse to you.

Sir Anthony Shirley.

An Englishman whats his name.

Seruant.

He calls himselfe Kempe.

[*Enter Kempe.*]

Sir Anthony Shirley.

Kemp, bid him come in, welcome honest Will, and how doth all thy fellowes in England.

Kempe.

Why like good fellowes when they haue no money, liue vpon credit.

Sir Anthony Shirley.

And what good new Plays haue you.

* In the second play of the Coventry series, Adam says,

Se us nakyd be for and be hynde,

* * *

Woman ley this leff on thi pryvyte,
And with this leff I shall hyde me.

Kempe.

Many idle toyes, but the old play that Adam and Eue acted in bare action vnder the figge tree drawes most of the Gentlemen*.

In whatever light we may be disposed to view Miracle-plays, there can be no doubt that the public exhibition of them was attended with several beneficial effects. They were very useful in the civilisation of the people, from their bringing together all classes, and giving them a taste for other amusements than those which required only strength and prowess, and must moreover have been highly valuable in an age when few could read, as a means of instructing the people in the truths of Christianity.

* This extract is taken from a reprint of this play in *Bibliographical Memoranda*, p. 347. *Bristol* 1816. Of this work only one hundred copies were published, and it is much to be regretted that this custom of reprinting only a very limited number of scarce books, often only twenty-five, prevails so generally, as it tends to make these works excessively expensive, and very-difficult to procure.

CHESTER

MIRACLE-PLAYS.

THE DELUGE.

Deus.

A God that all the World have wrought
Heaven, Earth, and all of nought,
I see my people, in deede and thought,
Are fowle rotted in synne.
  My Ghost shall not lenge in man,
That through fleshlie liking is my fone
But till vi skore yeares be gone,
To loke if they will blynne.
  Manne that I made I will destroy;
Beast, worme, and fowle to flie:
For on earthe they doe me noye,
The folke yt is thereon.
  For it barmes me so hartfullie
The malyce now that can multeply,
That sore me greves, inwardlie,
That ever I made manne.
  Therfore Noe, my servant free,
That righteous man art, as I see,
A shipp sone thou shalt make the,
Of trees drye and light.

Little chambers therein thou make,
And byndinge slich also thou take:
Wthin and out, thou ne slake
To anoynte it through all thy might.
300 Cubytes it shall be longe,
And so of breadeth, to make it strong,
Of heighte so, the mest thou fonge,
Thus measure it about.
One Window worch through thy might,
One cubyte of length and breadeth make it:
Upon the syde a dore shall fit,
For to come in and out.
Eatinge places thou make also,
Three rowfed chambers, one or two:
For wth water I thinke to stowe
Man that I can make.
Destroyed all the World shall be,
Save thou, thy Wife, thy sonnes thre;
And all their Wives, also, wth the,
Shall saved be for thy sake.

Noe.

Ah Lord! I thanke the, lowd and still,
That to me art in such will;
And spares me and my house to spill,
As now I sothlie fynd.
Thy bydding, Lord, I shall fulfill,
And never more the greeve, ne grill,
That suche grace has sent me till,
Among all mankinde.
Have done yow men and women all;
Helpe, for ought that may befall,
To worke this shipp, chamber and hall,
As God hath bydden vs doe.

Sem.

Father, I am already bowne,
Anne axe I have, by my crowne!

As sharpe as any in all this towne,
For to goe thereto.

Ham.

I have a hatchet, wonder kene,
To byte well, as may be scene,
A better grownden, as I wene,
Is not in all this towne.

Japhet.

And I can well make a pyn,
And wth this hammer knocke yt in;
Goe and worche, wthout more dyme,
And I am ready bowne.

Uxor Noe.

And we shall bring tymber, to,
For women nothing els doe;
Women be weake to undergoe
Any great travayle.

Uxor Sem.

Here is a good hackstoke;
On this you must hew and knoch:
Shall non be idle in this flocke,
Ne now may no man fayle.

Uxor Ham.

And I will goe to gather slicke,
The shipp for to cleane and piche:
Anoynted it must be, every stich,
Board, tree, and pyn.

Uxor Japhet.

And I will gather chippes here
To make a fire for yow, in feere,
And for to dight yor dynner,
Against yow come in.

[*Tunc faciunt signa quasi laborarent cum diversis instrumentis.*]

Noe.

Now, in the name of God, I will begin
To make the shippe that we shall in,
That we be ready for to swym
At the coming of the floode.
These hurdes I joyne together,
To keep vs safe from the wedder,
That we may rome both hither and thider,
And safe be from this floode.
Of this tree will I have the mast
Tyde wth gables that will last;
Wth a sayle yarde for each blaste,
And each thing in the kinde.
With topeas he and bew sprytt,
Wth coardes and ropes I hold all meete
To sayle forth at the next weete.
This shipp is at an ende.

Noe.

Wife, in this castle we shall be keped;
My childer and thou I wold in leaped!

Vxor Noe.

In faith, Noe, I had as lief thou had slepped,
for all thy frankishfare,
For I will not doe after thy red.

Noe.

Good Wife doe as I the bydd.

Vxor Noe.

By Christ not, or I see more neede,
Though thou stand all the day and rave.

Noe.

Lord, that women be crabbed aye!
And never are meke, that dare I saye.
This is well sene by me to daye,
In witness of you each one.
Good wife, let be all this beere
That thou makes in this place here,

For all they were thou art master;
And so thou art, by St. John!

Deus.

Noe, take thou thy meanye,
And in the shippe hye that you be,
For none so righteous man to me
Is now on earth lyvinge.

Of cleane beastes wth thee thou take
Seaven and seaven, or thou slake,
Hee and shee make to make
Belyve in that thou bringe.

Of beastes uncleane two and two,
Male and female, without moe;
Of cleane fowles seaven alsoe,
The hee and shee together.

Of fowles uncleane two, and no more;
Of beastes as I said before:
That shall be saved throughe my lore,
Against I send the wedder.

Of all meates that must be eaten
Into the ship loke there be getten,
For that no way may be foryeten,
And doe all this by deene.

To sustayne man and beastes therein,
Aye, till the waters cease and blyn.
This world is filled full of synne,
And that is now well seene.

Seaven dayes be yet cominge,
You shall have space them into bringe;
After that, it is my lyking
Mankinde for to noye.

Forty dayes and forty nightes,
Rayne shall fall for their unrightes,
And that I have made through my mighte,
Now thinke I to destoye.

Noe.

Lord, at youre byddinge I am bayne,
Sith non other grace will gayne,
Hit will I fulfill fayne,
For gracious I the fynde.

A hundred wynters and twenty
This shipp making tarried have I:
If, through amendment, any mercye
Wolde fall vnto mankinde.

Have done, you men and women all;
Hye you, lest this water fall,
That each beast were in his stall
And into ship broughte.

Of cleane beastes seaven shall be,
Of vncleane two, this God bade me;
This floode is nye well may we see,
Therefore tary you noughte.

Sem.

Syrr, here are lyons, libardes in,
Horses, mares, oxen, and swyne,
Goates, calves, sheepe, and kine,
Here sitten thou may see.

Ham.

Camels, afses, men may finde,
Buck, doe, harte and hynde,
And beastes of all manner kinde,
Here bene, as thinckes mee.

Japhet.

Take here cattes and doggs to,
Otter, fox, fulmart also;
Hares, hopping gaylie, can yee
Have cowle here for to eate.

Vxor Noe.

And here are beares, wolfes sett,
Apes, owles, marmoset;

Weesells, squirrles, and ferret,
Here they eaten their meate.

Vxor Sem.

Yet more beastes are in this house!
Here cattes maken in full crowse;
Here a ratten, here a mouse,
They stand nye together.

Vxor Ham.

And here are fowles les and more,
Hearnes, cranes, and byttour,
Swans, peacocks, have them before!
Meate for this wedder.

Vxor Japhet.

Here are cocks, kites, crowes,
Rookes, ravens, many rowes;
Cuckoes, curlewes, whoso knows,
Each one in his kinde.
And here are doves, diggs, drakes,
Redshankes, running through ye lakes,
And each fowle that ledden makes,
In this shipp men may finde.

In the stage direction the sons of Noah are enjoined to mention aloud the names of the animals which enter; a representation of which, painted on parchment, is to be carried by the actors.

Noe.

Wife, come in, why standes thou there?
Thou art ever forward, that dare I sweare:
Come on Gods half, tyme yt were,
For feare lest that we drowne.

Vxor Noe.

Yea Syr, set vp yor sayle,
And rowe forth wth evill heale,
For, wthout any fayle,
I will not out of this towne.

But I have my gossips everichan,
One foote further I will not gone;
They shall not drowne, by St. John!
And I may save their lyfe.
They loved me full well, by Christ!
But thou wilt let them in thy chist,
Els rowe forth, Noe, whither thou list,
And get thee a new wife.

Noe.

Sem, some loe thy mother is wraw;
Forsooth, such another I do not know!

Sem.

Father, I shall sett her in, I trow,
Without any fayle.
Mother, my father after thee send,
And bydds thee into yonder ship wend:
Loke vp and se the wynde,
For we be ready to sayle.

Vxor Noe.

Sonne, goe againe to him, and say,
I will not come therein to daye!

Noe.

Come in, wife, in twenty devills waye;
Or els stand wthout.

Ham.

Shall we all fetche her in?

Noe.

Yea, sonnes, in Christs blessinge and myne,
I wolde you hyde you betyme,
For of this flood I am in doubte.

Japhet.

Mother, we pray yow altogether,
For we are here, yor childer;
Come into the ship fore feare of the wedder,
For his love that you boughte.

Uxor Noe.

That will I not for yo[r] call,
But if I have my gossips all.

Gossip.

The flood comes in full fleetinge fast,
On every side it breadeth in hast;
For feare of drowning I am agast:
Good gossip, let me come in!
Or let us drincke, or we depart,
For often tymes we have done soe;
For at a time thou drinckes a quarte,
And so will I or that I goe.

Sem.

In feyth, mother, yet you shall,
Whether you will or not!

[*Tunc ibit.*]

Noe.

Welcome, wife, into this boate!

Uxor Noe.

And have thou that for thy note!

[*Et dat alapam victa.*]

Noe.

Aha! marry this is hote!
It is good to be still.
A childer! methinkes this boate removes!
Our tarrying here hugelie me greves!
Over the lande the water spredes!
God doe as he will!
Ah, great God! thou art so good!
Now all this world is on a flood!
As I see well in sighte.
This window will I steake anon,
And into my chamber will I gone,
Till this water, so greate one,
Be slaked throughe thy mighte.

Noah, according to the stage directions, is now to shut the windows of the ark, and retire for a short time. He is then to chaunt the psalm, *Salva me, Domine!* and afterwards to open them and look out.

Now forty dayes are fullie gone,
Send a raven I will anone;
If aught were earth, tree, or stone,
Be drye in any place.
And if this fowle come not againe,
It is a signe, soth to sayne,
That drye it is on hill or playne,
And God hath done some grace.

A raven is now despatched.

Ah Lord! wherever this raven lie,
Somewhere is drye well I see;
But yet a dove, by my lewtye,
After I will sende.
Thou wilt turn againe to me,
For of all fowles that may flye,
Thou art most meke and hend.

The stage direction enjoins here that another dove shall be ready with an olive branch in its mouth, which is to be dropt, by means of a cord, into the hand of Noah.

Ah, Lord! blessed be thou aye,
That me hast comfort thus to daye!
By this sight, I may well saye,
This flood beginnes to cease.
My sweete doue to me brought hase
A branch of olyue from some place;
This betokeneth God has done vs some grace,
And is a signe of peace.
Ah, Lord! honoured most thou be!
All earthe dryes now I see;

But yet tyll thou commande me,
Hence will I not hye.
All this water is alwaye,
Therefore, as sone as I maye
Sacryfice I shall doe in faye
To The devoutlye.

Deus.

Noe, take thy wife anone,
And thy childer every one,
Out of the shippe thou shalt gone,
And they all with thee.
Beastes, and all that can flie,
Out anon they shall hye,
On earth to grow and multeplye:
I will y^t yt be soe.

Noe.

Lord, I thank the, through thy might,
Thy bydding shall be done in hight,
And, as fast as I may dighte,
I will doe the honoure.
And to the offer sacryfice,
Therefore comes in all wise,
For of these beastes that bene hise
Offer I will this stower.

[*Tunc egrediens archâ cum tota familia sua accipiet animalia sua et volucres, et offeret ea et mactabit.*]

Lord God, in majesty,
That such grace has graunted me,
When all was borne safe to be,
Therefore now I am boune.
My wife, my childer, my meanye,
With sacryfice to honour the
With beastes, fowles, as thou may se,
I offer here right sone.

Deus.

Noe, to me thou arte full able,
And thy sacryfice acceptable,
For I have found the true and stable,
On the now must I myn.
Warry earth will I no more,
That mans synne yt greves sore,
For of youth manfull yore
Has byn enclyned to synne.
You shall now grow and multeply,
And earth you edefie:
Each beast and fowle yt may flie
Shall be afrayd for yow.
And fishe in sea yt may flytte
Shall susteyne yow — I yow bebite:
To eate of them yow ne lett
That cleane bene you may knowe.
There as yow have eaten before
Grasse and rootes, sith you were bore,
Of cleane beastes, les and more,
I geve you leave to eate.
Safe bloode and fishe bothe in feare
Of wrong dead carren that is here,
Eates not of that in no manere,
For that aye you shall lett.
Manslaughter also yow shall flee,
For that is not pleasant to mee,
That shedes bloode, he or shee,
Ought where amonge mankinde.
That shedes bloode, his bloode shall be,
And vengence haue, that men shall se;
Therefore now beware now all yee
You fall not in that synne.
And forwarde now with yow I make,
And all thy seede, for thy sake,

Of suche vengence for to slake,
For now I have my will.
  Here I behet the a behest,
That man, woman, fowle, ne beaste,
With water, while the worlde shall last,
I will no more spill.
  My bowe betwene yow and me
In the firmament shall bee,
By verey tokens, that you may se,
That such vengence shall cease.
  That man, ne woman, shall never more,
Be wasted by water, as is before,
But for synne, that greveth sore,
Therefore this vengence was.
  Where cloudes in the welkin bene,
That ilke bowe shall be sene,
In tokennge that my wrath or tene,
Shold never this wroken bee.
  The stringe is turned toward yow,
And toward me bend is the bowe,
That such wedder shall never showe,
And this behet I the.
  My blessinge now I geve the here,
To the, Noe, my servant dere,
For vengence shall no more appeare;
And now farewell, my darling deere!

ANTICHRIST.

Antichristus.

De celso throno poli, pollens clarior sole,
Age vos monstrare, descendi vos judicare.
Reges et principes sunt subditi sub me venientes.
Sitis sapientes, vos semper in me credentes,
Et faciam flentes gaudere atque dolentes.
Sic omnes gentes gaudebunt in me sperantes.
Descendo presens rex pius et perlustrator;
Princeps eternus vocor, Christus vester salvator.
  All lordes in lande now belighte
That will be ruled throughout the righte,
Your savyour now, in your sighte,
Here may you safely see.
  Messias, Christe, and most of mighte,
That in the law was you beheight,
All mankynde to joye, to dighte,
Is comen, for I am hee.
  Of me was spoken, in prophesye
Of Moyses, David, and Esay;
I am he they call Messy,
Forebyer of Israell.
  Those that leeven on me steadfastly
I shall them save from anoy;
And joy, righte as have I,
Wth them I think to deal.
  But one hath ligged me here in lande,
Jesu he hight, I understande;
To further falsehood he cane founde,
And farde with fantayse.
  His wikednes he woulde not wounde,
Tell he was taken and put in bande,

And slayne throughe vertue of my sounde;
This is soth seekerly.
My people of Jewes he could twayne,
That there lande came the never in;
Then one them now must I myne,
And restore them agayne.
To buylde this temple will I not blyne,
As God honoured be therein:
And endlesse wayle I shall them wyne,
All that to me bene hayne.
One thinge me glades, be you boulde,
As Danyell the prophett before me tolde,
All women in worlde me love shoulde,
And there fayrenes to founde.
What say you kings, that here bene lente?
Are not my wordes at your assente?
That I am Christe omnipotente,
Leeve you not this eich one?

Primus Rex.

We leeven, Lorde, without let,
That Christe is not comen yet;
Yf thou be he, thou shal be set
In temple as God alone.

Secundus Rex.

Yf thou be Christe, called Messy,
That from our bale shall us lye,
Doe before us, masterye,
A signe that we may see.

Tercius Rex.

Then will I leeve that it is soe,
Yf thou doe wounders or thou goe;
Soe that thou save us from wo,
Then honoured shalte thou be.

Quartus Rex.

Houle have we leeved many a yeare,
And of our weyninge many a weare;

And thou be Christe nowe comen here,
Then maye thou stynte all stryffe.

Antichristus.

That I am Christe, and Christe will be,
By verye signes you shall see;
For dead men through my postee
Shall rise from death to life.
Now will I torne all, through my mighte,
Trees downe, the rootes uprighte;
That is marwayl to your sighte,
That frute growing upon.
Soe shall the groe and multeplye,
Through my mighte and my masterye;
I put you out of heresye,
Ty leeve me upon.
And bodyes that bene dead and slayne,
Yf I maye rayse them up agayne,
Then honour me with mighte and mayne,
Then shall no man you greeve.
Forsoth, then, after will I dye,
And rise agayne, throughe my postee;
Yf I maye doe this marvelously,
I red ye one me leeve.
Men buryed in graves you maye see,
What mastery, is now hope ye
To rayse them up, throughe my postee,
And all throughe myne accorde.
Whether I in my godhead be
By very signes you shall see:
Rise up, dead men, and honour me,
And know me for your Lorde.

[*Here the dead rise from their graves.*]

Primus Mortuus.

O lorde, to the I aske mercye!
I was dead but nowe live:

Now wott I well and witterly,
That Christe is hether come.

Secundus Mortuus.

Hym honour we and all men,
Devoutly kneelinge one our ken;
Worshipped be thou there, amen!
Christ our name is comen.

Antichristus.

That I shall fulfill wholly wrytten,
You shall wott and knowe well it;
For I am wall, weale, and wytt,
And lorde of every lande.

And as the prophet, Sophany,
Speaketh of me, full witterly,
I shall rehearse readely,
That clearke shall understande.

Now will I die that you shall see,
And rise agayne, through my postee;
I will in grave that you put me,
And worshipp me alone.

For in this temple a tombe is made,
There in my bodye shalbe layde;
Then will I rise as I have sayde;
Take teene to me eich one.

And after my resurreccion,
Then will I sit in greate renowne,
And my ghost send to you downe
In forme of fier, full sone.

I dye! I dye! now ame I dead.

Primus Rex.

Now, seyth this worthy lorde is dead,
And his grave is wth us leade,
To take his bodye, it is my read,
And bury it in a grave.

Secundus Rex.

For soth, and soe to us he sayde,
In a tombe he woulde be layde;
Now goe we forth all in abreade,
From disease he maye us save.

[*Then they pass over to Antichrist.*]

Tercius Rex.

Take we the bodye of this sweete,
And bury it low under the greete;
Now lorde comforte us! we the beseeke!
And sende us of thy grace.

Quartus Rex.

And yf he rise sone throughe his mighte,
From death to life, as he beheighte,
Hym will I honour daye and nighte,
As God in every place.

[*They now ascend from the tomb to the surface of the earth.*]

Primus Rex.

Now wott I well that he is dead,
For now in grave we have him layde;
Yf he rise, as he hath sayde,
He is full of great mighte.

Secundus Rex.

I cannot leeve hym upon,
But yf he rise hym selfe alone,
As he hath sayde to many one,
And shew hym here in sighte.

Tercius Rex.

Tell that my savyour be risen agayne,
In fayth my harte maye not be fayne,
Tell I hym see with joye.

Quartus Rex.

I must mourne with all my mayne,
Tell Christe be risen up agayne;

And of that mirrackle make us feigne,
Rise up, lorde, that we may see!

[Here Antichrist rises from the dead.]

Antichristus.

I rise, now reverence doe to me,
God gloryfyed created of degree,
Yf I be Christe, now leave you me
And worke after my wyse.

Primus Rex.

O lorde, welcome mayst thou be!
That thou art good now leeve we;
Therefore goe sit up in thy see,
And keep our sacryfice.

[Here they go over to Antichrist, and sacrifice to him.]

Secundus Rex.

For soth in seat thou shalte be set,
And honoured with laude greate,
As Moyses law that lasteth yet,
As he hath sayde before.

Tercius Rex.

O gracious lorde! goe siht downe then,
And we shall kneel upon our ken
And worshippe the, as thyne owne men,
And worke after thy lorde.

[Here Antichrist ascends the throne.]

Quartus Rex.

Hether we be comen, with good intente,
To make our sacryffice, lorde exelente!
With this lambe that I have here hente,
Kneelinge the before.

Antichristus.

I Lorde, I God, I High Justice,
I Christe that made the dead to rise;
Here I receive your sacryffice,
And blesse you fleshe and fell.

I will now sende my Holy Ghost,
You kinges also you I tell
To knowe me love, of mighte most
Of heaven, earth and hell.

[*Here his ghost descends.*]

Severales Reges.

A God, a Lorde, mickle of mighte,
This Holy Ghost is in us pighte;
Me thinkes my haste is very lighte
Seth it came into me.

Primus Rex.

Lorde, we thee honour day and night;
For thou shewest us in sighte,
Right as Moyses us beheighte,
Honoured must thou be.

Antichristus.

Yet worthy workes, to your will,
Of phrophesye I shall fulfill,
As Danyell phrophesyed untill
That landes should devyse.
You kinges I shall advaunce you all,
And because your regions be but small,
Cities, castells, shall you befall,
With townes and towers gaye.
And the gyftes I shal beheight
You shall have, as is good righte,
Hense ere I goe out of your sighte,
Eich one shall knowe his dole.
To the I gyve Lomberdy;
And to the Demarke and Hongarye;
And take thou Pontus and Italy;
And Rome it shal be thyne.

Secundus Rex.

Grante mercye, Lorde, your gyfts to daye,
Honour we will the alwaye;

For we were never so riche, in faye,
Nor non of all our kyne.

Antichristus.

Therefore, be true and steadfast aye,
And truely leeves on my law,
For I will harken one you to daye,
Stydfast yf you I fynde.

Enocke.

All mighty God, in majesty,
That made the heaven and earth to be,
Fier, water, stonne, and tree,
And man through thy mighte.
The poyntes of thy privity,
Any earthly man to see,
Is impossible, as thinkes me,
Or any worldly wighte.
Gracious Lorde, that art soe good,
That who soe longe in fleshe and blonde,
Hath granted life and heavenly food,
Let never our thought be defiled.
But geve us, Lorde, mighte and mayne,
Or wee of this shrew be slayne,
To converte thy people agayne,
That he hath thus defiled.
Synce first the worlde begane,
Through helpe of high heavenly Kinge,
I have lived in greete likeinge
In Parradiz wth out anoye.
Tell we harde takeinge
Of this theefes cominge,
That now on earth is reigninge,
And doth Godes folkes destroye.
To Parradiz taken I was that tyde,
This thefes cominge to abyde,
And Hely my brother here by syde
Was after sente to me.

With this champion we must chide,
That now in worlde walketh wyde,
To disprove his pompe and pride,
And payer all his postee.

Helyas.

O Lorde, that madest all thinge,
And longe hath lente us livinge,
Let never the devills power springe,
That man hath hym with in.
God gyve you grace, bouth oulde and younge,
To know deceate in his doinge,
That you may come to that likeinge
Of blys that never shal blyne.
I warne you all men, witterly,
This is Enocke, I am Hely,
Bene comen his errours to destroy,
That he to you now shewes.
He calles hym self Christe and Messi,
He lyes, for soth, apertely;
He is the Devill, you to anoye,
And for non other hym knowe.

Primus Rex.

Amen, what speake ye of Hely
And Enocke, the bene bouth in company,
Of our bloude the bene witterly,
And we bene of their kyne.

Quartus Rex.

We readen in bookes of our law,
And they to heaven were drawe,
And yet bene there is the common sawe,
Wrytten as men in aye fynde.

Enocke.

We bene those men, for soth, I wrys,
Comen to tell you doe amysse,
And bringe your soules to heaven blisse,
Yf y^t^ were any boote.

Helyas.

This devilles lyme that comen is,
That sayth heaven and earth is his;
Nowe we be ready, leeve you this,
Agaynst hym for to mote.

Primus Rex.

Yf that we here wytt mone
By profles of disputacion
That you have skill and reason,
With you we will abyde.

Secundus Rex.

Yf your skills may doe hym downe,
To dye with you we will be boune,
In hope of salvacion,
Whatsoever betyde.

Enocke.

To doe hym downe we shall assaye
Through mighte of Jesee, borne of a maye,
By righte and reason, as you shall say,
And that shall well here.

And for that cause hether we be sente
By Jesu Christe, omnipotente,
And that you shall not albe shente,
He bought you all full deare.

Be glade therefore and make good cheare, —
And I doe reade as I doe leare, —
For we be comen in good mannere,
To save you every one.

And dreade you not for that false feynde;
For you shall see hym cast behynde,
Or we departe, or from hym wynde,
And shame shall light hym one.

[*Here Enoch and Elijah shall pass over to Antichrist.*]

Saye, thou verye devilles lyme,
That sitts soe grysely and so gryme,

From hym thou came and shall to hym,
For many a soule thou deceives.
  Thou haste deceived men many a daye
And made the people to thy paye,
And bewiched them into a wronge waye
Wickedly wth thy wyles.

Antichristus.

  False features from me you fley!
Ame not I most in majesty?
What men dare name them thus to me,
Or make such distaunce?

Helyas.

  Fye one the feature! fye one thee!
The devilles owne nurry!
Through hym thou preachest and haste posty
A while, through sufferaunce.

Antichristus.

  O, ye ypocrytes that soe cryen!
Lossels lordens, soe lewdly lyen!
To spill my lawe, you spine!
That speach is good to spare.
  You that my true fayth defyne!
And needles my folke deiryne,
From hense hastely you hyne!
To you comes sorrowe and care.

Enocke.

  Thy sorrowe and care come one thy head!
For falsely, through thy wicked read,
Thy people is put to payne.
I woulde thy body were from thy head
Twenty myles from it lead,
Tell I brought yt againe.

Antichristus.

  But I shall teach you curteseye,
Your sairjour to knowe anon in hye!

False theffes, wth your heresye,
And yf you dare abyde —

Helyas.

Yes, for soth, for all thy pride,
Through grace of God all right,
Here we porpose for to abyde:
And all the worlde that is soe wyde
Shall wounder one the one every syde,
Sone in all mens sighte.

Antichristus.

Out one you theefles! bonth two,
Eich man maye see you be soe,
Alby your arraye,
Muffled in mantles non such I know,
I shall make you lowte full lowe,
Or I departe you froe,
To know me Lorde for aye.

Enocke.

We be no theefles we the tell,
Thou false feynde, comen from hell!
With thee we porpose for to mell,
My fellowe and I, in feare.
To knowe thy power and thy mighte,
As we these kinges, have be height,
And there to we be ready dighte,
That all men nowe maye heare.

Antichristus.

My mighte is moste I tell to thee,
I died, I rose, through my postee.
That all these kinges saw with theyr eye,
And every man and wiff.
And myrrackles and marveyles, I did, also,
I consell you therefore bonth two
To worshipp me, and no moe,
And let us nowe no more stryve.

Helyas.

They were no myrrackles, but maweless things,
That thou showest unto these kings,
Through thy feyndes crafte.
And as the flower now springs
Fayleth fayth and beings
So thy *joye* it reignes
That shalbe frome the rafte.

Antichristus.

Out one the theefle that sitts soe still!
Why wylt thou not speake them till.

Docter.

O lorde master, what shall I say then?

Antichristus.

I beshew both thy . . . .
Arte thou nowe for to kene,
I fayth, I shall the greeve.
Of my Godhead I made thee wise,
And set the ever at mickle price,
Now I woulde feele thy good advise,
And heare what thou woulde saye.
These losells they woulde me greeve,
And nothinge one me they wille leeve,
But ever be ready me to reprove,
And all the people of my law.

Docter.

O Lorde thou arte soe mickle of mighte,
Me thinke thou should mey chide no feight;
But curse them all, through thy mighte,
Then shal they fare full yll.
For those thou blesses they shall well speed,
And those thou curses they are but dead;
This is my consell and my read
Yender heretykes for to spill.

Antichristus.

The same I porposed, leeve thou to me,
All thinges I know through my postee,
But yet thy wytt I thought to se
What was thy intente.
Yt shall donne, right witterly,
The sentence geven full openly
With my mouth truely
Upon them shal be bente.
My curse I geve you to amende
Your meales,
From your heade unto your heeles,
Walke you forth, in twenty devills way!

Enocke.

Yea thou shalt never come inclysse,
For falsely with thy wyles,
The people is put in payne.

Antichristus.

Out one you theefles! why fare you this?
Whether had you rather have paine or bles,
I maye you save from all amysse.
I made the daye and eke the nighte,
And all thinges that is one earth growinge;
Flowers freshe that fayer can springe;
Also I made all other thinge —
The starres that be so brighte.

Helyas.

Thou lyest! vengence one thee fall!
Out one thee, wretch! wroth thee I shall!
Thou callest thee hinge and lorde of all!
A feeynde is the within!

Antichristus.

Thou lyest falsely, I thee tell!
Thou wylt be damned into hell.
I made the man of fleshe and fell,
And all that is lyveinge.

For other godes have you nowe,
Therefore worshippe me alone,
The wch hath made the water and stone,
And all at my lykeing.

Enocke.

For soth, thou lyest falsely;
Thou art a feynde comen to anoye
Godes people that standeth us by.
In hell I woulde thou were!

Helyas.

Fye on the fellow! fye on the! Fye;
For all thy wichcrafte and sorcerye!
To mote with the I am readye,
That all this people maye here.

Antichristus.

Out one you harlotts! whense come ye?
Where have you any other god but me?

Enocke.

Yes Christe, God in Trenity,
Thou false feature attaynte —
That sent his sonne from heaven see,
That for mankynde dyed one roode tree,
That shall sone make the to flee,
Thou feature false and faynte!

Antichristus.

Rybbaldes ruled out of raye!
What is the Trenety for to saye?

Helyas.

Thre personesas thou leeve maye
In one Godhead in free.

Father and Sonne, that is no ney,
And the Holy Ghost, styrringe aye,
That is one God verey,
Bene all thre named here.

Antichristus.

Out one you theefles! what sayen yee?
Will ye have one God and Thre?
How dare you soe saye?
Madmen therefore leeve one me
That am one God, soe is not hee,
Then maye you live in joye and lee,
All this lande I dare laye.

Enocke.

Ney tyrante, understand thou this
Without begyninge his Godhead is,
And also without endinge is,
Thus fully leeven we.
And thou that ingendered was amysse,
Haste begyninge and noro this bliss,
An ende shall have, no dreade there is,
Full fowle as men shall se.

Antichristus.

Wreches gowles, you be blente!
Gode sonne I am, from hym sente!
How dare you mayuteyne your intente,
Seith he and I be one?
Have I not synce I came hym froe,
Made the dead to rise and goe,
And to men I sent my ghoste alsoe
That leeved me upon.

Helyas.

Fye one the, fellow! fye one the! fye!
For through his mighte and his mastry,
By sufferaunce of God Almighty,
The people is blente through the.
Yf those men be raysed witterly,
Without the devills fantasye,
Here shalbe provyd perfectly,
That all men shall se.

Antichristus.

A fooles I red you leeve me upon,
To the people every eich one,
To put them out of doubte.
Therefore I red you hastely,
Converted to me most mightely, —
I shall you save from anoye,
And that I ame aboute.

Enocke.

Now of thy myrrackles woulde I se.

Helyas.

Therefore comen hether here we,
Doe what is thy great postee,
And some thereof to leeve.

Antichristus.

Some maye you se, yf you will abyde,
For I will neither feight ney chide;
Of all the worlde that is soe wyde
Therein is not my peace.

Enocke.

Bringe forth these men here in our sighte
That thou hast raysed agaynst the righte,
Yf thou be soe mickle of mighte
To make them eate and drinke.
For very god we will the knowe,
Such a signe if thou wylt show,
And doe thee reverence one a row,
All at thy lykeinge.

Antichristus.

Wreches dampned al be yee,
But nought for that it falleth me,
As gracious God abydinge be,
Yf you will mende your life.
You dead men rise, through my postee;
Come eate and drinke that men maye se,

And prove me worthy of dyety,
Soe shal we stynte al stryffe.

Primus Mortuus.

Lorde, thy bydinge I will doe aye,
And for to eate I will assaye.

Secundus Mortuus.

And I will al that I maye,
Will doe thy bydinge here.

Helyas.

Have here bread bouth two,
But I must blesse yt or I goe,
That the feynde, mankyndes foe,
One yt have no power.
This bread I blesse with my hande,
In Jesus name, I understande
The wbch is lorde of sea and lande,
And hinge in heaven soe hye.
In nomine Patris, that all hath wrought, —
Et Filii Virginis, that deare us bought, —
Et Spiritus Sancti, is all my thought, —
One God and persons thre.

Primus Mortuus.

Alas! put that breade out of my sighte,
To loke one yt I ame not lighte;
That printe that is upon yt pighte,
That putts me to greate feare.

Secundus Mortuus.

To loke one yt I ame not lighte,
That bread to me it is soe brighte,
And is my foe bouth daye and nighte,
And putts me to greate dreade.

Enocke.

Nowe, you men that hath done amysse,
You see well what his power is,
Convertes to hym I red, I wys
That you one rood hath boughte.

Tercius Rex.

And nowe we know appeartely
We have bene broughte in heresye,
Wth you to death we will for thy,
And never more torne our thoughte.

Quartus Rex.

Nowe, Enocke and Hely, yt is no ney,
You have taunted the tyrrant this same daye,
Blessed be Jesu, borne of a maye,
One hym I leeve upon.

Primus Rex.

Thou feature fere wth fantasye,
Wth sorcerye, wichcrafte and nigremy
Thou hast us led in heresye,
Fye one thy workes eich one.

Secundus Rex.

Jesu, for thy mickle grace,
Forgeve us al our trespasse,
And bring us to thy heavenly place,
As thou art God and man.

Nowe ame I wise made through thy mighte,
Blessed be thou Jesu daye and nighte!
This greesly groome greetes hym to feighte,
To slea us here anon.

Tercius Rex.

Of our lyves let us not reach,
Though we be slayne of such a wrech,
For Jesu his sake that maye us leech,
Our soules to bringe to blisse.

Quartus Rex.

That was well sayde, and soe I assente
To dye, for soth is my intente,
For Christes sake, omnipotente,
In cause that is righte wise.

Antichristus.

A false features torne you nowe!
You shalbe slayne, I make a vowe;
And those traytors that soe turned you,
I shall make them unfeayne.

That all other by very sighte
Shall knowe that I ame most of mighte;
For wth this sworde nowe will I feighte,
For al you shalbe slayne.

[*Here Antichristus kills them.*]

Michaell.

Antichristus nowe is comen this daye,
Reigne no longer thou ney maye,
He that hath led thee allwaye,
Nowe hym thou must goe to.

No more men shalbe slayne by the,
My Lorde will dead that thou be,
He that gyven the this postee
Thy soule shall under soe.

In synne ingendered fyrst thou was;
In synne leade thy life thou hast;
In synne nowe an ende thou made,
That marred hath many one.

Thre yeares and halfe one, witterly,
Thou hast had leeve to destroye
Godes people wickedly,
Through thy fowle read.

Nowe thou shalt knowe and witt, in hye,
That more is Godes majesty,
Than eke the devills and thyne thereby,
For nowe thou shalt be dead.

Thou hast ever served Sathanas,
And had his power in every place;

Therefore thou getts no other grace,
With hym thou must gone.

[*Here Michaell shall kill Antichristus, and Antichristus shall call aloud, Help! help! help!*]

Antichristus.

Helpe, Sathanas and Luciffier!
Belzabubb, bolde Balacheire!
Ragnell, Ragnell, thou art my deare!
Nowe face I wounder evill.

Alas! alas! where is my power?
Alas! my wittes is in a were!
Nowe bodye and soule bouth in feare,
And all goeth to the devill.

[*Here Antichristus shall die, and two devils shall come.*]

Primus Demon.

Anon, master, anon, anon!
From hell grounde I harde the grone.
I thought not to come my selfe alone,
For worshippe of thyne estate.

With us to hell thou shalbe gone,
For thy death we make greate mone,
To wyne more soules into our pond,
But now y^{t} is too late.

Secundus Demon.

With me thou shalbe, from me thou come,
Of me shall come thy last dome,
For thou hast well deserved;
And, through my mighte and my postee,
Thou hast lived in dignitye,
And many a soule deceived.

Primus Demon.

This bodye was gotten by myne assente
In cleane hordome, verament,
Of mother wombe or that he wente,
I was hym wth in.

And taughte hym aye, with myne intente,
Synne by wch he shalbe shente;
For he did my commandemente,
His soule shall never blyne.

Secundus Demon.

Nowe fellow, in fayth, greate mone we maye make,
For this lorde of estate that standeth us instead,
Many a fatt morsell we had for his sake
Of soules that have bene saved in hell by the head.
[*Here the devils carry Antichristus away.*]

Enocke.

A Lorde that al shall leade,
And bouth deeme the quiche and dead;
That reverence the thou one them read,
And them through righte releeved.

I was dead and righte here slayne,
But through thy mighte, Lorde, and thy mayne,
Thou hast me raysed up againe,
Thee will I love and leeve.

Helyas.

Yea, Lorde, blessed must thou be;
My fleshe gloryffyed now I se;
Witt ney sleight againste the
Conspired may be by no way.

Al that leeve in thee stedfastly
Thou helpes, Lorde, from al anoye;
For dead I was and nowe lyve I;
Honoured be thou aye!

Michaell.

Enocke and Hely come you anon;
My Lorde will that you with me gone
To heaven blisse, bouth bloude and bone,
Ever more there to be.

You have bene lange, for you bene wise,
Dwellinge in earthly parradize,
But to heaven where hym selfe is,
Nowe shall you goe with me.

[*Here the Archangel shall lead them to heaven, and shall sing «Gaudete.»*]

Finis — Deo Gracias!

COVENTRY

MIRACLE-PLAYS.

JOSEPH'S JEALOUSY.

Joseph.

How dame, how! vndo your dor! vndo!
  Ar ye at hom? why speke ye notht?

Susannah.

Who is ther? why cry ye so?
  Telle us your heraid: wyl ye ought?

Joseph.

Vndo yowr dor! I sey yow to,
  For to com in is all my thought.

Mary.

It is my spowse, that spekyth us to,
  Ondo the dor, his wyl were wrought.
Well come home, my husbond der!
  How have you ferd, in fer countre?

Joseph.

To gete our levynge, with owtyn dwere,
  I have sore laboryd, for the aid me.

Mary.

Husbond, ryght gracyously, now come he ye;
  It solacyth me sore, sothly, to se yow in syth.

Joseph.

Me merveylyth, wyff! surely your face I can not se,
But as the sonne with his bemys in the is most bryth.

Mary.

Husbond, it is, as it plesyth our Lord, that grace of hy grew.
Who that evyr beholdyth me, veryly,
They schal be grettly steryd to vertu;
For this gyfte, and many moo, good lord gramercy!

Joseph.

How hast thou ferde, jentyl mayde,
Whyl I have ben out of loıde?

Mary.

Sekyr, ser; beth nowth dysmayde,
Byth aftyr the wyl of Goddys sonde.

Joseph.

That semyth evyl, I am afrayd;
Thi wombe to hyge doth stonde;
I drede me sore I am betrayd,
Sum other man the had in honde,
Heıs, sythe, that I went.
Thy wombe is gret, it gynnyth to ryse,
Than has thou begownne a synnfull gyse,
Thy self thou art thus schent.
Now, dame, what thinge menyth this?
With childe thou gynnyst ryth gret to gon;
Sey me, Mary, this childys fadyr who is?
I pray the telle me, and that aıon?

Mary.

The fadyr of hevyn, and se, it is,
Other fadyr hath he non:
I dede nevyr forfete with man, I wys,
Wherefore, I pray yow, amende yowr mon:
This childe is Goddys, and yours.

Joseph.

Goddys childe! thou lyist, in faye,
God dede nevyr rape so with maye.

* * * *

But yit I say, Mary, whoos childe is this?

Mary.

Goddys and yours, I sey, I wys.

Joseph.

Ya, ya! all olde men, to me take tent,
And weddyth no wyff, in no kynnys wyse,
That is a yonge wench, be my asent,
For doute and drede and swych servyse.
Alas! Alas! my name is shent:
All men may me now dyspyse,
And seyn olde cokwold! thi bowe is bent
Newly now, after the frensche gyse.
Alas, and welaway!
Alas, dame! why dedyst thou so?
For this synne, that thou hast do,
I the forsake, and from the go,
For onys evyr, and dy.

Mary.

Alas gode spowse! why sey ye thus?
Alas dere hosbund amende your mod!
It is no man, but swete Jhus,
He wyll be clad in flesch and blood,
And of your wyff be born.

Saphor.

For sothe the Angel thus seyd he,
That Goddys sone, in trynite,
For mannys sake, a man wolde be,
To save that is forlorn.

Joseph.

An Angel! allas, alas! fy for schame!
Ye syn now, in that ye do say;

To puttyn an Angel in so gret blame.
Alas, alas! let be do way;
It was sum boy began this game,
That clothyd was clene and gay,
And ye geve hym now an Angel name.
Alas, alas! and welaway,
That evyr this game be tydde!
A dame! what thought haddyst thou?
Her may all men this proverbe trow,
That many a man doth bete the bow,
Another man hath the brydde.

Mary.

A gracyous God! in hefne trone!
Comforte my spowse in this hard cas;
Mercyful God amend his mone,
As I dede nevyr so gret trespas.

Joseph.

Lo, lo, sers! what told I yow,
That it was not for my prow,
A wyff to take me to,
And that is wel sene now;
For Mary, I make God a vow
Is grett with childe, lo!
Alas! why is it so?
To the busshop I wole it telle,
That he the lawe may here do,
With stonys her to qwelle.
Nay, nay, yet God forbede!
That I shuld do that vengeabyl dede.
But if I wyst, welaway!
I knew nevyr with her, so God me spede,
To ky of thynge, in word nor dede,
That towchyd velany.
Nevyr the less what for thy,
Thow she be meke and mylde,

With owth mannys compayny,
She myght not be with childe.
But I ensure me was it nevyr:
Thow yet she hath not done her devyr,
Rather than I shuld pleyny opynly,
Certeynly, yett, had I levyr
Forsake the countre for evyr,
And nevyr come in her compayny.
For, and men knew this velany,
In reproff thei wolde me holde,
And yett many bettyr than I,
Ya! hath ben made cokolde.
Now, alas! whedyr schal I gone?
I wot nevyr whedyr, nor to what place;
For often tyme sorrowe comyth sone,
And longe it is or it pace.
No comfort may I have here.
I wys, wyff, thou dedyst me wronge,
Alas I taryed from the to longe,
All men have pety enime amonge,
For to my sorrowe is no cher.

Mary.

God! that in my body art sesyd,
Thou knowist my husbond is dysplesyd,
To se me in this plight;
For unknowlage he is desesyd,
And therfor help that he were esyd,
That he myght knowe the ful profyght;
For I have levyr abyde respyt,
To kepe thi sone in priuite,
Graunted by the holy spyryt,
Than that it shulde be opyned by me.

God appears and instructs an Angel to desire Joseph will abide with Mary, she being pregnant by God himself.

Angel.

Joseph! Joseph! thou wepyst shyrle,
From thi wyff why comyst thou owte?

Joseph.

Good ser! lete me wepe my fyle;
Go forthe that wey, and lett me nowght.

The *Angel* requests him to return and cheer her: —

Sche is a ful clene maye,
I tolle ye God wyl of her be born,
And sche clene mayd as she was beforn,
To save mankynd that is forlorn;
Go-chere her, therefor, I say.

Joseph.

A! Lord God! benedicite!
Of thi gret comforte I thank the,
That thou sent me this space;
I myght wel a wyst parde,
So good a creature as sche,
Wold nevyr a done trespace

* * * *

Joseph then returns to Mary, and under a feeling of repentance and delight, says,

Alas! for joy, I qwedyr and qwake!
Alas! what hap now was this!
A mercy! mercy! my jentyl make,
Mercy! I have seyd al amys;
All that I have seyd her I forsake,
Your swete fete now let me kys.

Mary.

Nay lett be; my fete not thou them take;
My mowth ye may kys, I wys,
And welcome on to me.

Joseph.

Gramercy! my owyn swete wyff!
Gramercy! myn hert! my love! my lyff!

Schal I nevyr more mak suche stryff,
Betwyx me and the!

He tells her he is convinced: —

Had thou not ben a vertuous wyff,
God wold not a ben the with inne.

Joseph assures Mary that hereafter he will serve her, and worship the child; yet he expresses curiosity: —

And therefor telle me, and nothynge withhoulde,
The holy matter of your concepcion.

Mary relates, that the Angel Gabriel greeted her, and said,

God shulde be borne of my bode,
The fendys powste for to felle,
Thorowe the Holy Gost, as I well se:
Thus God, in me, wyl byde and dwelle.

Joseph expresses satisfaction, thanks God, is reconciled to Mary, and the performance concludes.

THE TRIAL OF MARY AND JOSEPH.

Primus Detractor.

A! A! serys, God save you all!
Here is a fayr pepyl, in good fay.

* * * * *

To reyse blawdyr is al my lay,
Bakbyter is my brother of blood.
Dede he ought come hedyr in al this day;
Now wolde God that he wer here,
And, be my trewth, I dare wel say,
That, if we tweyn, togedyr apere,
Mor slawndyr we to schal arere,
Within an howre, thorwe outh this town,
Than evyr ther was this thowsand yer,
And ellys I shrewe you, bothe vp and down.
Now, be my trewth, I have a syght,
Euyn of my brother, lo wher he is: —
Welcom, der brother! my trowth I plyght,
Yowr jentyl mowth let me now kys.

Secundus Detractor.

Gramercy! brother, so have I blys;
I am ful glad we met this day.

Primus Detractor.

Ryght so am I, brother, I wys,
Moch gladder than I kan say.
But yitt good brother, I yow pray,
Telle, al these pepyl, what is yowr name:
For yf thei knew it, my lyf I lay,
Thei wole yow wurchep, and spek gret fame.

Secundus Detractor.

I am bakbyter, that spyllyth all game,
Bothe kyd and knowyn, in many a place.

Primus Detractor.

Be my trowth, I seyd the same;
  And yet sum seyden thou shulde have evyl grace.

Secundus Detractor.

Herk! reyse sclaundyr: canst thou owth telle
  Of any newe thynge that wrought was late?

Primus Detractor.

Within a shorte whyle a thynge befelle,
  I trowe thou wylt lawgh ryghtt wel therate,
For, be trowth, ryght mekyl hate,
  If it be wyst, therof wyl growe.

Secundus Detractor.

If I may reyse ther with debate,
  I schal not spare the seyd to sowe.

Primus Detractor.

Syr, in the tempyl, a mayd ther was,
  Calde mayd Mary; the trewth to tell,
Sche seruyd so holy, with inne that plas,
  Men seyd sche was fedde with holy Angell;
Sche made a vow with man nevyr to melle,
  But to leve chast, and clene virgine,
Howevyr it be, her wombe doth swelle,
  And is as gret as thyne or myne.

They discourse for some time upon this news, but in terms not befitting modern refinement.

The Bishop, Abizachar, enters with two Doctors of Law. They listen to part of the slander, and at last the *Bishop* says,

I charge you serys of your fals cry,
  For sche is sybbe of my owyn blood.

Secundus Detractor.

Syb of thi kyn thow that she be,
  All gret with chylde her wombe doth swelle;
Do calle her hedyr, thi self schal se,
  That it is trewthe that I thee telle.

Primus Detractor.

Ser, for yowr sake, I schal kepe cowncelle,
  Yow for to greve I am ryght loth,
But list, syrs, lyst, what seyth the belle?
  Our fayr mayd now gret with childe goth.

Principalis Doctor Legum.

Make good heed, sers, what ye doth say,
  Avyse yow wele what ye present,
If this be fownde fals, anothyr day
  Ful sore ye schal yowr tale repent.

Secundus Detractor.

Ser, the mayd, forsothe, is good, and gent,
  Both comely, and gay, and a fayr wench;
And, feetly, with help, sche can consent,
  To set a cokewolde on the hye benche.

Episcopus.

This verey talys my hert doth greve,
  Of hir to here such fowle dalyawnce,
If she be fowndyn in such repreve,
  She schal sore rewe her governawns.
Sym Somnor, in hast wend thou thi way,
  Byd Joseph, and his wyff, be name
At the coorte to apper this day,
  Here hem to pourge of her defame;
Sey that I here of hem grett schame,
  And that doth me gret hevynes,
If thei be clene, withowtyn blame,
Byd hem come hedyr, and shewe wyttnes.

Denunciator.

All redy, ser, I schal hem calle,
  Here at yowr coorte for to apper,
And, yf I may hem mete with all,
  I hope ryght sore thei schal ben her.
Awey, sers! let me com nerne;
  A man of wurchep here comyth to place.

Of curtesy, me semyth, ye be to lerne,
  Do of yow bodys, with an evyl grace!
Do me sum wurchep befor my face,
  Or, be my trowth, I shall yow make
If that I rolle yow up in my race,
  For fer I schal do yowr limbs qwake,
But yit sum mede, and ye me take,
  I wyl withdrawe my gret rough toth.
Gold, or sylvyr, I wyl not forsake,
  But evyn as all Somnors doth.
A, Joseph! good day, with thi fayr spowse;
  My lorde, the buschop, hath for yow sent,
It is hym tolde that in thi house
  A cockolde is —

Mary.

Of God, in hevyn, I take wyttnes,
  That synful werk was nevyr my thought,
I am a mayd yit, of pure clennes,
  Lyke as I was into this werd brought.

Denunciator.

Othyr wyttnes shall non be sought;
  Thou art with childe, eche man may se;
I charge yow bothe ye tary nought,
  But, to the buschop, com forth, with me.

Joseph.

To the buschop, with yow, we wende;
  Of our purgacion have we no dowth.

Mary.

Almighty God shal be our frende,
  When the trewthe is tryed owth.

Denunciator.

Ha! on this wyse, excusyth her, every scowte,
  When her owyn synne hem doth defame:

But lowly therin thei gyn to lowth,
  Whan thei be gylty, and fowndyn in blame.
Therfore come forth cokewolde —

Denunciator upbraids them further, and brings them before the Bishop, whom he thus addresses: —

My lord, the buschop; here haue I brought
  This goodly copyl, at yowr byddyng;
And, as me semyth, as be here, fraught
  Fayr chylde, lullay, sone must she syng.

Primus Detractor.

To her a credyl ye wolde brynge,
  Ye myght saue mo1y in her purse,
Becawse she is yowr cosyn, — thinge,
  I pray yow, ser, lete her nevyr far the wers.

Episcopus.

Alas, Mary! what hast thou wrought?
  I am a schamyd evyn for thi sake.

* * * *

Tell me who hath wrought this wranke,
  How hast thou lost thi holy name?

Mary.

My name, I hope, is saff and sownde,
  God to wyttnes I am a mayd.

* * * *

Of fleschly lust and gostly wownde
  In dede nor thought I nevyr asayd.

Secundus Doctor Legum.

Herke thou, Joseph; I am afrayd
  That thou hast wrought this opyn synne:
This woman thou hast thus betrayd,
  With gret flaterynge, or sum fals gynne.

Secundus Detractor.

Now, be my trowth, ye hytte the pynne,
  With that purpose in feyth I holde,
Tell now how thou thus hir dudyst wynne,
  Or knowlych thi self for a cockewold?

Joseph.

Sche is, for me, a trewe clene mayde,
  And I, for hir, am clene also;
Of fleschly synne I nevyr asayde,
  Sythyn that sche was weddyd me to.

Episcopus.

Thou schalt not schape from vs, yitt so,
  Fyrst thou shalte tellyn us another lay:
Streyt to the awter thou shalt go,
  The drynge of vengeawns ther to asay.
Here is the botel of Goddys vengeauns:
  This drynk shall be now thi purgacion:
This hath suche vertu, by Goddys ordenauns,
  That what man drynk of this potacion,
And goth straightway in processyon,
  Here in this place this awter abowth,
If he be gylty, sum maculacion,
  Pleyn in his face, schal shewe it owth.

[*Hic JOSEPH bibit et sepcies circumit altare dicens —*

This drynk I take, with meke entent,
  As I am gyltles, to God I pray;
Lord! as thou art omnypotente,
  On me then shewe the trowth this day.

[*Modo bibit.*]

About this awter I take the way;
  O gracyous God help thi servaunt,
As, I am gyltles, ageyn you may;
  Thi hand of mercy, this tyme, me graunt.

Denunciator.

This olde shrewe may not wele gon.
  Longe he taryeth to go abowth;

Lyft up thi feet, set forth thy ton,
  Or, be my trewth, thou getyst a clowte.

Joseph is sorely upbraided and taunted, by Denunciator and the Detractors, whilst he paces round the altar.

Joseph.

A, gracyous God! help me this tyde,
  Ageyn this pepyl, that doth me defame:
As I nevyr more dede towche her syde,
  This day help me, from werdly schame,
Aboute this awter to kepe my fame.
  vij tymes I haue gon rowid abowte,
If I be wurthy to suffyr blame,
  O, ryghtful God! my synie shewe owghte.

Episcopus.

Joseph; with herte, thaık God, thi lorde,
  Whos hey mercy doth the excuse;
For thi purgacion we schal recorde,
  With hyr, of syıie, thou dedyst nevyr muse;
But, Mary, thi self mayst not refuse,
  All grett with chlyde we se the stonde;
What mystyz man dede the mysvse?
  Why hast thou synned ageyn thi husbonde?

Mary.

I trespacyd nevyr, with erthely wyght,
  Therof I hope, throwe Goddys sonde,
Her to be purgyd, befor yowr syght,
  From all synie cleie, lyke as my husbonde;
Take me the botel, out of yowr hoıde;
  Her schal I drynke, beforn yowr face,
Abowth this awter than schal I fonde
  vij tymes to go, by Godys grace.

Secundus Doctor Legum.

With Goddys hyg myght loke thou not rape,
Of thi purgacion wel the avyse;
Yf thou be gylty thou mayst not schape,
Bewar evyr of God that ryghtful justyce.
If God with vengeauns set on the his syse,
Not only thou, but all thi kyn is schamyd,
Bettyr it is to telle the trewth devyse,
Than God for to greve, and of hym be gramyd

Mary drinks of the water of vengeance, and walks around the altar, saying a prayer to God, which she concludes thus: —

Gabryel me, with wordys, he be forn,
That ye, of your goodnes, woulde become my chylde;
Help now of your hygness, my wurchep be not lorn,
A dere sone! I pray yow, help yowr modyr mylde.

Mary receives no harm from the potation, and the *Bishop,* in astonishment, declares, that

Sche is clene mayde, both modyr and wyff!

The Detractors suspecting some deceit, express their dissatisfaction.

Primus Detractor.

Be my fadyr sowle, here is gret gyle,
Because sche is syb of yowr kynreed:
The drynk is chaungyd, by sum fals wyle,
That sche no shame shulde haue this steed.

The Bishop orders Detractor to drink of the same cup.

Primus Detractor.

Syr, in good feyth, a draught I pulle,
If these to drinkers have not all spent.

He instanly becomes frantic from the draught; the Bishop and all present ask pardon of Mary for their suspicion and detraction, which she grants; she and Joseph congratulate each other; and the piece concludes.

THE

PAGEANT

OF

THE COMPANY OF SHEARMEN AND TAILORS,

IN COVENTRY.

Although the Transcriber of this Pageant in 1534, complacently announces that it is «nevly correcte", we must nevertheless regret the loss of older copies; for the orthography of «Robert Croo" is so illiterate and confused, as not to exhibit the language of his times in a fair and appropriate, dress. The Speech of the « *Nonceose* " in French is particularly corrupted.

THE NATIVITY.

Isaye.

The sofferent thatt seithe evere seycrette,
He saue you all and make you perfett and stronge:
And gevenes grace wt his marce forto mete,
For now in grett mesere mankynd ys bownd.
The sarpent hathe gevin vs soo mortall a wonde,
That no creature ys abull vs forto reyles
Tyll thye right vncion of Jvda dothe seyse;
Then schall moche myrthe and joie in cresse,
And the right rote in Isaraell sprynge,
Thatt schall bryng forthe the greyne off whollenes:
And owt of danger he schall vs bryng
In to thatt reygeon where he ys kyng:
Wyche abowe all othur far dothe a bownde,
And thatt cruell Sathan he schall confownde.
Where fore I cum here apon this grownde,
To comforde eyuere creature off birthe;
For I Isaye, the profet, hathe fownde
Many swete matters, whereof we ma make myrth
On this same wyse.

For thogh that Adam be demid to deythe
W^t all his childur, asse Abell and Seythe:
Yett *ecce virgo consepeet;*
Loo, where a reymede schall ryse!
Be holde a mayde schall conseyve a childe,
And gett vs more grace than eyner men had:
And hir meydin od nothing defylid:
Sche ys deputyd to beare the sun almyghte God.
Loo, sufferntis now ma you be glad,
For of this meydin all we ma be fayne;
For Adam, that now lyis in sorrois full sade,
Hir gloreose birth schall reydeme hym ageyn
From bondage and thrall.
Now be myrre eyuere mon,
For this dede bryffly in Isarael schalbe done,
And before the fathur in trone,
Thatt schall glade vs all.
More of this matter fayne wolde I meve,
But lengur tyme I haue not here for to dwell.
That lorde that ys merecfull his merce soo in vs ma prove,
For to sawe owre sollis from the darknes of hell,
And to his blys he vs bryng asse he ys bothe lord and kyng,
And shalbe eyuerlastyng *in secula seculos:* amen.

Gaberell.

Hayle! Mare, full of grace, oure Lord God ys w^t the
Aboue all wemen that eyuer wasse;
Lade blesside mote thow be.

Mare.

All myght fathur and kyng of blys,
From all dysses thu saue me now:
For inwardely my spretis trubbuld ys,
Thatt I am amacid and kno nott how.

Gaberell.

Dred the nothyng meydin of this:
From heyvin a howe hyddur am I sent.
Of ambassage from that kyng of blys,

Unto the lade and virgin reyuerent,
Salutyng the here asse most exselent,
Whose vertu aboue all othur dothe abownde;
Wherefore in the grace schalbe fownde:
For thow schalt conseyve apon this grownd
The second persone of God in trone;
He wylbe borne of the alone, wt owt sin thu schalt hym see.
Thy grace and thi goodnes wyl neyuer be gone,
But eyuer to lyve in vergenete.

Mare.

I marvell soore how thatt mabe:
Manes cumpany knev I neyuer yett,
Nor neyuer to do kast I me,
Whyle thatt owre lord sendith me my wytt.

Gaberell.

The wholle Gost in the schall lyght,
And schall do thy soll soo wt vertu,
From the fathur thatt ys on hyght:
These wordis turtill the be full tru.
This chylde that of the schalbe borne,
Ys the seconde persone in trenete;
He schall saue that wase forlorne,
And the fyndis powar, dystroie schall he;
These wordis, lade, full tru the bene,
And furthur, lade, here in thy noone lenage.
Be holde Eylesabeth thy cosyn clene,
The wyche wasse barren and past all age,
Amd now wt chyld sche hath bene
Syx monethis, and more asse schalbe sene;
Where for discomforde the not Mare,
For to God onpossibull nothyng mabe.

Mare.

Now and yt be thatt lordis wyll,
Of my bodde to be borne and forto be;
Hys hy pleysuris forto full fyl,
Asse his one hande mayde I submyt me.

Gaberell.

Now blessid be the tyme sett,
That thu waste borne in thy degre:
For now ys the knott surely knytt,
And God conseyvide in trenete.
Now fare well lade off myghtis most,
Vnto the God hed I the be teyche.

Mare.

Thatt lorde the gyde in eyuere cost,
And looly he leyde me and be my leyche.

[*Here the Angell deptyth, and* **JOSOFF** *cumyth in and seyth:*—

Mare, my wyff soo dere!
How doo ye dame, and whatt chere
Ys wt you this tyde?

Mare.

Truly, husebonde, I am here,
Owre Lordis wyll forto abyde.

Josoff.

Whatt I troo thatt we be all schent:
Sey womon who hath byn here sith I went,
To rage wyth the.

Mare.

Syr, here wase nothur man nor mans eyvin,
But only the sond of owre Lorde God in heyvin.

Josoff.

Sey not soo womon, for schame ley be:
Ye be wt chyld soo wondurs grett,
Ye nede no more therof to tret,
Agense all right.
For sothe this chylde dame ys not myne,
Alas that eyuer wt my nynee
I suld see this syght.
Tell me womon whose ys this chyld?

Mare.

Non but youris husebond soo myld,
And thatt schalbe seyne.

Josoff.

But myne, allas! allas! why sey ye soo?
Wele awey womon, now may I goo
Be gyld as many a nothur ys!

Mare.

Na truly, sir, ye be not be gylde,
Nor yet w^{t} spott of syn I am not defylde;
Trust yt well huse bonde.

Josoff.

Huse bond in feythe, and that acold:
A weylle awey Josoff, as thow ar olde!
Lyke a fole now ma I stand and truse,
But in feyth, Mare, thu art in syn.
Soo moche ase I haue cheyrischyd the dame and all thi kyn,
Be hynd my bake to serve me thus:
All olde men insampull take be me;
How I am be gylid here may you see,
To wed soo yong a chyld.
Now fare well, Mare, I leyve the here alone,
Worthe the dam and thy warkis ycheone:
For I woll noo more be gylid be for frynd nor fooe.
Now of this ded I am soo dull,
And off my lyff I am soo full, no farthur ma I oo.

Angell j.

Aryse up Josoff, and goo whom ageyne
Vnto Mare thy wyff that ys soo fre;
To comford hir loke that thow be fayne,
For Josoff a cleyne meydin ys schee.
Sche hath conseyvid w^{t} owt any trayne
The seycond person in trenete:
Jhu schalbe hys name sarten,
And all thys world sawe schall be not agast.

Josoff.

Now, Lorde! I thanke the w^{t} hart full sad,
For of these tythyngis I am so glad,
Thatt all my care awey ys cast:

Wherefore to Mare I woll in hast.
A Mare! Mare! I knele full loo,
Forgeve me, swete wyff, here in this lond.
Marce, Mare! for now I kno
Of youre good gouernance and how yt doth stond:
Thoght thatt I dyd the mys name.
Marce, Mare! whyle I leve
Wyll I neyuer, swet wyff, the greve in ernyst, nor in game.

Mare.

Now thatt Lord in heyvin, sir, he you forgyve:
And I do for geve yow in hys name for euermore.

Josoff.

Now truly, swete wyff, to you I sey the same;
But now to Bedlem must I wynde,
And scho my self soo full of care,
And I to leyve you this grett behynd,
God wott the whyle dame how you schuld fare.

Mare.

Na hardely, husebond, dred ye nothyng,
For I woll walke w^{t} you on the wey.
I trust in God all myghte kyng
To spede right well in owre jurney.

Josoff.

Now I thanke you, Mare, of youre goodnes,
Thatt ye my wordis woll not blame;
And syth that to Bedlem we schall vs dresse,
Goo we to gedur in Goddis wholle name.
Now to Bedlem haue we leygis three,
The day ys ny spent, yt drawyth toward nyght:
Fayne at your es, dame, I wold that ye schulde be:
For you groue all werely, yt semyth in my syght.

Mare.

God haue marcy! Josoffe, my spowse, soo dere!
All profettis herto dothe beyre wyttnes,
The were tyme now draith nere
Thatt my chyld wolbe borne, wyche ys kyng of blis.

Vnto sum place, Josoff, kyndly me leyde,
Thatt I moght rest me wt grace in this tyde.
The lyght of the fathur ouer hus both spreyde,
And the grace of my sun wt vs here abyde.

Josoff.

Loo, blessid Mare! here schall ye lend,
Cheff chosyn of owre Lorde, and cleynist in degre;
And I for help to towne woll I wende.
Ys nott this the best dame. whatt sey ye?

Mare.

God haue marce! Josoff, my huse bond, soo meke!
And hartely I pra you goo now fro me.

Josoff.

Thatt schalbe done in hast, Mare, soo swete!
The comford of the wholle Gost leyve I wt the.
Now to Bedlem streyght woll I wynd,
To gett som helpe for Mare soo fre,
Sum helpe of wemen, God ma me send!
Thatt Mare, full off grace, pleysid ma be.

Pastor j.

Now God that art in trenete,
Thow sawe my fellois and me;
For I kno nott wheyre my scheepe nor the be,
Thys nyght yt ys soo colde.
Now ys yt nygh the myddis of the nyght,
These wedurs ar darke and dym of lyght,
Thatt of them can hy haue noo syght
Standyng here on this wold.
But now to make there hartis lyght,
Now will I full right stand apon this looe,
And to them cry wt all my myght:
Full well my voise the kno,
Wt hoo! fellois! hoo! hoo! hoo!

Pastor ij.

Hark, Sym, harke, I here owre brothur on the loe.
This ys hys woise, right well I knoo,

There fore toward hym lett vs goo,
And follo his woise a right.
See, Sym, se where he doth stond;
I am ryght glad we haue hym fond.
Brothur! where hast thow byn soo long,
And this nyght hit ys soo cold?

Pastor j.

E! fryndis! ther cam a pyrie of wynd w^{t} a myst suddenly,
Thatt forth off my weyis went I,
And grett heyvenes in made I,
And wase full sore afrayde;
Then forto goo wyst I nott whyddur,
But trawellid on this loo hyddur and thyddur;
I wasse so were of this cold weddur,
Thatt nere past wasse my myght.

Pastor iij.

Brethur, now we be past that fryght,
And hit ys far w^{t} in the nyght:
Full sone woll spryng the day lyght,
Hit drawith full nere the tyde.
Here awhyle lett vs rest,
And repast owreself of the best,
Tyll thatt the sun ryse in the est,
Let vs all here abyde.

[*There the* SCHEPPERDIS *drawys furth ther meyte, and doth eyte and drynk, and asse the drynk, the fynd the star and sey thus;* —

Brethur, loke vp and behold,
Whatt thyng ys yondur thatt schynith soo bryght,
Asse long ase eyuer I haue wachid my fold,
Yett sawe I neyuer soche a syght in fyld.
A ha! now ys cum the tyme that old fathurs hath told,
Thatt in the wynturs nyght soo cold,
A chyld of meydyn borne be he wold,
In whom all profeciys schalbe fullfyld.

Pastor j.

Truth y^t ys w^t owt naye,
Soo seyd the profett Isaye,
Thatt a chylde schuld be borne of a made soo bryght,
In wentur ny the schortist dey,
Or elis in the myddis of the nyght.

Pastor ij.

Loovid be God, most off myght!
That owre grace ys to see thatt syght:
Pray we to hym ase hit ys right,
Yff thatt hys wyll yt be,
Thatt we ma haue knoleyge of this syngnefocacion,
And why hit aperith on this fassion;
And eyuer to hym lett vs geve lawdacion,
In yerthe, whyle thatt we be.

[*There the Angelis syng* Glorea in exselsis Deo.]

Pastor iij.

Harke, the syng abowe in the clowdis clere;
Hard I neyuer of soo myrre a quere:
Now gentyll brethur draw we nere
To here there armony?

Pastor j.

Brothur, myrth and solas ys cum hus amony,
For be the swettnes of ther songe;
Goddis sun ys cum, whom we haue lokid for long,
Asse syngnefyith thys star that we do see.

Pastor ij.

Glore, *glorea in exselsis*, that wase ther songe;
How sey ye, fellois! seyd the not thus?

Pastor j.

Thatt ys welseyd, now goo we hence
To worschipe thatt chyld of hy manyffecence;
And that we may syng in his presence,
Et in tarra pax omynibus.

[*There the Schepperdis syngis* Ase I owt rodde, *and* ***JOSOFF*** *seyth:* —

Now Lorde this noise that I do here,
W^{t} this grett solemnete,
Gretly amendid hath my chere,
I trust hy nevis schortly wolbe.

[*There the Angellis syng* Gloria in cxselsis *ageyne.*]

Mare.

A! Josoff, husebond, cum heddur anon,
My chylde ys borne that ys kyng of blys.

Josoff.

Now welcum to me, the makar of mon,
W^{t} all the omage thatt I con;
Thy swete mothe here woll I kys.

Mare.

A! Josoff, husebond, my chyld waxith cold,
And we haue noo fyre to warme hym w^{t}.

Josoff.

Now in my armys I schall hym fold,
Kyng of all kyngis be fyld and be fryth:
He myght haue had bettur, and hym selfe wold,
Then the breythyng of these bestis to warme hym w^{t}.

Mare.

Now Josoff, my husbond, fet heddur my chyld,
The maker off man, and hy kyng of blys.

Josoff.

That schalbe done anon, Mare, soo myld!
For the brethyng of these bestis hath warmyd well I wys.

Angell j.

Hyrd men hynd drede ye nothyng,
Off thys star thatt ye do se;
For thys same morne Godis sun ys borne,
In Bedlem of a maydin fre.

Angell ij.

Hy you hyddur in hast;
Yt ys hys wyll ye schall hym see
Lyinge in a crybbe of pore reypaste,
Yett of Davithis lyne cumon ys hee.

Pastor j.

Hayle, mayde, modur, and wyff, soo myld!
Asse the Angell seyd, soo haue we fonde.
I haue nothyng to present w^t^ the chylde,
But my pype hold, take yt in thy hond;
Where in moche pleysure that I haue fond,
And now to oonowre thy gloreose byrthe,
Thow schallt yt haue to make the myrthe.

Pastor ij.

Now hayle be thow chyld, and thy dame,
For in apore loggyn here art thow leyde;
Soe the Angell seyde, and tolde vs thy name.
Holde, take thow here my hat on thy bedde,
And now off won thyng thow art well sped;
For weddur thow hast noo nede to complayne,
For wynde, ne sun, hayle, snoo, and rayne.

Pastor iij.

Hayle, be thow lorde ouer watur and landis,
For thy cumyng all we ma make myrthe;
Haue here my myttens to pytt on thi hondis,
Othur treysure haue I non to present the w^t^.

Mare.

Now, herdmen, hynd for youre comyng,
To my chylde schall I pra,
Asse he ys heyvin kyng, to grant you his blessyng,
And to hys blys that ye may wynd at your last day.

[*There the Schepperdis syngith ageyne, and goth forthe of the place, and the ij Profettis cumyth in and seyth thus;* —

Profeta j.

Novellis, novellis, of wondrfull mervellys!
Were hy and defuce vnto the heryng,
Asse scripture tellis these strange novellis to you I bryng.

Profeta ij.

Now hartely, syr, I desyre to knoo,
Yff hytt wolde pleyse you forto schoo
Of whatt maner a thyng.

Profeta j.

Were mystecall vnto youre heryng
Of the natevete off a kyng?

Profeta ij.

Of a kyng, wheice schuld he cum?

Profeta j.

From thatt reygend ryall, and mighty mancion,
The sede seylesteall and heyvinly vysedome;
The seycond person, aid Godis one sun,
For owre sake ys man be cum;
This godly spere desendid here,
In to a vergin clere sche on defyld,
Be whose warke obskevre
Owre frayle nature ys now begilde.

Profeta ij.

Why bathe sche a chyld?

Profeta j.

E! trust hyt well, and neuer the las,
Yet ys sche a mayde evin asse sche wasse,
And hir sun the kyng of Isaraell.

Profeta ij.

A wondur full marvell how thatt ma be,
And far dothe exsell all owre capasete,
How thatt the trenete of soo hy regallete,
Schuld be jonyd vnto owre mortallete.

Profeta j.

Of his one grett marce as ye schall se the exposyssion,
Throgh whose vmanyte all Adamis progene
Reydemyd schalbe owt of perdyssion;
Syth man did offend, who schuld amend,
But the seyd mon and no nothur;
For the wyche cawse he incarnate wold be,
And lyve in mesere asse manis one brothur.

Profeta ij.

Syr, vnto the deyite I beleve perfettle
Onpossibull to be there ys nothyng:

How be yt this warke vnto me ys darke,
In the opperacion or wyrkyng.

Profeta j.

Whatt more reypriff ys vnto belyff then to be dowtyng.

Profeta ij.

Yet dowtis oftymis hathe derevacion.

Profeta j.

Thatt ys be the meynes of comenecacion,
Of trawthis to haue a dev probacion,
Be the same dowts reysoning.

Profeta ij.

Then to you thys won thyng; —
Of whatt nobull and hy lenage ys schee,
Thatt myght this verabull princis modur be?

Profeta j.

Ondowtid sche ys cum of hy parrage,
Of the howse of Davith, and Salamon the sage,
And won off the same lyne joynid to hir be mareage,
Of whose trybe we do subscryve this chy[l]dis lenage.

Profeta ij.

And why in thatt wysse?

Profeta j.

For yt wasse the gysse
To conte the parant on the manys lyne,
And nott on the feymyne,
Amonst vs here in Isaraell.

Profeta ij.

Yett can I nott aspy, be no wysse,
How thys chylde borne schuldbe w[t] ow [t] naturis prejudyse.

Profeta j.

Nay no prejudyse vnto nature I dare well sey,
For the kyng of nature may hawe all at his one wyll.
Dyd not the powar of God make Aronis rod beyre frute
in on day?

Profeta ij

Truth yt ys in ded

Profeta j.

Then loke you and rede.

Profeta ij.

A! I preseyve the sede where apon thatt you spake;
Yt wasse for owre nede thatt he frayle nature did take,
And his blod he schuld schede amens forto make
For owre transegression,
Ase yt ys seyd in profece; — thatt of the lyne of Jude
Schuld spryng a right Messe,
Be whom all wee schalld haue reydemcion.

Profeta j.

S[r], now ys the tyme cum,
And the date there of run
Off his natevete.

Profeta ij.

Yett I beseke you hartele, that ye wold schoo me how
Thatt this straige nowelte were broght vnto you.

Profeta j.

This othur nyght soo cold,
Hereby apon a wolde,
Schepperdis wachyng there fold,
In the nyght soo far,
To them aperid a star,
And eyuer yt drev them nar;
Wyche star the did behold,
Bryghter the sey M folde,
Then the sun so clere
In his mydday spere;
And the these tythyngis tolde.

Profeta ij.

What seycretly?

Profeta j.

Na, na, hardely,
The made there of no conseil,
For the song ase lowde,

Ase eyuer the cowde,
Presyng the kyng of Isaraell.

Profeta ij.

Yett do I marvell,
In what pyle or castell,
These herdmen dyd hym see.

Profeta j.

Nothur in hallis, nor yett in bowris,
Borne wold he not be;
Nothur in castellis, nor yet in towris,
That semly were to se:
But att hys fathurs wyll,
The profeci to full fyll,
Be twyxt an ox and an as,
Ihu this kyng borne he was;
Heyvin he bryng us tyll!

Profeta ij.

Sr, a! but when these Schepperdis had seyne hym there,
In to whatt place did they repeyre?

Profeta j.

Forthe the went, and glad the were;
Going the did syng
Wt myrthe and solas, the made good chere,
For joie of thatt new tything.
And aftur asse I hard the tell,
He reywardid them full well,
He graunt them hevyn ther in to dwell.
In ar the gon wt joie and myrthe,
And there songe hit ys neowell.

[*There the Profettis gothe furthe, and Erod cumyth in and the Messenger.*]

Noncease.

Faytes pais, domnyis barons de grande reynowne!
Payis, seneoris schevaleris de nooble posance!
Pays, gentis homos companeonys petis egrance!
Je vos command dugard treytus sylance!

Payis tanque vottur nooble Roie syre ese peresance!
Que nollis perso ie ese non fawis perwynt dedfferance:
Nese harde de frappas, mayis gardus to cor paceance
Mayis gardus voter seneor to cor reyuerance;
Car elat vottur Roie tuto puysance. ·
Amon de leo pase, tos je vose cummande,
E lay Roie Erott——la, grandeaboly vos vmport.

Erode.

Qui statis in Jude et Rex Iseraell,
And the myghttyst conquerowre that eyuer walkid on grownd;
For I am evy i he thatt made bothe hevin and hell,
And of my myghte powar holdith vp this world rownd.
Magog and Madroke, bothe the did I confownde,
And wt this bryght bronde there bonis I brak on sund'r,
Thatt all the wyde worlde on those rappis did wond'r.
I am the cawse of this grett lyght and thund'r;
Yett ys throgh my fure that the soche noyse dothe make.
My feyrefull contena ice the clowdis so doth incumbur,
Thatt oftymis for dred ther of the verre yerth doth quake.
Loke when I wt males this bryght bro id doth. schake;
All the whole world from the north to the sowthe,
I ma them dystroie wt won worde of my mowthe.
To reycownt vnto you myn innevmerabull substance
Thatt were to moche for any to ig to tell;
For all the whole Orent ys vnd'r myn obbeydeance,
A id prynce am I of purgatorre, a id cheff capten of hell.
And those tyraneos trayturs be force ma I compell
Myne enmyis to vanquese, and evy i to dust them dryve,
A id wt a twynke of my ie iee not won to be lafte alyve.
Behold my contenance and my colur,
Bryghtur then the sun in the meddis of the dey!
Where can you haue a more grettur succur,
The i to behold my person that ys soo gaye;
My fawcun and my fassion wt my gorgis araye?
He thatt had the grace all wey ther on to thynke,
Lyve the myght all wey wt owt othur meyte or drynke;

And thys my tryomfande fame most hylist dothe a bownde,
Throgh owt this world in all reygeons abrod,
Reysemelyng the fauer of thatt most myght Mahownd;
From Jubytor be desent, and cosyn to the grett God,
And namyd the most reydowndid kyng Eyrodde,
Wyche thatt all pryncis hath vndur subjeccion,
And all there whole powar vndur my proteccion;
And therefore my barcode here callid Calcas,
Warne thow eyuer porte, thatt no schyppis a ryve,
Nor also aleond stranger throg my realme pas,
But the for there truage do pay markis fyve.
Now spede the forth hastele,
For the thatt wyll the contrare
Apon a galowse hangid schalbe;
And, be Mahownde, of me the gett noo grace.

Noncios.

Now, lord and mastur! in all the hast,
Thy worethe wyll ytt schall be wroght;
And thy ryall cuntreyis schalbe past,
In asse schort tyme asse can be thoght.

Erode.

Now schall owre regeons throgh owt be soght
In eyver place, bothe Est and West:
Yff any katyffis to me be broght
Yt schalbe nothyng for there best.
And the whyle thatt I do resst,
Trompettis, viallis, and othur armone,
Schall bles the wakyng of my maiste.

[Here Erod goth awey, and the iij Kyngis speykyth in the strete.]

Rex j.

Now blessid be God of his swet sonde,
For yondur a feyre bryght star I do see!
Now ys he commonn vs a monge
Asse the profettis seyd that yt schuld be.
Aseyd there schuld a babe be borne
Comyng of the rote of Jesse,

To sawe mankynd that wasse for lorne,
And truly come now ys he.
Reyuerence and worschip to hym woll I do,
Asse God and man thatt all made of noght.
All the profettis acordid and seyd evyn soo,
Thatt wt hys presseos blod mankynd schuld be boght.
He grant me grace be yonder star thatt I see,
And in to thatt place bryng me,
Thatt I ma hym worschipe wt umellete,
And se hys gloreose face.

Rex ij.

Owt off my wey I deme thatt I am,
For toocuns of thys cuntrey can I non see;
Now God thatt on yorth madist man,
Send me sum knolcyge where thatt I be.
Yondur me thynke a feyre bryght star I see,
The wyche be tocunyth the byrth of a chyld,
Thatt bedur ys cum to make man fre,
He borne of a mayde, and sche nothyng defyld;
To worschip thatt chyld ys myn in tent.
Forth now wyll I take my wey;
I trust sum cumpany God hath me sent,
For yondur I se a kyng labur on the wey;
To warde hym now woll I ryde.
Harke, cumly kyng, I you pray,
In to whatt cost wyll ye thys tyde,
Or weddur lyis yowre jurney?

Rex j.

To seke a chylde ys myne in tent,
Of whom the profettis bathe ment;
The tyme ys cum now ys he sent,
Be yondur star here ma [you] see.

Rex ij.

Sr, I prey you wt your lysence,
To ryde wt you vnto his presence;

To hym wyll I offur frank in sence,
For the hed of all whole churche schall he be.

Rex iij.

I ryde wanderyng in veyis wyde,
Ouer montens and dalis, I wot not where I am.
Now kyng of all kyngis send me soche gyde,
Thatt I myght haue knoleyge of this cuntreys name.
A yondur I se a syght be seymyng all afar,
The wyche be tocuns sum nevis ase I troo,
Asse me thynke a chyld peryng in a stare;
I trust he be cum thatt schall defend vs from woo.
To kyngis yundur I see, and to them woll I ryde,
Forto haue there cumpane I trust the wyll me abyde.
Hayle, cumly kyngis, augent!
Good surs, I pray you wheddur ar ye ment?

Rex j.

To seke a chylde ys owre in tent,
Wyche be tocuns yondur star asse ye ma see.

Rex ij.

To hym I purpose thys present.

Rex iij.

Surs, I pray you and thatt ryght vmblee,
W^{t} you thatt I ma ryde in cumpane;
To all myghte God now prey we,
Thatt hys pressiose persone we ma se.

[*Here Erode cumyth in ageyne, and the MESSENGERE seyth;* —

Hayle lorde, most off myght!
Thy commandement ys right.
In to thy land ys comyn thys nyght
iij kyngis, and w^{t} them a grett cumpany.

Erod.

Whatt make those kyngis in this cuntrey?

Noncios.

To seke a kyng and a chyld the sey.

Erode.

Of whatt age schuld he bee?

Noncios.

Skant twellve deyis old fulle.

Erod.

And wasse he soo late borne?

Noncios.

E! Syr, soo the schode me thys same dey in the morne.

Erod.

Now, in payne of deyth, bryng them me beforne;
And there fore, harrode, now hy the in hast,
In all spede thatt thow were dyght,
Or thatt those kyngis the cuntrey be past;
Loke thow bryng them all iij before my syght.
And in Jerusalem inquere more of thatt chyld?
But I warne the that thy wordis be mylde,
For there mast thow hede, and crafty wey
How to do his powere, and those iij kyngis shalbe begild.

Noncios.

Lorde, I am redde att youre byddyng,
To sarve the ase my lord and kyng,
For joye there of loo how I spryng,
Wt lyght hart and fresche gamboldyng,
Alofte here on this molde.

Erode.

Then sped the forthe hastely,
And loke thatt thow beyre the eyvinly:
And also I pray the hartely, thatt thow doo
Comand me bothe to yong and olde.

Nuncios.

Hayle, syr kyngis, in youre degre!
Erood, kyng of these cuntreyis wyde
Desyrith to speyke wt you all thre,
And for youre comyng he dothe abyde.

Rex j.

Syr, att his wyll we be ryght bayne.
Hy us brethur vnto thatt lordis place;

To speyke w^t hym we wold be fayne,
Thatt chyld thatt we seke, he grant vs of his grace!

Noncios.

Hayle, lorde w^t owt pere!
These iij kyngis here have we broght.

Erode.

Now welcum, syr kyngis, all in fere;
But of my bryght blesurs bassche ye noght.
S^r kyngis, ase I vndurstand
A star bathe gydid you into my land;
Where in grett harie ye haue founde,
Be reysun of hir beymis bryght;
Wherefore I pray you hartely,
The vere truthe thatt ye wold sertefy;
How long yt ys surely,
Syn of that star you had furst syght?

Rex j.

S^r kynge, the vere truthe sey.
And forto schoo you ase hit ys best,
This same ys evin the xii^{th} dey
Seyth yt aperid to vs to be west.

Erode.

Brethur, then ys there no more to sey,
But w^t hart and wyll kepe ye your jurney;
And cum whom by me this same wey,
Of your nevis thatt I myght knoo.
You schall tryomfe in this cuntre,
And w^t grett conquorde bankett w^t me:
And thatt chylde myself then woll I see,
And honor hym also.

Rex ij.

S^r, youre commandement we woll fulfyll,
And humbly abaye owreself there tyll;
He thatt weldith all thyng at wyll
The redde way hus teyche,
S^r kyng! thatt we ma pass your land in pes.

Erode.

Yes! and walke softely eyvin at your one es,
Youre pase porte for a C deyis,
Here schall you haue of clere cummand
Owre reme to labur any weyis,
Here schall you haue be spesschall grante.

Rex iij.

Now fare well kyng of hy, degre;
Humbly of you owre leyve we take.

Erode.

Then adev, Sr kyngis, all thre;
And whyle I lyve be bold of me;
There ys nothyng in this cuntre,
But for youre one ye schall yt take.
Now these iij kyngis ar gon on ther wey.
On wysely and on wyttely haue the all wroghte.
When the cum ageyne the schall dy thatt same dey,
And thus these vyle wreychis to deyth the schalbe broght;
Soche ys my lykyng.
He that agenst my lawys wyll hold,
Be he kyng or keysar, neyuer soo bold,
I shall them cast in to caris cold,
And to deyth I schall them bryng.

[*There Erode goth his weys, and the iij Kyngis cum in ageyne.*]

Rex j.

O blessid God, moche ys thy myght!
Where ys this star thatt gawe vs lyght?

Rex ij.

Now knele we downe here in this presence,
Be sekyng that lord of hy maugnefecens;
That we ma see his hy exsellence,
Yff that his swet wylbe.

Rex iij.

Yondur, brothur, I see the star,
Where by I kno he ys nott far;

Therefore, lordis, goo we nar
Into this pore place.

[*There the iij Kyngis gois in to the Jesen, to Mare, and hir child.*]

Rex j.

Hayle, Lorde thatt all this worlde hath wroght!
Hale, God and man to gedur in fere!
For thow hast made all thyng of noght,
Albe yt thatt thow lyist porely here.
A cupe full [of] golde here I haue the broght
In toconyng thow art wt owt pere.

Rex ij.

Hayle be thow, lorde of hy maugnyffecens!
In toconyng of presteod, and dyngnete of offece,
To the I offur a cupe full of in sence;
For yt be hovith the to haue soche sacrefyce.

Rex iij.

Hayle be thow, lorde longe lokid fore!
I haue broght the myre for mortalete,
In to cunyng thow schalt mankynd restore,
To lyff be thy deyth apon a tre.

Mare.

God haue merce, kyngis, of yowre goodnes!
Be the gydyng of the godhed hiddur are ye sent;
The provyssion of my swete sun your weyis whom reydres,
And gostely reywarde you for youre present.

Rex j.

Syr kyngis, aftur owre promes,
Whome be Erode, I mvst nedis goo.

Rex ij.

Now truly, berthur, we can noo las
But I am soo far wachid I wott not wat to do.

Rex iij.

Ryght soo am I, where fore I you pray,
Lett all vs rest vs awhyle upon this grownd.

Rex j.

Brethur, your seying ys right well vnto my pay;
The grace of thatt swet chylde saue vs all sownde.

Angell.

Kyng of Tawrus, Sr Jesper!
Kyıg of Arraby, Sr Balthasar!
Melchor kyng, of Aginare!
To you now am I sent.
For drede of Eyrode, goo you west whom
In to those perties when ye cum downe,
Ye schalbe byrrid w^t gret reynowne:
The wholle Gost thus knoleyge hath sent.

Rex j.

Awake, Sr Kyngis, I you praye,
For the voise of an Angell I hard in my dreme!

Rex ij.

Thatt ys full tru thatt ye do sey,
For he reyherssid owre names playıe.

Rex iij.

He bad thatt we schuld goo downe be west,
For drede of Eryrodis fawls be traye.

Rex j.

Soo forto do yt ys the best,
The child that we haue soght, gyde vs the wey!
Now fare well the feyrist of schapp soo swete,
And thankid be Jhu of his sonde,
Thatt we iij to gedur soo suddeıly schuld mete,
Thatt dwell soo wyde, and in strauıge lond,
And here make owre presentacion
Vnto this kyngis son clensid soo cleyne,
And to his modur for ovre saluacion;
Of moche myrth now ma we meyne,
Thatt we soo well hath done this obblacion.

Rex ij.

Now farewell, Sr Jaspar, brothur to you
Kyıg of Tawrus, the most worthe;

S[r] Balthasar, also to you I bow,
And I thanke you bothe of youre good cumpany,
Thatt we togeddur haue had.
He thatt made vs to mete on hyll,
I thanke hym now and eyuer I wyll;
For now may we goo owt yll,
And off owre offerynge be full fayne.

Rex iij.

Now syth thatt we mvst nedly goo
For drede of Erode, thatt ys soo wrothe,
Now fare well, brothur, and brothur also;
I take my leve here at you bothe
This dey on fote.
Now he thatt made vs to mete on playne,
And offurde to Mare in hir jeseyne;
He geve vs grace in heyvin a gayne
All to geyder to mete.

Nuncios.

Hayle, kyng most worthist in wede!
Hayle, manteinar of curterse throgh all this world wyde!
Hayle, the most myghtyst that eyuer bestrod a stede!
Ha[y]le, most monfullist mon in armor man to a byde!
Hayle, in thyne hoonowre!
Theese iij kyngis thatt forthe were sent,
And schuld haue cum ageyne before the here present,
Anothur wey, Lorde, whom the went
Contrare to thyn honoure.

Erode.

A nothur wey! — owt! owt! owt!
Hath those fawls traytvrs done me this ded?
I stampe, I stare, I loke all abowtt;
Myght I them take I schuld them bren at a glede!
I rent, I rawe, and now run I wode.
A! thatt these velen traytūrs hath mard thys my mode!
The schalbe hangid yf I ma cum them to.

[*Here Erode ragis in thys pagond, and in the strete also.*]

E! and thatt kerne of Bedlem, he schalbe ded,
And thus schall I for do his profece.
How sey you, Sr knyghtis, ys not this the best red,
Thatt all yong chyldur for this schuld be dede,
Wyth sworde to be slayne?
Then schall I, Erod, lyve in lede,
And all folke me dowt and drede,
And offur to me bothe gold, rychesse, and mede;
Thereto wyll the be full fayne.

Myles j.

My lorde, kyng Erode be name!
Thy wordis agenst my wyll schalbe,
To see so many yong chyldur dy, ys schame;
Therefore consell ther to gettis thu non of me.

Myles ij.

Well seyd, fello! my trawth I plyght;
Sr kyng! perseyve right well you may,
Soo grett a morder to see of yong frute,
Wyll make a rysyng in thi noone cuntrey.

Erode.

A rysyng! — owt! owt! owt!

[*There Erode ragis ageyne, and then seyth thus;* —

Owt, velen wrychis! har apon you I cry,
My wyll vtturly loke thatt yt be wroght,
Or apon a gallowse bothe you schall dy,
Be Mahownde, most myghtyste, thatt me dere hath boght!

Myles j.

Now, cruell Erode, syth we schall do this dede,
Your wyll nedefully in this realme moste be wroght;
All the chyldur of thatt age dy the most nede,
Now wt all my myght the schall be vpsoght.

Myles ij.

And I woll sweyre here apon your bryght sworde,
All the chyldur thatt I fynd sclayne the schalbe;
Thatt make many a modur to wepe

And be full sore aferde,
In owre armor bryght when the hus see.

Erode.

Now you have sworne forth that ye goo;
And my wyll thatt ye wyrke bothe be dey and nyght;
And then wyll I for fayne trypp lyke a doo;
But whan the be ded, I warne you, bryng ham be fore
my syght.

Angell.

Mare and Josoff! to you I sey,
Swete word from the fathur I bryng you full ryght; —
Owt of Bedlem in to Eygype forth goo ye the wey,
And wt you take the kyng full of myght,
For drede of Eroddis red.

Josoff.

A ryse up, Mare, hastely and sone!
Owre Lordis wyll nedys most be done,
Lyke ase the Angell vs bad.

Mare.

Mekely, Josoff, my one spowse,
Towarde that cuntrey let vs reypeyre.
Att Eygyp sum tocun off bowse,
God grant hus grace saff to cum there!

[*Here the Wemen cum in wythe there chyldur, syngyng them, and Mare and Josoff goth awey cleyne.*]

Woman j.

I lolle my chylde wondursly swete,
And in my barmis I do hyt kepe,
Be cawse thatt yt schuld not crye.

Woman ij.

Thatt babe thatt ys borne, in Bedlem, so meke,
He saue my chyld and me from velany!

Woman iij.

Be styll! be styll! my lyttul chylde!
That Lorde of lordis saue bothe the and me;

For Erode hath sworne w[t] wordis wyld,
Thatt all yong chyldur sclayne the schalbe.

Miles j.

Sey ye wyddurde, wyvis, wyddur ar ye a wey?
What beyre you in youre armis nedis mvst we see;
Yff the be man chyldur, dy the mvst thys dey,
For at Eroddis wyll all thyng mvst be.

Myles ij.

And I in handis wonys them hent,
Them forto sley noght woll I spare;
We most full fyll Erodis commandement,
Elis be we asse trayturs, and cast all in care.

Woman j.

S[r] knyghtis! of youre curtesse
Thys dey schame not youre chevaldre,
But on my child haue pytte,
For my sake in this tyde.
For a sympull sclaghtur yt were to sloo,
Or to wyrke soche a chyld woo,
Thatt can nodur speyke nor goo,
Nor neuer harme did.

Woman ij.

He thatt sleyis my chyld in syght,
Yff thatt my strokis on hym ma lyght,
Be he skwyar or knyght,
I hold hym but lost.
Se thow fawls losyngere,
A stroke schalt thow beyre me here,
And spare for no cost.

Woman iij.

Sytt he neyuer soo hy in saddull,
But I schall make his braynis addull,
And here w[t] my pott ladull,
W[t] hym woll I fyght.
I schall ley on hym athog, I wode were,
W[t] thys same womanly geyre;

There schall noo man steyre,
Wheddur thatt he be kyng or knyght.

Myles j.

Who hard eyuer soche a cry
Of wemen, thatt there chyldur haue lost,
And grettly reybukyng chewaldry,
Throgh owt this reme in eyuer cost,
Wyche many a mans lyff ys lyke to cost;
For thys grett wreyche thatt here ys done,
I feyre moche wengance ther off woll cum.

Myles ij.

E, brothur, soche talis may we not tell,
Where fore to the kyng lett vs goo,
For he ys lyke to beyre the bell,
Wyche wasse the cawser that we did soo;
Yett must the all be broght hym to,
Wt waynis and waggyns fully fryght:
I tro there wolbe a carefull syght.

Myles j.

Loo! Eyrode, kyng! here mast thow see
How many M' thatt we haue slayne.

Myles ij.

And nedis thy wyll full fyllid must be,
There ma no mon sey there ageyne.

Nuncios..

Eyrod, kyng! I schall the tell,
All thy dedis ys cum to noght;
This child ys gone in to Eygipte to dwell,
Loo! Sr, in thy one land what wondurs byn wroght.

Erod

Into Eygipte, alas! for woo,
Lengur in lande here I canot abyde;
Saddull my palfrey, for in hast wyll I goo
Aftur yondur traytturs now wyll I ryde,
Them for to sloo.

Now all men, hy fast,
In to Eygipte in hast;
All thatt cuntrey woll I tast,
Tyll I ma cum them to.

Fynes lude de Taylars and Scharmen.

T[h]ys matter
nevly correcte be Robart Croo,
the xiiijth dey of Marche;
fenyschid in the yere of owre Lorde God
MCCCCC and xxxiiij^{te}
then beyng Mayre, Mastur Palmur:
also Mastris of the seyd Fellyschipp, Hev. Corbett,
Randull Pynkard, and
John Baggely.

THEISE SONGES
BELONGE TO
THE TAYLORS AND SHEAREMENS PAGANT.

THE FIRST AND THE LASTE THE SHEPHEARDS SINGE,
AND THE SECOND OR MIDDLEMOST THE WOMEN SINGE.

THOMAS MAWDYCKE

die decimo tertio Mai; anno Domini quingentesimo nonagesimo primo. Prætor fuit civitatis Conventriæ D. Mathæus Richardson: tunc Consules Johannes Whitehead et Thomas Grauener.

SONG I.

As I out rode this enderes night,
Of thre ioli sheppardes I saw a sight,
And all a bowte there fold a star shone bright;
They sange, terli, terlow;
So mereli the sheppards ther pipes can blow.

SONG II.

Lully, lulla, thow littel tine child;
By, by, lully, lullay, thow littell tyne child;
By, by, lully, lullay.

O sisters too! how may we do,
For to preserve this day
This pore yongling, for whom we do singe
By, by, lully, lullay.

Herod, the king, in his raging,
Chargid he hath this day
His men of might, in his owne sight,
All yonge children to slay.

That wo is me, pore child for the!
And ever morne and day,
For thi parting nether say nor singe,
By, by, lully, lallay.

SONG III.

Doune from heaven, from heaven so hie,
Of angeles ther came a great companie,
Wt mirthe, and ioy, and great solemnitye
The sange, terly, terlow;
So mereli the sheppards ther pipes can blow.

TOWNELEY

MIRACLE-PLAYS.

PHARAO.

Pharao.

Peas, of payn that no man pas;
But kepe the course that I commaunde,
And take good hede of hym that has
Youre helthe alle holy in hys hande,
For kyng Pharro my fader was,
And led thys lordshyp of thys land;
I am hys hayre, as age wylle has,
Ever in stede to styr or stand.
Alle Egypt is myne awne
To leede aftyr my law,
I wold my myhte were knowne
And honoryd, as hit awe.
Fulle low he shalle be thrawne
That harkyns not my sawe,
Hanged hy and drawne,
Therfor no hoste ye blaw;
But, as for kyng, I commaund peasse,
To alle the people of thys empyre.
Looke no man put hym self in preasse,
Bot that wylle do as I desyre,

And of youre wordes look that ye seasse.
Take tent to me, youre soferand syre,
That may youre comfort most increasse,
And to my lyst howe lyfe and lyre.

Primus Miles.

My Lord, if any here were,
That wold not wyrk youre wylle;
If we myghte com thaym nere,
Fulle soyn we shuld theym spylle.

Pharao.

Thrughe out my kyngdom wold I ken,
And kun hym thank that wold me telle,
If any were so waryd men,
That wold my fors down felle.

Secundus Miles.

My Lord, ye have a maner of men
That make great mastres us emelle;
The Jues that won in Gersen,
Thay ar callyd chyldyr of Israel.
Thay multyplye fulle fast,
And sothly we suppose
That shalle ever last,
Oure lordshyp for to lose.

Pharao.

Why, how have thay syche gawdes begun?
Ar thay of myght to make sych frayes?

Primus Miles.

Yei, Lord, fulle felle folk ther was fun
In kyng Pharao, youre faders, dayes.
Thay cam of Josephe, was Jacob son,
He was a prince worthy to prayse;
In sythen in ryst have thay ay ron;
Thus ar thay lyke to lose youre layse,
Thay wylle confound you cleyn,
Bot if thay soner seasse.

Pharao.

What, devylle, is that thay meyn
That thay so fast incresse?

Secundus Miles.

How thay incres fulle welle we ken,
As oure faders dyd understand;
Thay were bot sexty and ten
When thay fyrst cam in to thys land;
Sythen have sojerned in Gersen
Four hundred wynter, I dar warand;
Now ar thay nowmbred of myghty men
Moo then ccc thousand,
Wythe outen wyfe and chyld,
Or hyrdes that kepe thare fee.

Pharao.

How thus myghte we be begyled!
Bot shalle it not be;
For wythe quantyse we shalle thaym quelle,
So that thay schalle not far sprede.

Primus Miles.

My Lord, we have hard oure faders telle,
And clerkes that welle couthe rede,
Ther shuld a man walk us amelle
That shuld fordo us and oure dede.

Pharao.

Fy on hym, to the devylle of helle,
Sych destyny wylle we not drede;
We shalle make mydwyfes to spylle them
Where any Ebrew is borne,
And alle menkynde to kylle them,
So shalle thay soyn be lorne.
And as for elder have I none awe,
Syche bondage shalle I to theym beyde,
To dyke and delf, bere and draw,
And to do all unhonest deyde;

So shalle these laddes be holden law,
In thraldom ever thare lyfe to leyde.

Secundus Miles.

Now, certes, thys was a sotelle saw,
Thus shalle these folk no farthere sprede.

Pharao.

Now help to bald theym downe,
Look I no fayntnes fynde.

Primus Miles.

Alle redy, Lord, we shalle be bowne,
In bondage thaym to bynde.

[*Tunc intrat Moyses cum virgâ in manu, etc,*]

Moyses.

Gret God, that alle thys warld began,
And growndyd it in good degre,
Thou mayde me, Moyses, unto man,
And sythen thou savyd me from the se,
Kyng Pharao had commawndyd than
Ther shuld no man chyld savyd be;
Agans hys wylle away I wan;
Thus has God showed hys might for me.
Now am I set to kepe,
Under thys montayn syde,
Byschope Jettyr shepe,
To better may betyde;
A, Lord, grete is thy myght!
What man may of yond mervelle meyn?
Yonder I se a selcowth syght,
Syche on in warld was never seyn;
A bush I se burnand fulle bryght,
And ever elyke the leyfes ar greyn,
If it be wark of warldely wyght,
I wylle go wyt wythoutyn weyn.

Deus.

Moyses! Moyses!

[*Hic properat ad rubum, et dicit ei Deus.* —

Moyses com not to nere,
Bot stylle in that stede thou dwelle,
And harkyn unto me here;
Take text what I the telle.
Do of thy shoyes in fere,
Wyth mowth as I the melle;
The place thou standes in there,
Forsoth, is halowd welle.
I am thy Lord, withouten lak,
To lengthe thi lyfe even as I lyst;
I am God that som tyme spake
To thyn elders, as thay wyst;
To Abraham, and Isaac,
And Jacob, I sayde shulde be blyst,
And multytude of them to make,
So that thare seyde shuld not be myst.
But now thys kyng, Pharao,
He hurtys my folk so fast,
If that I suffre hym so,
Thare seyde shuld soyne be past;
Bot I wylle not so do,
In me if thay wylle trast
Bondage to brynge thaym fro.
Therfor thou go in hast,
To do my message have in mynde
To hym, that me syche harme mase;
Thou speke to hym wythe wordes heynde,
So that he let my people pas
To wyldernes, that thay may weynde
To worshyp me as I wylle asse.
Agans my wylle if that thay leynd,
Ful soyn hys song shalle be, alas.

Moyses.

A, Lord! pardon me, wyth thy leyf,
That lynage luffes me noght;
Gladly thay wold me greyf,

If I syche bodworde broght.
Good Lord, lette som othere frast,
That has more fors the folke to fere.

Deus.

Moyses, be thou nott abast,
My bydyng shalle thou boldly here;
If thay wyth wrong away wold wrast,
Outt of the way I shalle the were.

Moyses.

Good Lord, thay wylle not me trast
For alle the othes that I can swere;
To neven sych noytes new
To folk of wykyd wylle,
Wyth outen tokyn trew,
Thay wylle not tent ther tylle.

Deus.

If that he wylle not understand
Thys tokyn trew that I shalle sent,
Afore the kyng cast down thy wand,
And it shalle turne to a serpent;
Then take the taylle agane in hand,
Boldly up look thou it hent,
And in the state thou it fand
Thou shal it turne by myne intent.
Sythen hald thy hand soyn in thy barme,
And as a lepre it shal be lyke,
And hole agane with outen harme;
Lo, my tokyns shal be slyke.
And if he wylle not suffre then
My people for to pas in peasse,
I shalle send venyance ix or ten,
Shalle sowe fulle sore or I seasse.
Bot ye Ebrewes, won in Jessen,
Shalle not be merkyd with that measse;
As long as thay my lawes wylle ken
Thare comforthe shalle ever increasse.

Moyses.

A, Lord, to luf the aght us welle
That makes thi folk thus free;
I shalle unto thaym telle
As thou has told to me.
Bot to the kyng, Lord, when I com,
If he aske what is thy name,
And I stand stylle, both deyf and dom,
How shuld I skape withoutten blame?

Deus.

I say the thus, *Ego sum qui sum*,
I am he that is the same;
If thou can nother muf nor mom,
I shalle sheld the from shame.

Moyses.

I understand fulle welle thys thyng;
I go, Lord, with alle the myght in me.

Deus.

Be bold in my blyssyng,
Thi socoure shalle I be.

Moyses.

A, Lord of luf, leyn me thy lare,
That I may truly talys telle:
To my freyndes now wylle I fare,
The chosyn childre of Israelle,
To telle theym comforthe of thare care,
In dawngere ther as thay dwelle.
God manteyn you evermare,
And mekylle myrthe be you emelle.

Primus Puer.

A, master Moyses, dere!
Oure myrthe is alle mowrnyng;
Fulle hard halden ar we here,
As carls under the kyng.

Secundus Puer.

We may mowrn, both more and myn,
Ther is no man that oure myrth mase;
Bot syn we ar alle of a kyn .
God send us comforth in thys case.

Moyses.

Brethere, of youre mowrnyng blyn,
God wylle delyver you thrughe his grace;
Out of this wo he wylle you wyn,
And put you to youre pleassyng place;
For I shalle carp unto the kyng,
And fownd fulle soyn to make you free.

Primus Puer.

God grant you good weyndyng,
And evermore with you be.

Moyses.

Kyng Pharao, to me take tent.

Pharao.

Why, boy, what tythynges can thou telle?

Moyses.

From God hym self hyder am I sent
To foche the chyldre of Israelle;
To wyldernes he wold thay went.

Pharao.

Yei, weynd the to the devylle of helle;
I gyf no force what he has ment;
In my dangere, herst thou, shalle thay dwelle;
And, fature, for thy sake,
Thay shalbe pent to pyne.

Moyses.

Then wylle God venyance take
Of the, and of alle thyn.

Pharao.

On me? fy on the lad, out of my land!
Wenys thou thus to loyse oure lay?

Say, whence is yond warlow with his wand
That thus wold wyle oure folk away?

Primus Myles.

Yond is Moyses, I dar warand,
Agans alle Egypt has beyn ay;
Greatt defawte with hym youre fader fand;
Now wylle he mar you if he may.

Pharao.

Fy on hym! nay, nay, that dawnce is done;
Lurdan, thou loryd to late.

Moyses.

God bydes the graunt my bone,
And let me go my gate.

Pharao.

Bydes God me? fals loselle, thou lyse!
What tokyn told he? take thou tent.

Moyses.

He sayd thou shuld dyspyse
Both me, and hys commaundement;
Forthy, apon thys wyse,
My wand he bad, in thi present,
I shuld lay downe, and the avyse
How it shuld turne to oone serpent.
And in hys holy name
Here I lay it downe;
Lo, syr, here may thou se the same.

Pharao.

A, ha, dog! the deville the drowne!

Moyses.

He bad me take it by the taylle,
For to prefe hys powere playn,
Then sayde, wythouten faylle,
Hyt shuld to a wand agayn.
Lo, sir, behold.

Pharao.

Wyth yl a haylle!
Certes this is a sotelle swayn;
Bot thyse boyes shalle abyde in baylle,
Alle thi gawdes shalle thaym not gayn;
Bot wars, both morne and none,
Shalle thay fare, for thi sake.

Moyses.

I pray God send us venjange sore,
And on thi warkes take wrake.

Primus Miles.

Alas, alas! this land is lorne!
On lyfe we may [no] longer leynd;
Syche myschefe is fallen syn morne,
Ther may no medsyn it amend.

Pharao.

Why cry ye so? laddes, lyst ye skorne?

Secundus Miles.

Syr kyng, syche care was never kend,
In no mans tyme that ever was borne.

Pharao.

Telle on, belyfe, and make an end.

Primus Miles.

Syr, the waters that were ordand
For men and bestes foyde,
Thrughe outt alle Egypt land,
Ar turnyd into reede bloyde;
Fulle ugly and fulle ylle is hytt,
That bothe freshe and fayre was before.

Pharao.

O, ho! this is a wonderfulle thyng to wytt,
Of all the warkes that ever wore.

Secundus Miles.

Nay, Lord, ther is anothere yit,
That sodanly sowys us fulle sore:

For todes and froskes may no man flyt,
Thay venom us so, bothe les and more.

Primus Miles.

Greatte mystes, sir, there is bothe morne and noyn,
Byte us fulle bytterly:
We trow that it be done
Thrughe Moyses, oure greatte enmy.

Secundus Miles.

My Lord, bot if this meyne may remefe;
Mon never myrthe be us amang.

Pharao.

Go, say to hym we wylle not grefe,
Bot thay shalle never the tytter gayng.

Primus Miles.

Moyses, my Lord gyffys leyfe
To leyd thi folk to lykyng lang,
So that we mend of oure myschefe.

Moyses.

Fulle welle, I wote, thyse wordes ar wrang;
Bot hardely alle that I heytt
Fulle sodanly it shalle be seyn:
Uncowth mervels shalbe meyt
And he of malyce meyn.

Secundus Miles.

A, Lord, alas, for doylle we dy!
We dar look oute at no dowre.

Pharao.

What, ragyd the dwylle of helle, alys you so to cry?

Primus Miles.

For we fare wars then ever we fowre;
Grete loppys over alle this land thay fly,
And where thay byte thay make grete blowre,
And in every place oure bestes dede ly.

Secundus Miles.

Hors, ox, and asse,
Thay falle downe dede, syr, sodanly.

Pharao.

We, lo, ther is no man that has
Half as myche harme as I.

Primus Miles.

Yis, sir, poore folk have mekylle wo,
To se thare catalle thus out east.
The Jues in Gessen fayre not so,
Thay have lykyng for to last.

Pharao.

Then shalle we gyf theym leyf to go
To tyme this perelle be on past;
Bot, or thay flytt oght far us fro,
We shalle them bond twyse as fast.

Secundus Miles.

Moyses, my Lord gyffes leyf
Thi meneye to remeve.

Moyses.

Ye mon hafe more myschefe
Bot if thyse talys be trew.

Primus Miles.

A, Lord, we may not leyde thyse lyfys.

Pharao.

What, dwylle, is grevance grofen agayn?

Secundus Miles.

Ye, sir, sich powder apon us dryfys,
Where it abides it makes a blayn;
Meselle makes it man and wyfe;
Thus ar we hurt with haylle and rayn.
Syr, mys in montanse may not thryfe,
So has frost and thoner thaym slayn.

Pharao.

Yei, bot how do thay in Gessen,
The Jues, can ye me say?

Primus Miles.

Of alle these cares no thyng thay ken,
Thay feylle noghte of our afray.

Pharao.

No? the ragyd, the dwylle, sytt thay in peasse?
And we every day in doute and drede?

Secundus Miles.

My lord, this care will ever encrese,
To Moyses have his folk to leyd;
Els be we lorne, it is no lesse,
Yit were it better that thai yede.

Pharao.

Thes folk shall flyt no far,
If he go welland wode.

Primus Miles.

Then wille it sone be war,
It were better thay yode.

Secundus Miles.

My lord, new harme is comyn in hand.

Pharao.

Yei, dwille, wille it no better be?

Primus Miles.

Wyld wormes ar layd over all this land,
Thai leyf no floure, nor leyf on tre.

Secundus Miles.

Agans that storme may no man stande;
And mekylle more mervelle thynk me,
Thatt these iij dayes has bene durand
Siche myst, that no man may other se.

Primus Miles.

A, my Lord!

Pharao.

Haghe!

Secundus Miles.

Grete pestilence is comyn;
It is like ful long to last.

Pharao.

Pestilence? in the dwilys name!
Then is oure pride over past.

Primus Miles.

My Lord, this care lastes lang,
And wille to Moyses have his bone:
Let hym go, els wyrk we wrang,
It may not help to hover ne hone.

Pharao.

Then wille we gif theym leyf to gang,
Syn it must nedes be doyn;
Perchauns we shalle thaym fang
And mar them or to morne at none.

Secundus Miles.

Moyses, my lord he says
Thou shalle have passage playn.

Moyses.

Now have we lefe to pas,
My freyndes, now be ye fayn;
Com furthe; now shalle ye weynd
To land of lykyng you to pay.

Primus Puer.

Bot kyng Pharao, that fals feynd,
He will us eft betray;
Fulle soyn he wille shape us to sheynd,
And after us send his garray.

Moyses.

Be not abast, God is oure freynd,
And alle oure foes wille slay;
Therfor com on with me,
Have done and drede you noght.

Secundus Puer.

That Lord blyst might he be,
That us from baylle has broght.

Primus Puer.

Siche frenship never we fand;
Bot yit I drede for perels alle,
The Reede See is here at hand,
Ther shal we byde to we be thralle.

Moyses.

I shalle make way ther with my wand,
As God has sayde, to sayf us alle;
On ayther syde the see mon stand,
To we be gone, right as a walle.
Com on wyth me, leyf none behynde,
Lo fownd ye now youre God to pleasse.

[*Hic pertransient mare.*]

Secundus Puer.

O, Lord! this way is heynd;
Now weynd us all at easse.

Primus Miles.

Kyng Pharao! thyse folk ar gone.

Pharao.

Say, ar ther any noyes new?

Secundus Miles.

Thise Ebrews ar gone, lord, everichon.

Pharao.

How says thou that?

Primus Miles.

Lord, that taylle is trew.

Pharao.

We, out tyte, that they were tayn:
That ryett radly shall thay rew;
We shalle not seasse to thay be slayn,
For to the see we shall thaym sew;
So charge youre chariottes swythe,
And fersly look ye folow me.

Secundus Miles.

Alle redy, lord, we ar fulle blythe
At youre byddyng to be.

Primus Miles.

Lord, at youre byddyng ar we bowne
Oure bodys boldly for to beyd;
We shalle not seasse, bot dyng alle downe,
To alle be dede withouten drede.

Pharao.

Heyf up youre hertes unto Mahowne,
He wille be nere us in oure nede;
Help, the raggyd dwylle, we drowne!
Now mon we dy for alle oure dede.

[*Tunc merget eos mare.*]

Moyses.

Now ar we won from alle oure wo,
And savyd out of the see;
Lovyng gyf we God unto,
Go we to land now merely.

Primus Puer.

Lofe we may that Lord on hyght,
And ever telle on this mervelle;
Drownyd he has Kyng Pharao myght,
Lovyd be that Lord Emanuelle.

Moyses.

Heven, thou attend, I say in syght;
And erthe my wordys, here what I telle.
As rayn or dew on erthe doys lyght
And waters, herbys, and trees fulle welle,
Gyf lovyng to Goddes mageste,
Hys dedys ar done, hys ways ar trew.
Honowred be he in trynyte,
To hym be honowre and verteu.

AMEN.

EXPLICIT PHARAO.

PASTORES.

Primus Pastor.

Lord, what these weders ar cold, and I am ylle happyd;
I am nere hande dold, so long have I nappyd;
My legys thay fold, my fyngers ar chappyd,
It is not as I wold, for I am al lappyd
In sorow.
In stormes and tempest,
Now in the eest, now in the west,
Wo is hym has never rest
Myd day nor morow.
Bot we sely shepardes, that walkys on the moore,
In fayth we are nere handes outt of the doore;
No wonder as it standys if we be poore,
For the tylthe of oure landes lyys falow as the floore,
As ye ken.
We are so hamyd,
For taxed and ramyd,
We ar mayde hand tamyd,
Withe thyse gentlery men.
Thus thay refe us oure rest, Oure Lady theym wary,
These men that ar lord fest thay cause the ploghe tary.
That men say is for the best we fynde it contrary,
Thus ar husbandes opprest, in point to myscary,
On lyfe.
Thus hold thay us hunder,
Thus thay bryng us in blonder,
It were greatte wonder,
And ever shuld we thryfe.
For may he gett a paynt slefe or a broche now on dayes,
Wo is hym that hym grefe, or onys agane says,
Dar no man hym reprefe, what mastry he mays,

And yit may no man lefe oone word that he says
          No letter.
He can make purveance,
With boste and bragance,
And alle is thrughe mantenance
          Of men that are gretter.
Ther shalle com a swane as prowde as a po,
He must borow my wane, my ploghe also,
Then I am fulle fane to graunt or he go.
Thus lyf we in payne, anger, and wo,
          By nyght and day;
He must have if he langyd,
If I shuld forgang it,
I were better be hangyd
          Then oones say hym nay.
It dos me good, as I walk thus by myn oone,
Of this warld for to talk in maner of mone:
To my shepe wylle I stalk and herkyn anone,
Ther abyde on a balk, or sytt on a stone
          Full soyne.
For I trowe, parde,
Trew men if thay be,
We gett more compane
          Or it be noyne.

Secundus Pastor.

Benste and Dominus! what may this bemeyne?
Why fares this warld thus oft have we not sene.
Lord, thyse weders ar spytus, and the weders fulle kene;
And the frost so hydus thay water myn eeyne,
          No ly.
Now in dry, now in wete,
Now in snaw, now in slete,
When my shone freys to my fete
          It is not alle esy.
Bot as far as I ken, or yit as I go,
We sely wodmen ure mekylle wo;

We have sorow then and then, it fallys oft so,
Sely Capyll, oure hen, both to and fro
She kakyls,
Bot begyn she to crok,
To groyne or to clok,
Wo is hym of oure cok,
For he is in the shekyls.
These men that ar wed have not alle thare wylle,
When they ar fulle hard sted thay syghe fulle stylle;
God wayte thay ar led fulle hard and fulle ylle,
In bower nor in bed thay say noght ther tylle,
This tyde.
My parte have I fun,
I know my lessun,
Wo is hym that is bun,
For he must abyde.
Bot now late in oure lyfys, a marvel to me,
That I thynk my hart ryfys siche wonders to see.
What that destany dryfys it shuld so be,
Som men wylle have two wyfys, and som men thre,
In store.
Som ar wo that has any;
Bot so far can I,
Wo is hym that has many,
For he felys sore.
Bot yong men of wowyng, for God that you boght,
Be welle war of wedyng, and thynk in youre thoght
„Had I wyst" is a thyng it servys of noght;
Mekylle stylle mowrnyng has wedyng home broght
And grefys,
With many a sharp showre,
For thou may cache in an owre
That shalle savour fulle sowre
As long as thou lyffys.
For, as ever red I pystylle, I have oone to my fere,
As sharp as thystylle, as rugh as a brere,

She is browyd lyke a brystylle, with a sowre, loten, chere;
Had she oones wett hyr whystyll she couth syng fulle clere
Hyr pater noster.
She is as greatt as a whalle,
She has a galon of galle,
By hym that dyed for us alle!
I wald I had ryn to I lost hir.

Primus Pastor.

God looke over the raw, fulle defly ye stand.

Secundus Pastor.

Yee, the deville in thi maw, so tariand,
Saghe thou awro of Daw?

Primus Pastor.

Yee, on a ley land
Hard I hym blaw, he commys here at hand,
Not far;
Stand tylle.

Secundus Pastor.

Qwhy?

Primus Pastor.

For he commys hope I.

Secundus Pastor.

He wylle make us both a ly~
Bot if we be war.

Tercius Pastor.

Crystes crosse me spede and Saint Nycholas,
Ther of had I nede, it is wars then it was.
Whoso couthe take hede, and lett the warld pas,
It is ever in drede and brekylle as glas,
And slythys.
This warld fowre never so,
With mervels mo and mo,
Now in weylle, now in wo,
And alle thyng wrythys.
Was never syn Noe floode sich floodes seyn,
Wyndes and ranys so rude, and stormes so keyn,

Som stamerd, som stod in dowte, as I weyn,
Now God turne alle to good, I say as I mene,
For ponder.
These floodes so thay drowne,
Both in feyldes and in towne,
And berys alle downe,
And that is a wonder.
We that walk on the nyghtys oure catelle to kepe,
We se sodan syghtes when othere men slepe:
Yet me thynk my hart lyghtes, I se shrewys pepe,
Ye ar two alle wyghtes, I wylle gyf my shepe
A turne.
Bot fulle ylle have I ment,
As I walk on this bent,
I may lyghtly repent,
My toes if I spurne.
A, sir, God you save, and master myne!
A drynk fayn wold I have and somwhat to dyne.

Primus Pastor.

Crystes curs, my knave, thou art a ledyr hyne.

Secundus Pastor.

What, the boy lyst rave, abyde unto syne
We have mayde it.
Ylle thryfte on thy pate!
Thoughe the shrew cam late
Yit is he in state
To dyne, if he had it.

Tercius Pastor.

Siche servandes as I, that swettys and swynkys,
Etys oure brede fulle drye, and that me forthynkys;
We are oft weytt and wery when master men wynkys,
Yit commys fulle lately both dyners and drynkys,
Bot nately.
Bothe oure dame and oure syre,
When we have ryn in the myre,

Thay can nyp at oure hyre,
        And pay us fulle lately.
Bot here my trouthe, master, for the fayr that ye make
I shalle do therafter wyrk, as I take;
I shalle do a lyttlle, sir, and emang ever lake,
For yit lay my soper never on my stomake
        In feyldys.
Wherto shuld I threpe?
With my staff can I lepe,
And men say «lyght chepe
        Letherly for yeldes."

Primus Pastor.

Thou were an ylle lad, to ryde on wowyng
With a man that had bot lytylle of spendyng.

Secundus Pastor.

Peasse boy I bad, no more janglyng,
Or I shall make the fulle rad, by the hevens kyng!
        With thy gawdys;
Wher ar oure shepe, boy, we skorne?

Tercius Pastor.

Sir, this same day at morne,
I them left in the corne,
        When thay rang lawdys;
Thay have pasture good, thay can not go wrong.

Primus Pastor.

That is right, by the roode, thyse nyghtes ar long,
Yit I wold, or we yode, oone gaf us a song.

Secundus Pastor.

So I thoght as I stode, to myrth us emong.

Tercius Pastor.

        I graunt.

Primus Pastor.

Lett me syng the tenory.

Secundus Pastor.

And I the tryble so hye.

Tertius Pastor.

Then the meyne fallys to me;
Lett se how ye chauntt.

[*Tunc intrat Mak in clamide se super togam vestitus.*]

Mak.

Now Lord, for thy naymes seven, that made both moyn and starnes
Welle mo then I can neven: thi wille, Lorde, of me tharnys;
I am alle uneven, that moves oft my harnes,
Now wold God I were in heven, for ther wepe no barnes
So stylle.

Primus Pastor.

Who is that pypys so poore?

Mak.

Wold God ye wyst how I foore!
Lo a man that walkes on the moore,
And has not alle his wylle.

Secundus Pastor.

Mak, where has thou gone? tell us tythyng.

Tercius Pastor.

Is he commen? then ylkon take hede to his thing.

[*Et accipit clamidem ab ipso.*]

Mak.

What, ich be a wyoman, I telle you, of the king;
The self and the same, sond from a greatt lordyng,
And siche.
Fy on you, goythe hence,
Out of my presence,
I must have reverence,
Why, who be iche?

Primus Pastor.

Why make ye it so qwaynt? Mak, ye do wrang.

Secundus Pastor.

Bot, Mak, lyst ye saynt? I trow that ye lang.

Tercius Pastor.

I trow the shrew can paynt, the dewylle myght hym hang!

Mak.

Ich shalle make complaynt, and make you alle to thwang
At a worde,
And tell evyn how ye doth.

Primus Pastor.

Bot Mak, is that sothe?
Now take outt that sothren tothe
And sett in a torde.

Secundus Pastor.

Mak, the dewille in your ee, a stroke wold I leyne you.

Tercius Pastor.

Mak, know ye not me? by God I couthe teyle you.

Mak

God looke you alle thre, me thought I had sene you.
Ye ar a fare compane.

Primus Pastor.

Can ye now mene you?

Secundus Pastor.

Shrew, jape;
Thus late as thou goys,
What wylle men suppoys?
And thou has an ylle noys
Of stelyng of shepe.

Mak.

And I am trew as steylle alle men waytt,
Bot a sekenes I feylle that haldes me fulle haytt,
My belly farys not weylle, it is out of astate.

Tercius Pastor.

Seldom lyys the dewylle dede by the gate.

Mak.

Therfore
Fulle sore am I and ylle,
If I stande stone stylle;
I ete not an nedylle
Thys moneth and more.

Primus Pastor.

How farys thi wyff? by my boode, how farys sho?

Mak.

Lyys walteryng, by the roode, by the fyere lo,
And a howse fulle of brude, she drynkys welle to,
Ylle spede othere good that she wylle do;
Bot so
Etys as fast as she can,
And ilk yere that commys to man,
She brynges furthe a lakan,
And som yeres two.
Bot were I not more gracyus, and rychere befar,
I were eten outt of howse, and of harbar,
Yit is she a fowlle dowse, if ye com nar:
Ther is non that trowse, nor knowys a war,
Then ken I.
Now wylle ye se what I profer,
To gyf alle in my cofer
To morne at next to offer
Her hed mas penny.

Secundus Pastor.

I wote so forwakyd is none in this shyre:
I wold slepe if I takyd les to my hyere.

Tercius Pastor.

I am cold and nakyd, and wold have a fyere.

Primus Pastor.

I am wery for rakyd, and run in the myre.
Wake thou!

Secundus Pastor.

Nay, I wylle lyg downe by,
For I must slepe traly.

Tercius Pastor.

As good a manys son was I
As any of you.
Bot, Mak, com heder, betwene shalle thou lyg downe.

Mak.

Then myght I lett you bedene: of that ye wold rowne,
No drede.

Fro my top to my too
Manus tuas commendo
Pontio Pilato,
Cryst crosse me spede.
[*Tunc surgit, pastoribus dormientibus, et dicit:*
Now were tyme for a man, that lakkys what he wold,
To stalk prively than unto a fold,
And neemly to wyrk than, and be not to bold,
For he myght aby the bargan, if it were told
At the endyng.
Now were tyme for to reylle;
Bot he nedes good counselle
That fayn wold fare weylle,
And has bot lytylle spendyng.
Bot abowte you a serkylle, as rownde as a moyn,
To I have done that I wylle, tylle that it be noyn,
That ye lyg stone stylle, to that I have doyne,
And I shall say thertylle of good wordes a foyne.
On hight
Over youre heydes my hand I lyft,
Outt go youre een, fordo your syght,
Bot yit I must make better shyft,
And it be right.
Lord! what thay slepe hard, that may ye alle here;
Was I never a shepard, bot now wylle I lere.
If the flok be skard, yit shalle I nyp nere,
How drawes hederward: now mendes oure chere
From sorow:
A fatt shepe I dar say,
A good flese dar I lay,
Eft whyte when I may,
Bot this wille I borow.
How, Gylle, art thou in? Gett us som lyght.
Uxor Ejus.
Who makys sich dyn this tyme of the nyght?
I am sett for to spyn: I hope not I myght

Ryse a penny to wyn: I shrew them on hight.
So farys
A huswyff that has bene
To be rasyd thus betwene:
There may no note be sene
For sich smalle charys.

Mak.

Good wyff, open the hek. Seys thou not what I bryng?

Uxor.

I may thole the dray the snek. A, com in, my swetyng.

Mak.

Yee, thou thar not rek of my long standyng.

Uxor.

By the nakyd nek art thou lyke for to hyng.

Mak.

Do way:
I am worthy my mete,
For in a strate can I gett
More then thay that swynke and swette
Alle the long day,
Thus it felle to my lot, Gylle, I had sich grace.

Uxor.

It were a fowlle blott to be hanged for the case.

Mak.

I have skapyd, Jelott, oft as hard a glase.

Uxor.

"Bot so long goys the pott to the water," men says,
"At last
Comys it home broken."

Mak.

Welle knowe I the token,
Bot let it never be spoken;
Bot com and help fast.
I wold he were flayn; I lyst well ete:
This twelmothe was I not so fayn of oone shepe mete.

Uxor.

Com thay or he be slayn, and here the shepe blete?

Mak.

Then myght I be tane: that were a cold swette.
Go spar
The gaytt doore.

Uxor.

Yis Mak,
For and thay com at thy bak.

Mak.

Then myght I by for alle the pak
The dewille of the war.

Uxor.

A good bowrde have I spied, syn thou can none:
Here shalle we hym hyde, to thay be gone;
In my credylle abyde. Lett me alone,
And I shalle lyg besyde in chylbed and grone.

Mak.

Thou red;
And I shalle say thou was lyght
Of a knave childe this nyght.

Uxor.

Now welle is me day bright,
That ever I was bred.
This is a good gyse and a far cast;
Yit a woman avyse helpys at the last.
I wote never who spyse: agane go thou fast.

Mak.

Bot I com or thay ryse, els blawes a cold blast.
I wylle go slepe.
Yit slepys alle this meneye,
And I shalle go stalk prevely,
As it had never bene I
That caryed thare shepe.

Primus Pastor.

Resurrex à mortruis: have hald my hand.
Judas carnas dominus, I may not welle stand:
My foytt slepys, by Jesus, and I water fastand.
I thoght that we layd us fulle nere Yngland.

Secundus Pastor.

A ye!
Lord! what I have slept weylle;
As fresh as an eylle,
As lyght I me feylle
As leyfe on a tre.

Tercius Pastor.

Benste be here in. So my qwakys
My hart is outt of shyn, what so it makys.
Who makys alle this dyn? So my browes blakys,
To the dowore wylle I wyn. Harke felows, wakys!
We were fowre:
Se ye awre of Mak now?

Primus Pastor.

We were up or thou.

Secundus Pastor.

Man, I gyf God a vowe,
Yit yede he nawre.

Tercius Pastor.

Me thoght he was lapt in a wolfe skyn.

Primus Pastor.

So are many hapt now namely within.

Secundus Pastor.

When we had long napt; me thoght with a gyn
A fatt shepe he trapt, bot he mayde no dyn.

Tercius Pastor.

Be stylle:
Thi dreme makes the woode:
It is bot fantom, by the roode.

Primus Pastor.

Now God turne alle to good,
If it be his wylle.

Secundus Pastor.

Ryse, Mak, for shame! thou lyges right lang.

Mak.

Now Crystes holy name be us emang,
What is this for? Sant Jame! I may not welle gang.
I trow I be the same. A! my nek has lygen wrang
Enoghe.
Mekille thank, syn yister even.
Now, by Sant Strevyn!
I was flayd with a swevyn
My hart out of sloghe.
I thoght Gylle began to crok, and travelle fulle sad,
Welner at the fyrst cok, of a yong lad,
For to mend oure flok: then be I never glad.
I have tow on my rok, more then ever I had.
A, my heede!
A house fulle of yong tharmes,
The dewille knok outt thare harnes
Wo is hym has many barnes,
And therto lytylle brede.
I must go home, by youre lefe, to Gylle as I thoght.
I pray you look my slefe, that I steylle noght:
I am loth you to grefe, or from you take oght.

Tercius Pastor.

Go furth, ylle myght thou chefe, now wold I we soght,
This morne,
That we had alle oure store.

Primus Pastor.

Bot I wille go before,
Let us mete.

Secundus Pastor.

Whore?

Tercius Pastor.

At the crokyd thorne.

Mak.

Undo this doore! who is here? how long shalle I stand?

Uxor Ejus.

Who makys sich a bere? now walke in the wenyand.

Mak.

A, Gylle, what chere? it is I, Mak, youre husbande.

Uxor.

Then may we be here, the dewille in a bande,
        Syr Gyle.!
Lo, he commys with a lote
As he were holden in the throte.
I may not syt at my note,
        A hand lang while.

Mak.

Wylle ye here what fare she makys to get hir a glose,
And do noght but lakys and clowse hir toose.

Uxor.

Why, who wanders, who wakys, who comys, who gose?
Who brewys, who bakys? what makes me thus hose?
        And than
It is rewthe to be holde,
Now in hote, now in colde,
Fulle wofulle is the householde
        That wants a woman.
Bot what ende has thou mayde with the hyrdys, Mak?

Mak.

The last worde that thay sayde, when I turnyd my bak,
Thay wold looke that thay have thare shepe alle the pak.
I hope thay wylle not be welle payde, when thay thare shepe lak.
        Perde.
Bot how so the gam gose,
To me they wylle suppose,
And make a foulle noyse,
        And cry outt apon me.
Bot thou must do as thou hyght.

Uxor.

I accorde me thertylle.
I shalle swedylle hym right in my credylle.
If it were a gretter slyght, yit couthe I helpe tylle.
I wylle lyg downe stright. Com hap me.

Mak.

I wylle.

Uxor.

Behynde.
Com Colle and his maroo,
Thay wylle nyp us fulle naroo.

Mak.

Bot I may cry out haroo,
The shepe if thay fynde.

Uxor.

Harken ay when thay calle: thay wille com anone.
Com and make redy alle, and syng by thyn oone,
Syng lullay thou shalle, for I must grone,
And cry outt by the walle on Mary and John,
For sore.
Syng lullay on fast
When thou heris at the last;
And bot I play a fals cast
Trust me no more.

Tercius Pastor.

A, Colle, goode morne: why slepys thou nott?

Primus Pastor.

Alas, that ever was I borne! we have a fowlle blot.
A fat wedir have we lorne.

Tercius Pastor.

Mary, Godes forbott!

Secundus Pastor.

Who shuld do us that shorne? that were a fowlle spott.

Primus Pastor.

Some shrewe.
I have soght with my doges

Alle Horbery shroges,
And of xv hoges
Fond I bot oone ewe.

Tercius Pastor.

Now trow me if ye wille; by Sant Thomas of Kent!
Ayther Mak or Gylle was at that assent.

Primus Pastor.

Peasse, man, be stille; I sagh when he went.
Thou sklanders hym ylle; thou aght to repent.
Goode spede.

Secundus Pastor.

Now as ever myght I the,
If I shuld evyn here de,
I wold say it were he,
That dyd that same dede.

Tercius Pastor.

Go we theder I rede, and ryn on oure feete.
Shalle I never ete brede, the sothe to I wytt.

Primus Pastor.

Nor drynk in my heede with hym tylle I mete.

Secundus Pastor.

I wylle rest in no stede, tylle that I hym grete,
My brothere
Oone I wille hight:
Tylle I se hym in sight
Shalle I never slepe one nyght
Ther I do anothere.

Tercius Pastor.

Wille ye here how thay hak, oure syre, lyst, croyne.

Primus Pastor.

Hard I never none crak so clere out of toyne.
Calle on hym.

Secundus Pastor.

Mak! undo youre doore soyne.

Mak.

Who is that spak, as it were noyne?
On loft,
Who is that I say?

Tercius Pastor.

Goode felowse, were it day.

Mak.

As far as ye may,
Good, spekes soft
Over a seke womans heede, that is at maylle easse,
I had lever be dede or she had any dyseasse.

Uxor.

Go to an othere stede; I may not welle qweasse.
Ich fote that ye trede goys thorow my nese
So hee.

Primus Pastor.

Telle us, Mak, if ye may,
How fare ye, I say?

Mak.

Bot ar ye in this towne to day?
Now how fare ye?
Ye have ryn in the myre, and ar weytt yit:
I shalle make you a fyre, if ye wille syt.
A nores wold I hyre; thynk ye on yit,
Welle qwitt is my hyre, my dreme this is itt
A seson.
I have barnes if ye knew,
Welle mo then enewe,
Bot we must drynk as we brew,
And that is bot reson.
I wold ye dynyd ar ye yode: me thynk that ye swette.

Secundus Pastor.

Nay, nawther mendys oure mode, drynke nor mette.

Mak.

Why, sir, alys you oght bot goode?

Tercius Pastor.

Yes, our shepe that we gett,
Ar stollyn as thay yode. Oure los is grette.

Mak.

Syrs, drynkes.
Had I bene thore
Some shuld have boght it fulle sore.

Primus Pastor.

Mary, some men trowes that ye wore,
And that us forthynkes.

Secundus Pastor.

Mak, some men trowes that it shuld be ye.

Tercius Pastor.

Ayther ye or youre spouse; so say we.

Mak.

Now if ye have suspowse to Gille or to me,
Com and rype oure howse, and then may ye se
Who had hir.
If I any shepe fott,
Aythor cow or stott,
And Gylle, my wyfe, rose nott
Here syn she lade hir.
As I am and true and lele, to God here I pray,
That this be the fyrst mele that I shalle ete this day.

Primus Pastor.

Mak, as have I ceylle, aryse the, I say,
He lernyd tymely to steylle that couth not say nay.

Uxor.

I swelt.
Outt, thefys, fro my wonys!
Ye com to rob us for the nonys.

Mak.

Here ye not how she gronys?
Your hartys shuld melt.

Uxor.

Outt, thefys, fro my barne! negh hym not thore.

Mak.

Wyst ye how she had farne, youre hartys wold be sore.
Ye do wraig, I you warne, that thus commys before
To a woman that has farne; bot I say no more.

Uxor.

A my medylle!
I pray to God so mylde,
If ever I you begyld,
That I ete this chylde,
That lyges in this credylle.

Mak.

Peasse, woman, for Godes payn, and cry not so:
Thou spyllys thy braue, and makes me fulle wo.

Secundus Pastor.

I trow oure shepe be slayn, what finde ye two?

Tercius Pastor.

Alle wyrk we in vayn: as welle may we go.
But hatters
I can fynde no flesh,
Hard nor nesh,
Salt nor fresh,
Bot two tome platers.
Whik catelle bot this, tame nor wylde,
None, as have I blys, as lowde as he smylde.

Uxor.

No, so God me blys, and gyf me joy of my chylde.

Primus Pastor.

We have marked amys: I hold us begyld.

Secundus Pastor.

Syr, don.
Syr, oure lady hym save,
Is youre chyld a knave?

Mak.

Any lord myght hym have
This chyld to his son.
When he wakyns he kyppys, that joy is to se.

Tercius Pastor.

In good tyme to hys hyppys, and in cele.
Bot who was hys gossyppys, so sore rede?

Mak.

So fare falle thare lypps.

Primus Pastor.

Hark now, a le.

Mak.

So God thaym thank,
Parkyn, and Gybon Waller, I say,
And gentille John Horne, in good fay,
He made alle the garray,
With the greatt shank.

Secundus Pastor.

Mak, freyndes wille we be, for we are alle oone.

Mak.

We now I hald for me, for mendes gett I none.
Fare welle all thre: alle glad were ye gone.

Tercius Pastor.

Fare wordes may ther be, but luf ther is none
This yere.

Primus Pastor.

Gaf ye the chyld any thyng?

Secundus Pastor.

I trow not oone farthyng.

Tercius Pastor.

Fast agayne wille I flyng,
Abyde ye me there.
Mak, take it to no grefe, if I com to thi barne.

Mak.

Nay, thou does me greatt repreffe, and fowlle has thou farne.

Tercius Pastor.

The child wille it not grefe, that lytylle day starne.
Mak, with youre lefe, let me gyf youre barne,
Bot vj pence.

Mak.

Nay, do way: he slepys.

Tercius Pastor.

Me thynk he pepys.

Mak.

When he wakyns he wepys.
I pray you go hence.

Tercius Pastor.

Gyf me lefe hym to kys, and lyft up the clowtt.
What the dewille is this? he has a long snowte.

Primus Pastor.

He is markyd amys. We wate ille abowte.

Secundus Pastor.

Ille spon weft, iwys, ay commys foulle owte.
Ay, so?
He is lyke to oure shepe.

Tercius Pastor.

How, Gyb, may I pepe?

Primus Pastor.

I trow, kynde wille crepe
Where it may not go.

Secundus Pastor.

This was a qwantte gawde, and a far cast.
It was a hee frawde.

Tercius Pastor.

Yee, syrs, wast.
Lett bren this bawde and bynd hir fast.
A fals skawde hang at the last;
So shalle thou.
Wylle ye se how thay swedylle
His foure feytt in the medylle?
Sagh I never in a credylle
A hornyd lad or now.

Mak.

Peasse byd I: what! lett be youre fare;
I am he that hym gatt, and yond woman hym bare.

Primus Pastor.

What dewille shall he hatt? Mak, lo God Makys ayre.

Secundus Pastor.

Let be alle that. Now God gyf hym care,
I sagh.

Uxor.

A pratty child is he
As syttes on a womanys kne;
A dylly dowre, perde,
To gar a man laghe.

Tercius Pastor.

I know hym by the eere marke: that is a good tokyn.

Mak.

I telle you, syrs, hark: hys noys was broken.
Sythen told me a clerk, that he was forspokyn.

Primus Pastor.

This is a false wark. I wold fayn be wrokyn:
Gett wepyn.

Uxor.

He was takyn with an elfe;
I saw it myself.
When the clok stroke twelf
Was he forshapyn.

Secundus Pastor.

Ye two ar welle feft, sam in a stede.

Tercius Pastor.

Syn thay manteyn thare theft, let do thaym to dede.

Mak.

If I trespas eft, gyrd of my heede.
With you wille I be left.

Primus Pastor.

Syrs, do my reede.
For this trespas,
We wille nawther ban ne flyte
Fyght nor chyte,
Bot have done as tyte,

And cast hym in canvas.
Lord! what I am sore, in poynt for to bryst:
In fayth I may no more, therfor wylle I ryst.

Secundus Pastor.

As a shepe of vij. skore he weyd in my fyst.
For to slepe ay whore, me thynk that I lyst.

Tercius Pastor.

Now I pray you,
Lyg downe on this gréne.

Primus Pastor.

On these theftes yit I mene.

Tercius Pastor.

Wherto shuld ye tene?
Do as I say you.

[*ANGELUS cantat "Gloria in excelsis:" postea dicat,* —

Ryse, byrd men heynd, for now is he borne
That shall take fro the feynd that Adam had lorne:
That warloo to sheynd, this nyght is he borne.
God is made youre freynd: now at this morne,
He behestys;
At Bedlem go se,
Ther lyges that fre
In a cryb fulle poorely,
Betwix two bestys.

Primus Pastor.

This was a qwant stevyn that ever yit I hard.
It is a marvelle to nevyn thus to be skard.

Secundus Pastor.

Of Godes son of hevyn he spak up ward.
Alle the wod on a levyn me thoght that he gard
Appere.

Tercius Pastor.

He spake of a barne
In Bedlem I you warne.

Primus Pastor.

That betokyns yonder starne.
Let us seke hym there.

Secundus Pastor.

Say, what was his song? hard ye not how he crakyd it?
Thre brefes to a long.

Tercius Pastor.

Yee, mary, he hakt it.
Was no crochett wrong, nor no thyng that lakt it.

Primus Pastor.

For to syng us emong, right as he knakt it,
I can.

Secundus Pastor.

Let se how ye croyne.
Can ye bark at the mone?

Tercius Pastor.

Hold youre tonges, have done.

Primus Pastor.

Hark after, than.

Secundus Pastor.

To Bedlam he bad that we shuld gang:
I am fulle fard that we tary to lang.

Tercius Pastor.

Be mery and not sad: of myrth is oure sang,
Ever lastyng glad to mede may we fang,
Withoutt noyse.

Primus Pastor.

Hy we theder for thy;
If we be wete and wery,
To that chyld and that lady
We have it not to slose.

Secundus Pastor.

We fynde by the prophecy — let be youre dyn —
Of David and Isay, and mo then I myn;
Thay prophecyed by clergy, that in a vyrgyn
Shuld he lyght and ly, to slokyn oure syn

And slake it,
Oure kynde from wo;
For Isay sayd so,
Cite virgo
Concipiet a chyld that is nakyd.

Tercius Pastor.

Fulle glad may we be, and abyde that day
That lufly to se, that alle myghtes may.
Lord welle were me, for ones and for ay,
Myght I knele on my kne som word for to say
To that chylde.
Bot the angelle sayd
In a cryb was he layde;
He was poorly arayd,
Both mener and mylde.

Primus Pastor.

Patryarkes that has bene, and prophetes beforne,
Thay desyrd to have sene this chylde that is borne.
Thay ar gone fulle clene, that have thay lorne.
We shalle se hym, I weyn, or it be morne
To tokyn.
When I se hym and fele,
Then wote I fulle weylle
It is true as steylle
That prophetes have spokyn.
To so poore as we ar, that he wold appere,
Fyrst fynd, and declare by his messyngere.

Secundus Pastor.

Go we now, lett us fare: the place is us nere.

Tercius Pastor.

I am redy and yare: go we in fere
To that bright.
Lord! if thi wylles be,
We ar lewd alle thre,
Thou grauntt us somkyns gle
To comforth thi wight.

Primus Pastor.

Haylle comly and clene; haylle yong child!
Haylle maker, as I meyne, of a madyn so mylde!
Thou has waryd, I weyne, the warlo so wylde,
The fals gyler of teyn, now goys he begylde.
Lo, he merys;
Lo, he laghys, my swetyng,
A welfare metyng,
I have holden my hetyng,
Have a bob of cherys.

Secundus Pastor.

Haylle, sufferan savyoure, for thou has us soght!
Haylle frely foyde and floure, that alle thyng has wroght!
Haylle fulle of favoure, that made alle of noght!
Haylle! I kneylle and I cowre. A byrd have I broght
To my barne.
Haylle lytylle tyne mop,
Of our crede thou art crop!
I wold drynk on thy cop,
Lytylle day starne.

Tercius Pastor.

Haylle, derlyng dere, fulle of godhede!
I pray the be nere when that I have nede.
Haylle! swete is thy chere: my hart wold blede
To se the sytt here in so poore wede
With no pennys.
Haylle! put furthe thy dalle,
I bryng the bot a balle:
Have and play the with alle,
And go to the tenys.

Maria.

The fader of heven, God omnypotent,
That sett alle on seven, his son has he sent.
My name couthe he neven and lyght or he went.
I conceyvid hym fulle even, thrugh myght as he ment;
And new is he borne.

He kepe you fro wo:
I shalle pray hym so;
Telle furth as ye go,
    And myn on this morne.

Primus Pastor.

Farewelle, lady, so fare to beholde,
With thy chylde on thi kne.

Secundus Pastor.

Bot he lyges fulle cold.
Lord! welle is me: now we go, thou behold.

Tercius Pastor.

For sothe alle redy, it semys to be told
    Fulle oft.

Primus Pastor.

What grace we have fun.

Secundus Pastor.

Com furthe, now ar we won.

Tercius Pastor.

To syng ar we bun:
    Let take on loft.

EXPLICIT PAGINA PASTORUM.

CRUCIFIXIO.

Pilatus.

Peasse I byd everyeich wight;
Stand as stylle as stone in walle,
Whyles ye ar present in my syght,
That none of ye clatter ne calle;
For if ye do youre dede is dyght,
I warne it you both greatte and smalle,
With this brand burnyshyd so bright,
Therfor in peasse loke ye be alle.
What! peasse in the dwillys name!
Harlottes and dustards alle bedene,
On galus ye be maide fulle tame,
Thefes and mychers keyn;
Wille ye not peasse when I bid you?
By Mahownys bloode! if ye me teyn,
I shalle ordan sone for you,
Paynes that never ere were seyn,
And that anone:
Be ye so bold beggars, I warn you,
Fulle boldly shalle I bett you,
To helle the dwille shalle draw you,
Body, bak, and bone.
I am a lord that mekylle is of myght,
Prynce of alle Jury, sir Pilate I highte,
Next kyng Herode gryttyst of alle,
Bowys to my byddyng bothe greatt and smalle,
Or els be ye shentt:
Therfore stere youre tonges, I warn you alle,
And unto us take tent.

Primus Tortor.

Alle peasse, alle peasse, emang you alle!
And herkyns now what shalle befalle
Of this fals chuffer here;
That with his fals quantyse,
Has lett hym self as God wyse,
Emanges us many a yere.
He cals hym self a prophett,
And says that he can bales bete,
And make all thynges amende;
Bot or lang wytt we shalle,
Wheder he can bete his awne bale,
Or skapp out of oure hende.
Was not this a wonder thyng,
That he durst calle hym self a kyng
And make so greatt a lee?
Bot, by Mahowne! whyls I may lyf
Those prowde wordes shalle I never forgyf,
Tylle he be hanged on he.

Secundus Tortor.

His pride, fy, we sett at noght,
Bot ich man kest in his thoght,
And looke that we noght wante;
For I shalle fownde, if that I may,
By the order of knyghtede, to day,
To cause his hart pante.

Tercius Tortor.

And so shalle I with alle my myght,
Abate his pryde this ylk nyght,
And rekyn hym a crede.
Lo, he lettes he cowde none ylle,
Bot he can ay, when he wylle,
Do a fulle fowlle dede.

Quartus Tortor.

Yei felows, yei, as have I rest;
Emanges us alle I red we kest

To bryng this thefe to dede:
Looke that we have that we shuld nate,
For to hald this shrew strate.

Primus Tortor.

That was a nobylle red;
Lo, here I have a bande,
If nede be to hynde his hande;
This thwong, I trow, wille last.

Secundus Tortor.

And here oone to the othere syde,
That shalle abate his pride,
Be it be drawen fast.

Tercius Tortor.

Lo, here a hamere and nales also,
For to festen fast oure foo
To this tre fulle soyn.

Quartus Tortor.

Ye are wise, withoutten drede,
That so can help yourself at nede
Of thyng that shuld be done.

Primus Tortor.

Now dar I say hardely,
He shalle with alle his mawmentry
No longere us be telle.

Secundus Tortor.

Syn Pilate has hym tylle us geyn,
Have done, belyfe, let it be seyn
How we can withe hym melle.

Tercius Tortor.

Now ar we at the Monte of Calvarye,
Have done, folows, and let now se
How we can with hym lake.

Quartus Tortor.

Yee, for as modee as he can loke,
He wold have turnyd an othere croke
Myght he have had the rake.

Primus Tortor.

In fayth, syr, sen ye callyd you a kyng,
Ye must prufe a worthy thyng
That falles unto the were;
Ye must just in tornamente,
Bot ye sytt fast els ye be shent,
Els downe I shalle you bere.

Secundus Tortor.

If thou be Godes son, as thou tellys,
Thou can the kepe; how shuld thou ellys?
Els were it mervelle greatt;
And bot if thou can, we wille not trow
That thou has saide, bote make the mow
When thou syttes in yond sett.

Tercius Tortor.

If thou be kyng we shalle thank adylle,
For we shalle sett the in thy sadylle;
For fallyng be thou bold:
I hete the welle thou bydys a shaft,
Bot if thou sytt welle thou had better laft
The tales that thou has told.

Quartus Tortor.

Stand nere, felows, and let se
How we can hors oure kyng so fre,
By any craft;
Stand thou yonder on yond syde,
And we shalle se how he can ryde,
And how to weld a shaft.

Primus Tortor.

Syr, commys heder and have done,
And wyn apon youre palfray sone,
For he redy bowne:
If ye be bond to hym be not wrothe,
For be ye secure we were fulle lothe
On any wyse that ye felle downe.

Secundus Tortor.

Knit thou a knott, withe alle thi strength,
For to draw this arme on lengthe,
Tylle it com to the bore.

Tercius Tortor.

Thou maddes, man, bi this light!
It waytys, tylle ich mans sight,
Othere half span and more.

Quartus Tortor.

Yit drawe out this arme and fest it fast,
Withe this rope, that welle wille last,
And ilk man lay hand to.

Primus Tortor.

Yee, and bynd thou fast that band,
We shalle go to that other hand
And loke what we can do.

Secundus Tortor.

Do dryfe a naylle ther thrughe outt,
And then thar us nothyng doutt,
For it wille not brest.

Tercius Tortor.

That shalle I do, as myght I thryfe,
For to clynk and for to dryfe
Therto I am fulle prest;
So let it styk, for it is wele.

Quartus Tortor.

Thou says sothe, as have I cele,
Ther can no man it mende.

Primus Tortor.

Hald downe his knees.

Secundus Tortor.

That shalle I do.
His noryse yede never better to;
Lay on alle your hende.

Tercius Tortor.

Draw out hys lymmes, let se, have at.

Quartus Tortor.

That was welle drawen that that,
Fare falle hym that so puld!
For to have getten it to the marke
I trow lewde man, ne clerk,
Nothyng better shuld.

Primus Tortor.

Hald it now fast thor,
And oone of you take the bore,
And then may it not faylle.

Secundus Tortor.

That shalle I do witthoutten drede,
As ever myght I welle spede,
Hym to mekylle bayle.

Tercius Tortor.

So, that is welle, it wille not brest,
Bot let now se who dos the best
Withe any slegthe of hande.

Quartus Tortor.

Go we now unto the othere ende;
Felowse, fest on fast youre hende,
And pulle welle at this band.

Primus Tortor.

I red, felowse, by this wedyr,
That we draw alle ons togedir,
And loke how it wille fare.

Secundus Tortor.

Let now se and leyf youre dyn,
And draw we ilka syn from syn,
For nothyng let us spare.

Tercius Tortor.

Nay, felowse, this is no gam,
We wille no longere draw alle sam,
So mekille have I asspyed.

Quartus Tortor.

No, for as have I blys,
Som can twyk, who so it is,
Sekes casse on som kyn syde.

Primus Tortor.

It is better as I hope,
Oone by his self to draw this rope,
And then may we se
Who it is that ere while
Alle his felows can begyle
Of this companye.

Secundus Tortor.

Sen thou wille so have here for me;
How draw I, as myght thou the?

Tercius Tortor.

Thou drew right wele,
Have here for me half a foyte.

Quartus Tortor.

Wema, man! I trow thou doyte,
Thou flyt it never a dele;
Bot have for me here that I may.

Primus Tortor.

Welle drawen, son, bi this day!
Thou gose welle to thi warke.

Secundus Tortor.

Yit efte, whils thi hande is in,
Pulle ther at with som kyn gyn.

Tercius Tortor.

Yei, and bryng it to the marke

Quartus Tortor.

Pulle, pulle!

Primus Tortor.

Have now.

Secundus Tortor.

Let se.

Tercius Tortor.

A ha!

Quartus Tortor.

Yit a draght.

Primus Tortor.

Therto with alle my maght.

Secundus Tortor.

A, ha, hold stille thore.

Tercius Tortor.

So felowse! looke now belyfe
Whiche of you can best dryfe,
And I shalle take the bore.

Quartus Tortor.

Let me go therto, if I shalle
I hope that I be the best mershalle
For [to] clynke it right;
Do rase hym up now when we may,
For I hope he and his palfray
Shalle not twyn this nyght.

Primus Tortor.

Come hedir, felowse, and have done,
And help that this tre sone
To lyft with alle youre sleght.

Secundus Tortor.

Yit let us wyrk a whyle,
And no man now othere begyle
To it be broght on heght.

Tercius Tortor.

Felowse, fest on alle youre hende
For to rase this tre on ende,
And let se who is last.

Quartus Tortor.

I red we do as that he says,
Set we the tre on the mortase,
And ther wille it stand fast.

Primus Tortor.

Up with the tymbre.

Secundus Tortor.

A, it heldys.
For hym that alle this warld weldys,
Put fro the with thi hande.

Tercius Tortor.

Hald even emanges us alle.

Quartus Tortor.

Yee, and let it into the mortase falle,
For then wille it best stande.

Primus Tortor.

Go we to it and be we strong,
And rase it, be it never so long,
Sen that it is fast bon.

Secundus Tortor.

Up with the tymbre fast on ende.

Tercius Tortor.

A felowse, fare falle youre hende!

Quartus Tortor.

So sir, gape agans the son!

Primus Tortor.

A felow, war thi crowne!

Secundus Tortor.

Trowes thou this tymbre wille oght downe?

Tercius Tortor.

Yit help that it were fast.

Quartus Tortor.

Sogh hym welle and let us lyfte.

Primus Tortor.

Fulle shorte shalbe hys thryfte.

Secundus Tortor.

A, it standes up lyke a mast.

Jesus.

I pray you pepylle, that passe me by,
That lede youre lyfe so lykandly,

Heyse up youre hertes on highte;
Behold if ever ye saw body
Suffer and bett thus blody,
Or yit thus dulfully dight;
In warld was never no wight
That suffred half so sare.
My mayn, my mode, my myght,
Is noght bot sorow to sight,
And comfurthe none bot care;
My folk, what have I done to the,
That thou alle thus shalle tormente me?
Thy syn by I fulle sore.
What have I grevyd the? answere me,
That thou thus nalys me to a tre,
And alle for thyn erroure:
Where shalle thou seke socoure?
This mys how shalle thou amende,
When that thou thy saveoure
Dryfes to this dyshonoure,
And nalys thrughe feete and hende?
Alle creatoures that kynde may kest,
Beestys, byrdes, alle have thay rest,
When thay ar wo begon;
Bot Godes son, that shuld be best,
Has not where apon his hede to rest,
Bot on his shulder bone:
To whome now may I make my mone
When thay thus martyr me,
And sakles wille me slone,
And bete me bloode and bone,
That my brethere shuld be?
What kyndnes shuld I kythe theym to?
Have I not done that I aght to do,
Maide the to my lyknes?
And thou thus ryfes me rest and ro,
And lettes thus lightly on me, lo

Siche is thy catyfnes;
I have the kyd kyndnes, unkyndly thou me quytys;
Se thus thi wekydnes, loke how thou me dyspytys.
Gyltles thus am I put to pyne,
Not for [my] mys, man, bot for thyne,
Thus am I rent on rode;
For I that tresoure wold not tyne
That I markyd and made for myne;
Thus by I Adam blode
That sonken was in syn,
With none erthly good
Bot with my flesh and blode
That lothe was for to wyn.
My brethere that I cam forto by
Has hanged me here, thus hedusly,
And freyndes fynde I foyn;
Thus have thay dight me drerely,
And alle by spytt me spytusly,
As helples man in won.
Bot Fader that syttes in trone
Forgyf thou them this gylt,
I pray to the this boyn,
Thay wote not what thay doyn,
Nor whom thay have thus spylt.

Primus Tortor.

Yis, what we do fulle welle we knaw.

Secundus Tortor.

Yee, that shalle he fynde within a thraw.

Tercius Tortor.

Now, with a myschaunce tylle his cors,
Weny s he that we gyf any force
What dwille so ever he aylle?

Quartus Tortor.

For he wold tary us alle day
Of his dede to make delay
I telle you, sansfaylle.

Primus Tortor.

Lyft us this tre emanges us alle.

Secundus Tortor.

Yee, and let it into the mortase falle,
And that shalle gar hym brest.

Tercius Tortor.

Yee, and alle to ryfe hym lym from lym.

Quartus Tortor.

And it wille breke ilk jo ıte in hym;
Let se now who dos best.

Maria.

Alas the doyle I dre! I drowpe, I dare in drede;
Whi hynges thou, son, so hee? my baylle begynnes to brede.
Alle blemyshed is thi ble, I se thi body blede,
In warld, son, were never we so wo as I in wede.
My foode that I have fed,
In lyf longyng the led,
Fulle stratly art thou sted ·
Emanges thi foo men felle:
Sich sorow forto se,
My dere bar ı, on the,
Is more mowrnyng to me
Then any tong may telle.
Alas! thi holy hede
Has not wheron to held,
Thi face with blode is red
Was fare as floure in feylde;
How shuld I stand in sted
To se my barne thus blede,
Bete as blo as lede,
A ıd has no lym to weylde?
Festynd both handes a ıd feete
With nalys fulle unmete,
His woundes wryngyng wete,
Alas, my childe, for care!

For alle rent is thi hyde,
I se on aythere syde
Teres of blode downe glide
Over alle thi body bare,
Alas that ever I shuld byde and se my feyr thus fare!

Johannes.

Alas, for doylle, my lady dere!
Alle for changid is thy chere,
To see this prynce withouten pere
Thus lappyd alle in wo:
He was thi foode, thi faryst fone,
Thi luf, thi lake, thi luffsom son,
That high on tre thus hynges alone
With body blak and blo;
Alas!
To me and many mo a good master he was.
Bot, lady, sen it is his wille
The prophecy to fulfylle,
That mankynde in sy[n] not spille,
For them to thole payn;
And with his ded raunson to make,
As prophetys beforn of hym spake,
For thi I red thi sorowe thou slake,
Thi wepyng may not gayn
In sorowe;
Oure boytt he byes fulle bayn,
Us alle from bale to borowe.

Maria.

Alas! thyn een as cristalle clere, that shone as son in sight,
That lufly were in lyere, lost thay have thare light
And wax alle faed in fere, alle dym then ar thay dight,
In payn has thou no pere, that is withoutten pight.
Swete son, say me thi thoght;
What wonders has thou wroght
To be in payn thus broght,
Thi blissed blode to blende?

A son, think on my wo,
Whi wille thou fare me fro?
On mold is no man mo
That may my myrthes amende.

Johannes.

Comly lady, good and couthe, fayn wold I comforth the;
Me mynnys my master with mowth told unto his menyce
That he shuld thole fulle mekille payn and dy apon a tre,
And to the lyfe ryse up agayn, apon the thryd day shuld it be
Fulle right;
For thi, my lady swete,
Stynt a while of grete,
Oure hale then wille he hete
As he before has hight.

Maria.

My sorow it is so sad no solace may me safe,
Mowrnyng makes me mad, none hope of help I hafe;
I am redles and rad, for ferd that I mon rafe,
Noghte may make me glad to I be in my grafe.
To deth my dere is dryffen,
His robe is alle to ryffen,
That of me was hym gyffen
And shapen withe my sydes:
Thise Jues and he has stryffen
That alle the hale he bydes.
Alas! my lam so mylde, whi wille thou fare me fro
Emang thise wulfes wylde, that wyrke on the this wo?
For shame who may the shelde, for freyndes has thou fo?
Alas! my comly childe, whi wille thou fare me fro?
Madyns, make youre mone,
And wepe ye, wyfes, everyichon,
Withe me, most wriche, in wone,
The childe that borne was best:
My harte is styf as stone,
That for no baylle wille brest.

Johannes.

A, lady, welle wote I thi hart is fulle of care
When thou thus openly sees thi childe thus fare;
Luf gars hym rathly, hym self wille he not spare
Us alle fro baylle to by, of blis that ar fulle bare
For syn;
My leve lady, for thy of mowrnyng loke thou blyn.

Maria.

Alas! may ever be my sang, whyls I may lyf in leyd,
Me thynk now that I lyf to lang to se my barne thus blede;
Jues wyrke with hym alle wrang, wherfor do thay this dede?
Lo so hy thay have hym hang, thay let for no drede;
Whi so?
His fomen is he emang, no freynde he has bot fo.
My frely foode now farys me fro, what shalle worthe on me?
Thou art warpyd alle in wo and spred here on a tre
Fulle hee;
I mowrne, and so may mo, that sees this payn on the.

Johannes.

Dere lady, welle were me
If that I myght comforthe the,
For the sorow that I se
Sherys myn harte in sonder;
When that I se my master hang
With bytter paynes and strang,
Was never wight with wrang
Wroght so mekille wonder.

Maria.

Alas! dede, thou dwellys to lang, whi art thou hid fro me?
Who kend the to my childe to gang? alle blak thou makes his ble;
Now witterly thou wyrkes wrang, the more I wille wyte the,
Bot if thou wille my harte stang that I myght with hym dee
And byde.
Sore syghyng is my sang, for thyrlyd is his hyde,
A, dede, what has thou done? with the wille I moytt sone;

Sen I had childer none bot oone, best under son or moyn,
Freyndes I had fulle foyn, that gars me grete and grone
Fulle sore.
Good Lord, graunte me my boyn, and let me lyf no more!
Gabrielle! that good som tyme thou can me grete,
And then I understud thi wordes that were so swete,
Bot now thay meng my moode, for grace thou can me hete
To bere alle of my bloode a childe oure baylle shuld bete
With right.
Now hynges he here on rude, where is that thou me hight?
Alle that thou of blys hight me in that stede
From myrthe is faren omys, and yit I trow thi red;
Thy councelle now of this, my lyfe how shalle I lede
When fro me gone is he that was my hede
In hy?
My dede now comen it is. my dere son, have mercy!

Jesus.

My moder mylde, thou chaunge thi chere,
Cease of thi sorow and sighyng sere,
It syttes unto my hart fulle sore;
The sorow is sharp I suffre here,
Bot doylle thou drees, my moder dere,
Me marters mekille more.
Thus wille my fader I fare
To lowse mankynde of bandys,
His son wille he not spare
To lowse that bon was are
Fulle fast in feyndes bandes.
The fyrst cause, moder, of my comyng
Was for mankynde myscarying,
To salf thare sore I soght;
Therfor, moder, make none mowrnyng
Sen mankynde thrugh my dyyng
May thus to blis be boght.
Woman, wepe thou right noght,
Take ther Johne unto thi chylde,

Mankynde must nedes be boght;
And thou kest, cosyn, in thi thoght,
Johne, lo ther thi moder mylde!
Blo and blody thus am I bett,
Swongen with swepys and alle to swett,
Mankynde, for thi mysdede;
For my luf lust when wold thou lett,
And thi harte sadly sett,
Sen I thus for the have blede?
Sich lyf, for sothe, I led that unothes may I more,
This suffre I for thi nede,
To marke the, man, thi mede:
Now thyrst I wonder sore.

Primus Tortor.

Noght bot hold thi peasse,
Thou shalle have drynke with in a resse,
My self shalbe thy knave;
Have here the draght that I the hete,
And I shalle warand it is not swete
On alle the good I have.

Secundus Tortor.

So syr, say now alle youre wille,
For if ye couthe have halden you stylle
Ye had not had this brade.

Tercius Tortor.

Thou wold alle gaytt be kyng of Jues,
Bot by this I trow thou rues
Alle that thou has sayde.

Quartus Tortor.

He has hym rused of greatt prophes,
That he shuld make us tempylles,
And gar it clene downe falle;
And yit he sayde he shuld it rase
As welle as it was within thre dayes.
He lyes, that wote we alle:
And for his lyes in great dispyte

We wille departe his clothyng tyte,
Bot he can more of arte.

Primus Tortor.

Yee, as ever myght I thryfe,
Soyn wille we this mantylle ryfe,
And iche man take his parte.

Secundus Tortor.

How, wold thou we share this clothe?

Tercius Tortor.

Nay forsothe, that were I lothe,
Then were it alle gate spylt;
Bot assent thou to my saw,
Let us alle cutt draw,
And then is none begylt.

Secundus Tortor.

How so befallys now wylle I draw,
This is myn by comon law,
Say not ther agayn.

Primus Tortor.

Now sen it mon no better be,
Chevithe the with it for me,
Me thynk thou art full fayne.

Secundus Tortor.

How felowse, se ye not you skraw?
It is writen yonder within a thraw,
Now sen that we drew cut.

Tercius Tortor.

There is no man that is on lyfe
Bot it were Pilate, as might I thrife,
That durst it there have putt.

Quartus Tortor.

Go we fast, and let us loke
What is wretyne on yond boke,
And what it may bemyn.

Primus Tortor.

A the more I lohe theron,
A the more I thynke I ſon;
Alle is not worthe a beyn.

Secundus Tortor.

Yis ſor sothe, me thynk I se
Theron writen langage thre,
Ebrew and Latyn,
And Grew me thynk writen theron,
For it is hard for to expowne.

Tercius Tortor.

Thou red, by Apollyon!

Quartus Tortor.

Yee, as I am a trew knyght,
I am the best Latyn wryght
Of this company;
I wille go withoutten delay
And telle you what it is to say,
Behald, syrs, witterly,
Yonder is wretyn Jesus of Nazareyn,
He is kyng of Jues, I weyn.

Primus Tortor.

A, that is writene wrang.

Secundus Tortor.

He callys hym so, bot he is none.

Tercius Tortor.

Go we to Pilate and make oure mone,
Have done and dwelle not lang.
Pilate, yonder is a fals tabylle,
Theron is wryten noght bot fabylle,
Of Jues he is not kyng,
He callys hym so, bot he not is,
It is falsly writen, iwys,
This is a wrangwys thyng.

Pilatus.

Boys, I say what melle ye you?
As it is writen shalle it be now,
I say certaine;
Quod scriptum scripsi,
That same wrote I,
What gadlyng gruches ther agane?

Quartus Tortor.

Sen that he is a man of law he must nedys have his wille:
I trow he had not writen that saw without som propre skylle.

Primus Tortor.

Yee, let it hang above his hede,
It shalle not save hym fro the dede,
Noght that he can write.

Secundus Tortor.

Now ill a hale was he borne.

Tercius Tortor.

Ma fa, I telle his lyfe is lorne,
He shalle be slayn as tyte.
If thou be Crist, as men the calle,
Com downe emanges us alle,
And thole not thise missaes.

Quartus Tortor.

Yee, and help thi self that we may se,
And we shalle alle trow in the,
What soever thou says.

Primus Tortor.

He callys hym self good of myght,
Bot I wold se hym be so wight
To do siche a dede;
He rasyd Lazare out of his delfe,
Bot he can not help hym selfe,
Now in his great nede.

Jesus.

Hely, Hely, lamazabatany!
My God, my God! wherfor and why
Has thou forsakyn me?

Secundus Tortor.

How, here ye not, as welle as I,
How he can now on Hely cry
Apon this wyse?

Tercius Tortor.

Yee, ther is none Hely in this countre
Shalle delyver hym from this menyeye,
On no kyns wyse.

Quartus Tortor.

I warand you now at the last
That he shalle soyn yelde the gast,
For brestyn is his galle.

Jesus.

Now is my passyon broght tylle ende,
Fader of heven in to thyn hende
I betake my saulle!

Primus Tortor.

Let oone pryk hym withe a spere,
And if that it do hym no dere
Then is his lyfe nere past.

Secundus Tortor.

This blynde knyght may best do that.

Longeus.

Gar me not do bot I wote what.

Tercius Tortor.

Not but put up fast.

Longeus

A! Lord, what may this be?
Ere was I blynde, now may I se;
Godes son, here me, Jesu!
For this trespason me thou rew.

For, lord, othere men me gart,
That I the stroke unto the hart,
I se thou hynges here on hy,
And dyse to fulfylle the prophecy.

Quartus Tortor.

Go we hens, and leyfe hym here,
For I shalle be his borghe to yere
He felys no more payn;
For Hely ne for none othere man
Alle the good that ever he wan,
Gettes not his lyfe agayne.

Josephus.

Alas, alas, and walaway!
That ever shuld I abyde this day
To se my master dede;
Thus wykydly as he is shent,
With so bytter tormamente,
Thrughe fals Jues red.
Nychodeme, I wold we yede
To sir Pilate, if we myght spede
His body for to crave;
I wille fownde with alle my myght,
For my servyce to ask that knyght,
His body for to grave.

Nichodemus.

Josephe, I wille weynde with the
For to do that is in me,
For that body to pray;
For oure good wille and oure travale
I hope that it mon us avaylle
Here after ward som day.

Josephus.

Sir Pilate, God the save!
Graunte me that I crave,
If that it be thi wille.

Pilatus.

Welcom Josephe myght thou be,
What so thou askys I graunte it the,
So that it be skylle.

Josephus.

For my long servyce, I the pray,
Graunte me the body, say me not nay,
Of Jesus dede on rud.

Pilatus.

I graunte welle if he ded be,
Good leyfe shalle thou have of me,
Do wyth hym what thou thynk gud.

Josephus.

Gramercy, sir, of youre good grace,
That ye have graunte me in this place,
Go we oure way:
Nychodeme, come me furthe with,
For I my self shalle be the smythe
The nales out for to dray.

Nichodemus.

Josephe, I am redy here
To go withe the with fulle good chere,
To help the at my myght;
Pulle furthe the nales on aythere syde,
And I shalle hald hym up this tyde,
A, lord, so thou is dight.

Josephus.

Help now, felow, with alle thi myght,
That he were wonden and welle dight,
And lay hym on this bere;
Bere we hym furthe unto the kyrke,
To the tombe that I gard wyrk,
Sen fulle many a yere.

Nichodemus.

It shalle be so with outten nay.
He that dyed on Gud Friday
And crownyd was withe thorne
Save you alle that now here be,
That Lord that thus wold dee
And rose on Pasche morne.

EXPLICIT CRUCIFIXIO CHRISTI.

EXTRACTIO ANIMARUM

AB INFERNO.

Jesus.

My fader me from blys has send
Tille erthe for mankynde sake,
Adam mys for to amend,
My deth nede must I take:
I dwellyd ther thyrty yeres and two,
And som dele more, the sothe to say,
In anger, pyne, and mekylle wo,
I dyde on cros this day.
Therfor tille helle now wille I go,
To chalange that is myne,
Adam, Eve, and othere mo,
Thay shalle no longer dwelle in pyne;
The feynde theym wan withe trayn,
Thrughe fraude of earthly fode,
I have theym boght agan
With shedyng of my blode.
And now I wille that stede restore,
Whiche the feynde felle fro for syn,
Som tokyn wille I send before,
Withe myrthe to gar thare gammes begyn.
A light I wille thay have
To know I wille com sone,
My body shalle abyde in grave
Tille alle this dede be done.

Adam.

My brether, herkyn unto me here,
More hope of helth never we had,

Four thousand and six hundred yere
Have we bene here in darknes stad;
Now se I tokyns of solace sere,
A gloryous gleme to make us glad,
Wherthrughe I hope that help is nere,
That sone shalle slake oure sorowes sad.

Eve.

Adam, my husband heynd,
This menys solace certan,
Siche lighte can on us leynd
In paradyse fulle playn.

Isaias.

Adam, thrugh thi syn
Here were we put to dwelle,
This wykyd place within,
The name of it is helle;
Here paynes shalle never blyn
That wykyd ar and felle,
Love that lord withe wyn
His lyfe for us wold selle.

[*Et cantent omnes «Salvator mundi,» primum versum.*]

Adam, thou welle understand,
I am Isaias, so Crist me kende,
I spake of folk in darknes walkand,
I saide a light shuld on them lende;
This light is alle from Crist commande,
That he tille us has bedir sende,
Thus is my poynt proved in hand,
As I before to fold it kende.

Simeon.

So may I telle of farlys feylle,
For in the tempylle his freyndes me fande,
Me thoght dayntethe with hym to deylle,
I halsyd hym homely with my hand,
I saide, Lord, let thi servandes leylle
Pas in peasse to lyf lastande,

Now that myn eeyn has sene thyn hele
No longer lyst I lyf in lande.
This light thou has purvayde
For theym that lyf in lede,
That I before of the have saide
I se it is fulfillyd in dede.

Johannes Baptista.

As a voice cryand I kend
The wayes of Crist, as I welle can,
I baptisid hym with bothe myn hende
In the water of flume Jordan;
The Holy Gost from heven discende
As a white dowfe downe on me than,
The Fader voyce oure myrthes to amende
Was made to me lyke as a man;
"Yond is my son," he saide,
"And whiche pleasses me fulle welle,"
His light is on us layde,
And commys oure karys to kele.

Moyses.

Now this same nyght lernyng have I,
To me, Moyses, he shewid his myght,
And also to another oone, Hely,
Where we stud on a hille on hyght,
As whyte as snaw was his body,
His face was like the son for bright,
No man on mold was so mighty
Grathly durst loke agans that light,
And that same lighte here se I now
Shynyng on us, certayn,
Where thrughe truly I trow
That we shalle sone pas fro this payn

Rybald.

Sen fyrst that helle was mayde and I was put therin
Siche sorow never ere I had, nor hard I siche a dyn,

My hart begynnys to brade, my wytt waxys thyn,
I drede we can not be glad, thise saules mon fro us twyn;
How, Belsabub! bynde thise boys, siche harow was never
hard in helle.

Belzabub.

Out, Rybald! thou rores, what is betyd? can thou oght telle?

Rybald.

Whi, herys thou not this ugly noyse?
Thise lurdans that in lymbo dwelle,
They make menyng of maıy joyse,
And muster myrthes theym emelle.

Belzabub.

Myrth? nay, nay! that poyıt is past,
More hope of helthe shalle they never have.

Rybald.

That cry on Crist fulle fast,
And says he shalle thaym save.

Belzabub.

Yee, though he do not, I shalle,
For thay ar sparyd in specyalle space,
Whils I am prynce and pryncypalle,
Thay shalle never pas out of this place;
Calle up Astarot aıd Anaballe,
To gyf us counselle in this case;
Telle Berith aıd Bellyalle
To mar theym that siche mastry mase;
Say to sir Satan oure syre,
And byd hym bryng also
Sir Lucyfer lufly of lyre.

Rybald.

Alle redy, lord, I go.

Jesus.

*Attolite portas, principes, vestras et elevamini portæ æter-
nales, et introibit rex gloriæ.*

Rybald.

Out, harro, out! what deville is he
That callys hym kyng over us alle?
Hark Belzabub, com ne,
For hedusly I hard hym calle.

Belzabub.

Go spar the yates, ylle mot thou the!
And set the waches on the walle,
If that brodelle com ne
With us ay won he shalle;
And if he more calle or cry,
To make us more debate,
Lay on hym hardely,
And make hym go his gate.

David.

Nay, withe hym may ye not fyght,
For he is king and conqueroure,
And of so mekille myght,
And styf in every stoure;
Of hym commys alle this light
That shynys in this howre;
He is fulle fers in fight,
Worthi to wyn honoure.

Belzabub.

Honoure! harsto, harlot, for what dede
Alle erthly men to me ar thrálle,
That lad that thou callys lord in lede
He had never harbor, house, ne halle;
How, sir Sathanas, com nar
And hark this cursid rowte!

Sathanas.

The dewille you alle to har!
What ales the so to showte?
And me, if I com nar,
Thy brayn bot I bryst owte.

Belzabub.

Thou must com help to spar,
We ar beseged abowte.

Sathanas.

Besegyd aboute! whi, who durst be so bold
For drede to make on us a fray?

Belzabub.

It is the Jew that Judas sold
For to be dede this othere day.

Sathanas.

How, in tyme that tale was told,
That trature travesses us alle way;
He shalle be here fulle hard in hold,
Bot loke he pas not I the pray.

Belzabub.

Pas! nay, nay, he wille not weynde
From hens or it be war,
He shapys hym for to sheynd
Alle helle or he go far.

Sathanas.

Fy, fature, therof shalle he faylle,
For alle his fare I hym defy;
I know his trantes fro top to taylle,
He lyffes by gawdes and glory.
Therby he broght furthe of oure baylle
The lathe Lazare of Betany,
Bot to the Jues I gaf counsaylle
That thay shuld cause hym dy:
I entered there into Judas
That forward to fulfylle,
Therfor his hyere he has
Alle wayes to won here stylle.

Rybald.

Sir Sathan, sen we here the say
Thou and the Jues were at assent,

And wote he wan the Lazare away
That unto us was taken to tent,
Hopys thou that thou mar hym may
To muster the malyce that he has ment?
For and he refe us now oure pray
We wille ye witt or he is went.

Sathanas.

I byd the noght abaste
Bot boldly make you bowne,
Withe toyles that ye intraste,
And dyng that dastard downe.

Jesus.

Attolite portas principes vestras, etc.

Rybald.

Outt, harro! what harlot is he
That says his kyngdom shalbe cryde?

David.

That may thou in sawter se,
For of this prynce thus ere I saide;
I saide that he shuld breke
Youre barres and bandes by name,
And of youre warkes take wreke;
Now shalle thou se the same.

Jesus.

Ye prynces of helle open youre yate,
And let my folk furthe gone,
A prynce of peasse shalle enter therat
Wheder ye wille or none.

Rybald.

What art thou that spekys so?

Jesus.

A kyng of blys that hight Jesus.

Rybald.

Yee, hens fast I red thou go,
And melle the not with us.

Belzabub.

Oure yates I trow wille last,
Thay ar so strong I weyn,
Bot if oure barres brast
For the thay shalle not twyn.

Jesus.

This stede shalle stande no longer stokyn;
Open up and let my pepille pas.

Rybald.

Out, harro! oure baylle is brokyn,
And brusten ar alle oure bandes of bras.

Belzabub.

Harro! oure yates begyn to crak,
In sonder, I trow, thay go,
And helle, I trow, wille all to shak;
Alas, what I am wo!

Rybald.

Lymbo is lorn, alas!
Sir Sathanas com up;
This wark is wars then it was.

Sathanas.

Yee, hangyd be thou on a cruke;
Thefys, I bad ye shuld be bowne
If he maide mastres more
To dyng that dastard downe,
Sett hym bothe sad and sore.

Belzabub.

So sett hym sore that is sone saide,
Com thou thi self and serve hym so;
We may not abyde his bytter brayde,
He wold us mar and we were mo.

Sathanas.

Fy, fature! wherfor were ye flayd?
Have ye no force to flyt hym fro?
Loke in haste my gere be grayd,
My self shalle to that gadlyng go.

How, thou belamy, abyde,
Withe alle thi boste and beyr,
And telle me in this tyde
What mastres thou makes here.

Jesus.

I make no mastry bot for myne,
I wille theym save, that shalle the sow.
Thou has no powere theym to pyne,
Bot in my pryson for thare prow
Here have thay sojornyd, not as thyne,
Bot in thi waryd, thou wote as how.

Sathanas.

Why, where has thou bene ay syn
That never wold neghe theym nere or now?

Jesus.

Now is the tyme certan
My Fader ordand herfor,
That they shuld pas fro payn
In blys to dwelle for ever more.

Sathanas.

Thy fader knew I welle by syght,
He was a wright his meett to wyn,
Mary me mynnys thi moder hight,
The utmast ende of alle thy kyn,
Say who made the so mekille of myght?

Jesus.

Thou wykyd feynde lett be thi dy[n],
My Fader wonnes in heven on hight,
In blys that never more shalle blyn:
I am his oonly son his forward to fulfylle,
Togeder wille we won in sonder when we wylle.

Sathanas.

Goddes son! nay then myght thou be glad
For no catelle thurt the crave;
Bot thou has lyffed ay lyke a lad,
In sorow, and as a sympille knave.

Jesus.

That was for the hartly luf I had
Unto man's saulle it forto save,
And forto make the masyd and mad,
And for that reson rufully to rafe.
My Godhede here I hyd
In Mary, moder myne,
Where it shalle never be kyd
To the ne none of thyne.

Sathanas.

How now? this wold I were told in towne,
Thou says God is thi syre;
I shalle the prove by good reson
Thou moyttes as man dos into myre.
To breke thi byddyng they were fulle bowne,
And soyn they wroght at my desyre,
From paradise thou putt theym downe,
In helle here to have thare hyre;
And thou thi self, by day and nyght,
Taght ever alle men emang,
Ever to do reson and right,
And here thou wyrkys alle wrang.

Jesus.

I wyrk no wrang, that shalle thou wytt,
If I my men fro wo wille wyn;
My prophettes playnly prechyd it,
Alle the noytes that I begyn;
They saide that I shuld be that ilke
In helle where I shuld entre in,
To save my servandes fro that pytt
Where dampnyd saullys shalle syt for syn.
And ilke true prophete taylle
Shalle be fulfillid in me;
I have thaym boght fro baylle,
In blis now shalle thay be.

Sathanas.

Now sen thou lyst to legge the lawes
Thou shalbe tenyd or we twyn,
For those that thou to witnes drawes
Fulle even agans the shalle begyn;
As Salaman saide in his sawes,
Who that ones commys helle within
He shalle never owte, as clerkes knawes,
Therfor, belamy, let be thy dyn.
Job thi servande also
In his tyme can telle
That nawder freynde nor fo
Shalle fynde relese in helle.

Jesus.

He sayde fulle soythe, that shalle thou se,
In helle shalbe no relese,
Bot of that place then ment he
Where synfulle care shalle ever encrese.
In that baylle ay shalle thou be,
Where sorowes seyr shalle never sesse,
And my folk that wer most fre
Shalle pas unto the place of peasse;
For thay were here with my wille,
And so thay shalle furthe weynde,
Thou shalle thi self fulfylle,
Ever wo withoutten ende.

Sathanas.

Whi, and wille thou take theym alle me fro?
Then thynk me thou ar unkynde;
Nay, I pray the do not so,
Umthynke the better in thy mynde,
Or els let me with the go;
I pray the leyfe me not behynde.

Jesus.

Nay, tratur, thou shalle won in wo,
And tille a stake I shalle the bynde.

Sathanas.

Now here I how thou menys emang
With mesure and malyce for to melle,
Bot sen thou says it shalbe lang,
Yit som let alle wayes with us dwelle.

Jesus.

Yis, witt thou welle, els were greatt wrang,
Thou shalle have Caym that slo Abelle,
And alle that hastes theym self to hang,
As dyd Judas and Architophelle;
And Daton and Abaron and alle of thare assent,
Cursyd tyranttes ever ilkon that me and myn tormente.
And alle that wille not lere my law
That I have left in land for new
That makes my commyng knaw,
And alle my sacramentes persew;
My deth, my rysyng, red by raw,
Who trow thaym not thay ar untrewe,
Unto my dome I shalle theym draw,
And juge thaym wars then any Jew.
And thay that lyst to lere my law and lyf therby
Shalle never have harmes here, bot welth as is worthy.

Sathanas.

Now here my hand, I hold me payde,
Thise poyntes ar playnly for my prow,
If this be trew as thou has saide
We shalle have mo then we have now;
Thise lawes that thou has late here laide
I shalle theym lere not to alow,
If thay myn take thay ar betraide,
And I shalle turne theym tytte I trow.
I shalle walk eest, I shalle walk west,
And gar theym wyrk welle war.

Jesus.

Nay feynde, thou shalbe feste,
That thou shalle flyt no far.

Sathanas.

Feste? fy! that were a wykyd treson!
Belamy, thou shalle be smytt.

Jesus.

Deville, I commaunde the to go downe
Into thi sete where thou shalle syt.

Sathanas.

Alas! for doylle and care
I synk into helle pyt.

Rybald.

Sir Sathanas, so saide I are,
Now shalle thou have a fytt.

Jesus.

Com now furthe my childer alle,
I forgyf you youre mys;
Withe me now go ye shalle
To joy and endles blys.

Adam.

Lord, thou art fulle mekylle of myght,
That mekys thi self on this manere,
To help us alle as thou had us hight,
When bothe forfett I and my fere;
Here have we dwelt withoutten light
Four thousand and six hundreth yere,
Now se we by this solempne sight
How that mercy makes us dere.

Eva.

Lord, we were worthy more tornamentes to tast,
Thou help us lord of thy mercy, as thou of myght is mast.

Johannes.

Lord, I love the inwardly,
That me wold make thi messyngere,
Thi commyng in erthe to cry,
And teche thi fayth to folk in fere;
Sythen before the forto dy,
To bryng theym bodword that be here,

How thay shuld have thi help in hy,
Now se I alle those poyntes appere.

Moyses.

David, thi prophette trew,
Of tymes told unto us;
Of thi commyng he knew,
And saide it shuld be thus.

David.

As I saide ere yit say I so,
Ne derelinquas, domine,
Animam meam in inferno;
Leyfe never my saulle, Lord, after the,
In depe helle whedur dampned shalle go,
Suffre thou never thi payntes to se
The sorow of thaym that won in wo,
Ay fulle of fylthe and may not fle.

Moyses.

Make myrthe bothe more and les,
And love oure lord we may,
That has broght us fro bytternes
In blys to abyde for ay.

Ysaias.

Therfor now let us syng
To love oure lord Jesus,
Unto his blys he wille us bryng,
Te Deum laudamus.

EXPLICIT EXTRACTIO ANIMARUM AB INFERNO.

JUDITIUM.

. . . . . .

Fulle darfe has bene oure dede, for thi commen is oure care,
This day to take oure mede, for nothyng may we spare.
Alas! I harde that horne that callys us to the dome,
Alle that ever were borne thider behofys theym com;
May nathere land ne se us fro this dome hide,
For ferde fayn wold I fle, bot I must nedes abide;
Alas! I stand great aghe to loke on that Justyce,
Ther may no man of laghe help with no quantyce.
Vokettys ten or twelfe may none help at this nede,
Bot ilk man for his self shalle answere for his dede.
Alas, that I was borne!
I se now me beforne,
That Lord with woundes fyfe;
How may I on hym loke,
That falsly hym forsoke,
When I led synfulle lyfe?

Tercius Malus.

Alas! carefulle catyfes may we ryse,
Sore may we wryng oure handes and wepe,
For cursid and sore covytyse
Dampnyd be we in helle fulle depe;
Wroght we never of Godes servyce,
His comaundements wold we not kepe,
Bot oft tymes maide we sacrifice
To Sathanas when othere can slepe.
Alas! now wakyns alle oure were,
Oure wykyd warkes can we not hide,
Bot on oure bakes we must theym bere,
That wille us soroo on ilka syde.

Oure dedys this day wille do us dere,
Oure domys man here we must abide,
And feyndes, that wille us felly fere,
Thare pray to have us for thare pride.
Brymly before us be thai broght,
Oure dedes that shalle dam us bidene;
That eyre has harde, or harte thoght,
That mowthe has spokyn, or ee sene,
That foote has gone, or hande wroght,
In any tyme that we may mene,
Fulle dere this day now bees it boght.
Alas, unborne then had I bene!

Quartus Malus.

Alas, I am forlorne! a spytus blast here blawes,
I harde welle bi yonde horne, I wote wherto it drawes;
I wold I were unborne, alas! that this day dawes,
Now mon be dampnyd this morne my warkys, my dedes, my sawes.
Now bees my curstnes kyd, alas! I may not layn
Alle that ever I dyd, it bees put up fulle playn.
That I wold fayn were hyd, my synfulle wordes and vayn
Fulle new now mon be rekynyd up to me agayn.
Alas! fayn wold I fle for dedes that I have done,
Bot that may now not be, I must abyde my boyn,
I trowed never to have sene this dredfulle day thus soyn;
Alas! what shalle I say when he sittes on his trone?
To se his woundes bledande this is a dulfulle case,
Alas! how shalle I stand or loke hym in the face,
So curtes I hym fand that gaf me life so lang a space,
Mi care is alle command, alas! where was my grace?
Alas! catyffes unkynde, where on was oure thoght?
Alas! where on was oure mynde, so wykyd warkes we wroghte?
To se how he was pynde, how dere oure luf he boght,
Alas! we were fulle blynde, now ar we wars then noght.
Alas! my covetyse, myne ylle wille, and myn ire,
Mi neghbur to dispise most was my desyre;

I demyd ever at my devyse, me thoght I had no peyre,
With my self sore may I grise, now am quyt my hyre.
Where I was wonte to go and have my wordes at wille,
Now am I set fulle thro and fayn to hold me stille;
I went both to and fro, me thoght I did never ille,
Mi neghburs for to slo or hurt withoutten skille.
Wo worthe ever the fader that gate me to be borne!
That ever he let me stir bot that I had bene forlorne;
Warid be my moder, and warid be the morne
That I was borne of hir, alas, for shame and skorne!

Primus Angelus, cum gladio.

Stand not togeder, parte in two,
Alle sam shalle ye not be in blys,
Oure lord of heven wille it be so,
For many of you has done amys;
On his right hand ye good shalle go,
The way to heven he shalle you wys;
Ye wykid saules ye weynd hym fro,
On his left hande as none of his.

Jesus.

The tyme is commen, I wille make ende,
My Fader of heven wille it so be,
Therfor tille erthe now wille I weynde,
My selfe to sytt in majestie;
To dele my dome I wille discende,
This body wille I bere with me,
How it was dight man's mys to amende
Alle man's kynde ther shalle it se.

Primus Dæmon.

Oute, haro, out, out! harkyn to this horne,
I was never in dowte or now at this morne,
So sturdy a showte sen that I was borne
Hard I never here abowte, in erneste ne in skorne.
A wonder;
I was bonde fulle fast
In yrens for to last,

Bot my handes thai brast
And shoke alle in sonder.

Secundus Dæmon.

I shoterde and shoke, I herd siche a rerd,
When I harde it I qwoke for alle that I lerd,
Bot to swere on a boke I durst not aperd,
I durst not loke for alle medille erd
Fulle paylle;
Bot gyrned and grast,
My force did I frast,
Bot I wroghte alle wast,
It myghte not avaylle.

Primus Dæmon.

It was like to a trumpe, it had sich a sownde,
I felle on a lumpe for ferd that I swonde.

Secundus Dæmon.

There I stode on my stumpe I stakerd that stownde,
There chachid I the crumpe, yit held I my grounde
Halfe nome.

Primus Dæmon.

Make redy oure gere,
We ar like to have were,
For now dar I swere
That domysday is comme;
For alle oure saules ar wente and none ar in helle.

Secundus Dæmon.

Bot we go we ar shente, let us not dwelle,
It sittes you to tente in this mater to melle,
As a pere in a parlamente what case so befelle;
It is nedefulle
That ye tente to youre awne,
What draght so be drawne,
If the courte be knawen
The juge is right dredfulle.

Primus Dæmon.

For to stande this tome thou gars me grete.

Secundus Dæmon.

Let us go to this dome up Watlyn Strete.

Primus Dæmon.

I had lever go to Rome; yei thryse on my fete,
Then forto grefe yonde grome, or with hym for to mete;
For wysely
He spekys on trete,
His paustee is grete,
Bot begyn he to threte
He lokes fulle grisly:
Bot fast take oure rentals, hy, let us go hence!
For as this fals the great sentence.

Secundus Dæmon.

Thai ar here in my dals, fast stand we to fence,
Agans thise dampnyd saules without repentence,
And *just.*

Primus Dæmon.

How so the gam crokys,
Examyn oure bokys.

Secundus Dæmon.

Here is a bag fulle, lokys,
Of pride and of lust,
Of wraggers and wrears, a bag fulle of brefes,
Of carpars and cryars, of mychers and thefes,
Of lurdans and lyars that no man lefys,
Of flytars, of flyars, and renderars of reffys,
This can I,
Of alkyn astates
That go bi the gatys,
Of poore pride, that God hates,
Twenty so many.

Primus Dæmon.

Peasse, I pray the, be stille, I laghe that I kynke,
Is oghte ire in thi bille and then shalle thou drynke?

Secundus Dæmon.

Sir, so mekille ille wille that thay wold synke
Thare foes in a fyere stille; bot not alle that I thynke
Dar I say,
Bot before hym he prase hym,
Behynde he myssase hym,
Thus dowbille he mase hym,
Thus do thai today.

Primus Dæmon.

Has thou oght writen there of the femynyn gender?

Secundus Dæmon.

Yei, mo then I may bere of rolles forto render;
Thai ar sharp as a spere if thai seme bot slender,
Thai ar ever in were if thai be tender,
Ylle fetyld;
She that is most meke,
When she semys fulle seke,
She can raise up a reke
If she be welle netyld.

Primus Dæmon.

Thou art the best hyne that ever cam besyde us.

Secundus Dæmon.

Yei bot go we, master myne, yet wold I we hyde us,
Thai have blowen lang syne, thai wille not abide us,
We may lightly tyne, and then wille ye chide us
Togeder.

Primus Dæmon.

Make redy oure tolys,
For we dele with no folys.

Secundus Dæmon.

Sir, alle clerkys of oure scolys
Abowne furthe theder;
Bot, sir, I telle you before had domysday oght tarid
We must have biggid helle more, the warld is so warid.

Primus Dæmon.

Now gett we dowbille store of bodys myscarid
To the soules where thai wore, bothe sam to be harrid.

Secundus Dæmon.

Thise rolles
Ar of bakbytars,
And fals quest dytars,
I had no help of writars
Bot thise two dalles;
Faithe and trowthe, maffay, have no fete to stande,
The poore pepylle must pay if oght be in hande,
The drede of God is away and lawe out of lande.

Primus Dæmon.

By that wist I that domysday was at hande
In seson.

Secundus Dæmon.

Sir, it is saide in old sawes,
The longere that day dawes,
Wars pepille, wars lawes.

Primus Dæmon.

I laghe at thi reson;
Alle this was token domysday to drede,
Fulle oft was it spokyn, fulle few take hede,
Bot now shalle we be wrokyn of thare falshede,
For now bese unlokyn many dern dede
In ire;
Alle thare synnes shalle be knowen,
Othere men's, then thare owne.

Secundus Dæmon.

Bot if this draght be welle drawen
Don is in the myre.

Tutivillus.

Whi spyr ye not syr no questyons?
I am oone of youre order and oone of your sons;
I stande at my tristur when othere men shones.

Primus Dæmon.

Now thou art myn awne querestur,
I wote where thou wonnes;
Do telle me.

Tutivillus.

I was youre chefe tollare,
And sithen courte rollar,
Now am I master Lollar,
And of sich men I melle me;
I have broght to youre hande of saules, dar I say,
Mo than ten thowsand in an howre of a day;
Som at aylle howse I fande, and som of ferray,
Som cursid, som bande, som yei som nay;
So many
Thus broght I on blure,
Thus dyd I my cure.

Primus Dæmon.

Thou art the best sawgeoure
That ever had I any.

Tutivillus.

Here a rolle of ragman of the rownde tabille,
Of breffes in my bag, man, of synnes dampnabille,
Unethes may I wag, man, for wery in youre stabille
Whils I set my stag, man.

Secundus Dæmon.

Abide, ye ar abille.
To take wage;
Thow can of cowrte thew,
Bot lay downe the dewe
For thou wille be a shrew,
Be thou com at age.

Tutivillus.

Here I be gesse of many nyce hoket,
Of care and of curstnes, hethyng and hoket,
Gay gere and witles, his hode set on koket,
As prowde as pennyles, his slefe has no poket,

Fulle redles:
With thare hemmyd shoyn,
Alle this must be done,
Bot fyre is out at hye noyne
And his barnes bredeles.
A horne and a duch ax, his slefe must be flekyt,
A syde hede and a fare fax, his gowne must be spekytt,
Thus toke I youre tax, thus ar my bokys blekyt.

Primus Dæmon.

Thou art best on thi wax that ever was clekyt,
Or knowen;
With wordes wille thou fille us,
Bot telle thi name tille us.

Tutivillus.

My name is Tutivillus,
My horne is blawen;
Fragmina verborum Tutivillus colligit horum,
Belzabub algorum, Belial belium doliorum.

Secundus Dæmon.

What, I se thou can of gramory and som what of arte;
Had I bot a penny on the wold I warte.

Tutivillus.

Of femellys a quantite here fynde I parte.

Primus Dæmon.

Tutivillus, let se, Godes forbot thou sparte!

Tutivillus.

So *joly*,
Ilka las in a lande,
Like a lady nere hande,
So freshe and so plesande,
Makes men to foly.
If she be never so fowlle a dowde, with hir kelles and hir pynnes,
The shrew hir self can shrowde, both hir chekys and hir chynnes.

She can make it fulle prowde with japes and with gynnes,
Hir hede as hy as a clowde, bot no shame of hir synnes
Thai fele;
When she is thus paynt,
She makes it so quaynte,
She lokes like a saynt,
And wars then the deyle.
She is hornyd like a kowe . . . . . . fon syn,
The cuker hynges so side now, furrid with a cat skyn,
Alle thise ar for you, thay ar commen of youre kyn.

Secundus Dæmon.

Now, the best body art thou that ever cam here in.

Tutivillus.

An usage,
Swilk dar I undertake,
Makes theym breke thare wedlake,
And lif in syn for hir sake,
And breke thare awne spowsage.
Yet a poynt have I fon, I telle you before,
That fals swerers shalle hider com mo than a thowsand skore;
In sweryng thai grefe Godes son, and pyne hym more and more,
Therfor mon thai with us won in helle for ever more.
I say thus,
That rasers of the fals tax,
And gederars of greyn wax,
Diabolus est mendax
Et pater ejus.
Yit a poynte of the new gett to telle wille I not blyn,
Of prankyd gownes and shulders up set, mos and flokkes sewyd wyth in,
To use siche gise thai wille not let, thai say it is no syn,
Bot on sich pilus I me set and clap thaym cheke and chyn,
No nay.
David in his sawtere says thus,

That to helle shalle thay trus,
Cum suis adinventionibus,
For onys and for ay.
Yit of thise kyrkchaterars here ar a menee,
Of barganars and okerars and lufars of symonee,
Of runkers and rowners, God castes thaym out trulee
From his temple alle sich mysdoers, I each thaym then to me
Fulle soyn;
For writen I wote it is
In the Gospelle, withoutten mys,
Et eam fecistis
Speluncam latronum.
Yit of the synnes seven som thyng specialle
Now nately to neven, that ronnys over alle,
Thise laddes thai leven as lordes rialle,
At ee to be even picturde yn palle
As kynges;
May he dug hym a doket,
A kodpese like a pokett,
Hym thynk it no hoket
His taylle when he wrynges.
His luddokkys thai lowke like walk mylne clogges
His hede is like a stowke, hurlyd as hogges,
A welle blawen bowke thise fryggés as frogges,
This *j*elian jowke dryfys he no dogges
To felter,
Bot with youre yolow lokkys,
For alle youre many mokkes,
Ye shalle clym on helle crokkys
With a halpeny heltere.
And Nelle with hir nyfyls of crisp and of sylke,
Tent welle youre twyfyls your nek abowte as mylke;
With your bendys and youre bridyls of Sathan the whilke,
Sir Sathanas idyls you for tha ilke

This gille knave,
It is open behynde,
Before is it pynde,
Bewar of the west wynde
Youre smok lest it wafe.
Of ire and of envy fynde I herto,
Of covetyse and glotony and many other mo,
Thai calle and thai cry "go we now, go,
I dy here for dry," and ther syt thai so
All nyghte,
With hawvelle and jawvelle,
Syngyng of lawvelle,
Thise ar howndes of helle,
That is thare right.
In slewthe then thai syn, Goddes warkes thai not wyrke,
To belke thai begyn and spew that is irke,
His hede must be holdyn ther in the myrke,
Then deffes hym with dyn the bellys of the kyrke
When thai clatter;
He wisbys the clerke hanged
For that he rang it,
Bot thar hym not lang it,
What commys ther after.
And ye Janettes of the stewys; and lychoures on lofte
Your baille now brewys, avowtrees fulle ofte,
Youre gam now grewys, I shalle you set softe,
Your sorow enewes, com to my crofte
Alle ye;
Alle harlottes and horres,
And bawdes that procures,
To bryng thaym to lures,
Welcom to my see.
Ye lurdans and lyars, mychers and thefes,
Flytars and flyars that alle men reprefes,
Spolars, extorcyonars, welcom, my lefes!
Fals jurors and usurars to symony that clevys,

To telle,
Hasardars and dysars,
Fals dedes forgars,
Slanderars, bakbytars,
Alle unto helle.

Primus Dæmon.

When I harde many swilke, many spytus and felle,
And few good of ilke I had mervelle,
I trowid it drew nere the prik.

Secundus Dæmon.

Sir, a worde of counselle;
Saules cam so thyk now late unto helle
As ever,
Oure porter at helle gate
Is halden so strate,
Up erly and downe late,
He rystys never.

Primus Dæmon.

Thou art pereles of tho that ever yit knew I,
When I wille may I go if thou be by;
Go we now, we two.

Secundus Dæmon.

Sir, I am redy.

Primus Dæmon.

Take oure rolles also, ye knane the cause why,
Do com
And tent welle this day.

Secundus Dæmon.

Sir, as welle as I may.

Primus Dæmon.

Qui vero mala

Secundus Dæmon.

In ignem æternum.

Jesus.

Ilka creatoure take tente
What bodwarde I shalle you bryng.

This wykyd warld away is weite,
And I am commen as crownyd kyıg;
My fader of heven has me dowıe seıt,
To deme youre dedes and make endyng;
Commen is the day of Jugemente,
Of sorow may every synfulle syng.
The day is commen of catyfnes,
Alle those to care that ar uncleyn,
The day of batelle and bitternes,
Fulle long abideı has it beyı;
The day of drede to more and les,
Of joy, of tremlyng aıd of teyn,
Ilka wight that wykyd is
May say, alas this day is seyn!

[*Tunc expandit manus suas et ostendit eis vulnera sua:* —

Here may ye se my woundes wide
That I suffred for youre mysdede,
Thrughe harte, hede, fote, haıde and syde,
Not for my gilte bot for youre nede.
Behald both bak, body, and syde,
How dere I boght youre broder hede,
Thise bitter payıes I wold abide,
To by you blys thus wold I blede.
Mi body was skowrgid withoutten skille,
Also ther fulle throly was I threth,
Oı crosse thai haıg me on a hille,
Blo aıd blody thus was I bett,
With crowne of thorne thrastyn fulle ille,
A spere uıto my harte thai sett.
Mi harte blode sparid thai not to spille,
Man, for thi luf wold I not lett.
The Jues spytt on me spitusly,
Thai sparid me no more theı a thefe,
When thai me smote I stud stilly,
Agaıs thaym did I nokyns grefe.
Beholde, mankynde, this ilke am I,

That for the suffred sich myschefe,
Thus was I dight for thi foly,
Man, loke thi luf was me fulle lefe.
Thus was I dight thi sorow to slake,
Man, thus behovid the borud to be,
In alle my wo tooke I no wrake,
My wille it was for luf of the;
Man, for sorow aght the to qwake,
This dredful day this sight to se,
Alle this suffred I for thi sake,
Say, man, what suffred thou for me?

[*Tunc vertens se ad bonos, dicit illis,* —

Mi blessid barnes on my right hande,
Youre dome this day thar ye not drede,
For alle youre joy is now commande,
Youre life in lykyng shalle ye lede;
Commes to the kyngdom ay lastand,
That you is dight for youre good dede,
Fulle blithe may ye be there ye stand,
For mekille in heven bees youre mede.
When I was hungre ye me fed,
To slek my thrist ye war fulle fre,
When I was clothles ye me cled,
Ye wold no sorowe on me se;
In hard prison when I was sted
On my penance ye had pyte,
Fulle seke when I was broght in bed
Kyndly ye cam to comforth me.
When I was wille and weriest
Ye harberd me fulle esely,
Fulle glad then were ye of youre gest,
Ye plenyd my poverte fulle pitusly;
Belife ye broght me of the best,
And maide my bed there I shuld ly,
Therfor in heven shalle be youre rest,
In joy and blys to beld me by.

Primus Bonus.

Lord, when had thou so mekille nede?
Hungre or thrusty how myght it be?

Secundus Bonus.

When was oure harte fre the to feede?
In prison when myght we the se?

Tercius Bonus.

When was thou seke or wantyd wede?
To harbowre the when helpid we?

Quartus Bonus.

When had thou nede of oure fordede?
When did we alle this dede for the?

Jesus.

Mi blissid barnes, I shalle you say
What tyme this dede was to me done,
When any that nede had nyght or day,
Askyd you help and had it sone;
Youre fre harte saide theym never nay,
Erly ne late, myd day ne noȳn,
As ofte sithes as thai wold pray,
Thai thurte bot aske and have thare boyn.

[*Tunc dicet malis,* —

Ye cursid catyfs of Kames kyn,
That never me comforthid in my care,
Now I and ye for ever shalle twyn,
In doylle to dwelle for ever mare;
Youre bitter bayles shalle never blyn
That ye shall thole when ye com thare;
Thus have ye servyd for youre syn,
For derfe dedes ye have doyn are.
When I had myster of mete and drynke,
Catyfs, ye chaste me from youre yate,
When ye were set as syres on bynke
I stode ther oute wery and wate,
Yet none of you wold on me thynke,
To have pite on my poore astate,

Therfor to helle I skalle you synke,
Welle are ye worthy to go that gate.
When I was seke and soryest
Ye viset me noght, for I was poore;
In prison fast when I was fest
Wold none of you loke how I foore;
When I wist never where to rest
With dyntes ye drofe me from youre doore,
Bot ever to pride then were ye prest;
Mi flesh, my bloode, ye oft forswore.
Clothles, when that I was cold
That nere hande for you yode I nakyd,
Mi myschefe saghe ye many folde,
Was none of you my sorow slakyd,
Bot ever forsoke me yong and olde,
Therfor shalle ye now be forsakyd.

Primus Malus.

Lorde, when had thou, that alle has,
Hunger or thriste, sen thou God is?
When was that thou in prison was?
When was thou nakyd or harberles?

Secundus Malus.

When myght we see the seke, alas!
And kyd the alle this unkyndnes?

Tercius Malus.

When was we let the helples pas?
Whey dyd we the this wikydnes?

Quartus Malus.

Alas, for doylle this day!
Alas, that ever I it abode!
Now am I dampned for ay,
This dome may I not avoyde.

Jesus.

Catyfes, alas! ofte as it betyde
That nedefulle oght askyd in my name,

Ye hard them noght, youre eeres was hid,
Youre help to thaym was not at hame;
To me was that unkyndnes kyd,
Therfor ye bere this bitter blame,
To the lest of myne when ye oghte dyd,
To me ye dyd the self and same.

[*Tunc dicet bonis,* —

Mi chosyn childer, come to me,
With me to dwelle now shalle ye weynde,
Ther joy and blys ever shalle be,
Youre life in lykyng for to leynde.

[*Tunc dicet malis,* —

Ye warid wightes, from me ye fle,
In helle to dwelle withoutten ende,
Ther shalle ye noght bot sorow se,
And sit bi Sathanas the feynde.

Primus Dæmon.

Do now go furthe, trus, go we hyne,
Unto endles wo, ay lastand pyne,
Nay, tary not so, we get ado syne.

Secundus Dæmon.

Flyte hyder warde, ho, Harry Ruskyne
War oute!
The meyn shalle ye nebylle,
And I shalle syng the trebille,
A revant the deville
Tille alle this hole rowte.

Tutivillus.

Youre lyfes ar lorne and commen is youre care,
Ye may ban ye were borne the bodes you bare,
And youre faders beforne, so cursid ye ar.

Primus Dæmon.

Ye may wary the morne and day that ye ware
Of youre moder
First borne forto be,
For the wo ye mon dre.

Primus Dæmon.

Ilkon of you mon se
Sorow of oder;
Where is the gold and the good that ye gederd togedir?
The mery menee that yode hider and thedir?

Tutivillus.

Gay gyrdyls, jaggid hode, prankyd gownes, whedir?
Have ye wit or ye wode ye broght not hider
Bot sorowe,
And your synnes in youre nekkys.

Primus Dæmon.

I beshrew thaym that rekkys,
He comes to late that bekkys
Youre bodyes to borow.

Secundus Dæmon.

Sir, I wold cut thaym a skawte and make theym be knawen,
Thay were sturdy and hawte, great boste have thai blawne,
Youre pride and youre pransawte what wille it gawne?
Ye tolde ilk mans defawte and forgate youre awne.

Tutivillus.

Moreover
Thare neghburs thai demyd,
Thaym self as it semyd,
Bot now ar thai flemyd
From payntes to recover.

Primus Dæmon.

Thare neghburs thai towchid with wordes fulle ille,
The warst ay thai sowchid and had no skille.

Secundus Dæmon.

The pennys thai powchid and held thaym stille,
The negons thai mowchid and had no wille
For hart fare,
Bot riche and ille dedy,
Gederand and gredy,
Sor napand and nedy
Youre godes forto spare.

Tutivillus.

For alle that ye spard and dyd extorcyon,
For youre childer ye card, youre heyre and youre son
Now is alle in oure ward, youre yeres ar ron,
It is commen in vowgard youre dame malison,
To bynde it;
Ye set bi no cursyng,
Ne no siche smalle thyng.

Primus Dæmon.

No, bot prase at the partyng,
For now mon ye fynde it;
Youre leyfes and your females, ye brake youre wedlake,
Telle me now what it vales alle that mery lake?
Se so falsly it falys.

Secundus Dæmon.

Syr, I dar undertake
Thai wille telle no tales, bot-se so thai qwake
For moton,
He that to that gam gose,
Now namely on old tose.

Tutivillus.

Thou held up the lose
That had I forgotten.

Primus Dæmon.

Sir, I trow thai be dom som tyme were fulle melland,
Welle ye se how thai glom.

Secundus Dæmon.

Thou art ay telland,
Now shalle thai have rom in pyk and tar ever dwelland,
Of thare sorow no some, bot ay to be yelland
In oure fostre.

Tutivillus.

By youre lefe may we mefe you?

Primus Dæmon.

Showe furthe, I shrew you.

Secundus Dæmon.

Yet tonyght shalle I shew you
A mese of ille ostre.

Tutivillus.

Of thise cursid forsworne and alle that here leyndes,
Blaw, wolfes hede and outehorne, now namely my freyndes.

Primus Dæmon.

Illa haille were ye borne, youre awne shame you sheyndes
That shalle ye fynde or to morne.

Secundus Dæmon.

Com now with feyndes
To youre angre;
Youre dedes you dam,
Com, go we now sam,
It is commen youre gam,
Com, tary no longer.

Primus Bonus.

We love the, Lord, in alkyn thyng,
That for thyne awne has ordand thus,
That we may have now oure dwellyng
In heven blis giffen unto us;
Therfor fulle boldly may we syng
On oure way as we trus,
Make alle myrthe and lovyng
With *Te Deum laudamus.*

EXPLICIT JUDITIUM.

CANDLEMAS-DAY,

OR

THE KILLING OF THE CHILDREN OF ISRAEL.

THE NAMES OF THE PLEYERS.

The Poete.
Kyng Herowd.
Knyght j.
Knyght ij.
Knyght iij.
Knyght iiij
Watkyn, Messanger.
Symeon, the Bysshop.
Joseph.
Maria.
Anna, Prophetissa.
A Virgyn.
Angelus.
Mulier j.
Mulier ij.
Mulier iij.
Mulier iiij.

Jhan Parfre ded write thys booke.

The original of this play is preserved among the Digby MSS. in the Bodleian Library, Oxford, and has the date of 1512. No particulars are known of *Jhan Parfre*.

CANDLEMAS-DAY.

Poeta.

This solemne fest to be had in remenbraunce
Of blissed seynt Anne, moder to our lady,
Whos ryght discent was fro kyngs allyaunce,
Of Davyd and Salamon witnesseth the story;
Hir blissid doughter, that callid is Mary,
By Gods provision an husbond shuld have,
Callid Joseph, of nature old and drye,
And the moder unto Christ that all the world shall save.
  This glorious maiden doughter unto Anna,
In whos worship this fest we honour,
And by resemblaunce likenyd unto manna,
Wiche is in tast cœlestiall of savour,
And of Jerico the sote rose floure,
Gold Abryson callid in picture,
Chosyn for to bere mankynds savyour;
With a prerogative above eche creature.
  These grett thyngs remembred, after our entent
Is for to worshyppe oure lady and seynt Anne:
We be comen heder as servaunts diligent
Oure processe to shewe you as we can:

Wherfor of benevolence we pray every man,
To have us excused, that we no better doo,
An other tyme to emende it if we can,
Be the grace of God, if our cunnyng be ther too.
  The last yeer we shewid you, and in this place,
How the shepherds of Crist by the made letification,
And thre kynges that ycome fro the cuntrees be grace
To worshyp Jesu with enteer devotion:
And now we propose with hooll affection,
To procede in oure matter as we can,
And to shew you of oure ladies purification,
That she made in the temple, as the usage was than:
  And after that shall Herowd have tydyngs,
How the thre kyngs be goon hoom another way,
That were with Jesu, and made ther offryngs,
And promysed kynge Herowd, without delay
To come a geyn by him; this is no nay.
And whan he wist that thei were goon,
Like as a wodman he gan to fray,
And commaunded his knyght forth to go anoon
  In to Israell, to serche every towne and cite
For all the children that thei cowde ther fynde,
Of ij yeers age and under, sparyng neither bonde nor free,
But sle them all, either for foo or frende;
Thus he commaunded in his furious mynde;
Thought that Jesu shuld have be oon,
And yitt he failed of his froward mynde;
For, by Gods providaunce, our lady was in to Egypte gon.
  Frends, this processe we propose to pley as we can,
Before you all here in your presens,
To the honoure of God, oure lady, and seynt Anne;
Beseechyng you to geve us peseable audiens.
And ye menstrallis doth your diligens;
And ye virgynes, shewe sume sport and plesure,
These people to solas, and to do God reverens;
As ye be appoynted doth your besy cure.

Herowd.

Above all kynges under the clowdys cristall,
Royally I reigne in welthe without woo,
Of plesaunt prosperytie I lakke non at all;
Fortune I fynde, that she is not my foo,
I am kyng Herowd, I will it be knowen so,
Most strong and myghty in feld for to fyght,
And to venquyshe my enemyes that a geynst me do;
I am most be dred with my bronde bryght.
My grett goddes I gloryfye with gladnesse,
And to honoure them I knele up on my knee;
For thei have sett me in solas from all sadnesse,
That no conqueroure nor knyght is compared to me:
All the that rebelle a geyns me ther bane I will be,
Or grudge a geyns my godds on hyll or hethe;
All suche rebellers I shall make for to flee,
And with hard punyshements putt them to dethe.
What erthely wretches, what pompe and pride,
Do a geyns my lawes or withstonde myne entent,
Thei shall suffre woo and peyne thrugh bak and syde,
With a very myschaunce ther fleshe shal be all to rent;
And all my foes shall have suche commaundement
That they shalbe glad to do my byddyn ay,
Or ells thei shalbe in woo and myscheff permanent,
That thei shall fere me nyght and day.
My messanger, at my commaundement come heder to me,
And take hed what I shall to the say:
I charge the, loke a bought thurgh my cuntre
To aspye if ony rebell do a geynst our lay:
And if ony suche come in thy way,
Brynge hem in to our hygh presens,
And we shal se them correctid, or thei go hens.

Watkyn, the Messanger.

My lord, your commaundement I have fulfilled
Evyn to the uttermost of my pore power;
And I wold shew you more, so ye wold be contentid,
But I dare not, lest ye wold take it in anger:
For if it liked you not, I am sure my deth were nere;
And therfor, my lord, I wole hold my peas.

Herowd.

I warne the, thu traytor, that thu not seas
To observe every thyng thu knowest a geyns our reverence.

Messanger.

My lord, if ye have it in your remenbraunce,
Ther were iij straunger knyghts, but late in your presence,
That went to Bedlem to offre with due observaunce,
And promysed to come a geyn by you without variaunce;
But by ther bonys ten, thei be to you untrue,
For homeward an other wey thei doo sue.

Herod.

Now be my grett godds, that be so full of myght
I will be a vengid upon Israell, if this tale be true.

Messanger.

That it is, my lord, my trouth I you plight,
For ye founde me never false syn ye me knewe.

Herod.

I do perceyve, though I be here in my cheff cite,
Callid Jerusalem, my riche royall town,
I am falsly disceyved by straunge Knyghts thre:
Therfor, my knyghts, I warne you, without delacion,
That ye make serche thurgh oute all my region,
Withoute any tarieng my wille may be seen,
And sle all the children without excepcion
Of to yeers of age, that within Israell bene:
For within my self thus I have concluded,
For to avoide a wey all interrupcion,
Sythenes thes thre knyghts have me thus falsly deluded,
As in manner by froward collusion,

And a geyn resorted hom in to ther region:
But yitt, maugre ther herts, I shall avengid be:
Bothe in Bedlem and my provynces everychone,
Sle all the children to kepe my liberte.

Miles j.

My lord, ye may be sure that I shall not spare
For to fulfille your noble commaundement,
With sharpe swerde to perse them all hare,
In all cuntrees that be to you adjacent.

Miles ij.

And for your sake to observe your commaundement.

Miles iij.

Not on of them all our hands shall astert.

Miles iiij.

For we wole cruelly execute your judgement
With swerde and spere to perse them thurgh the hert.

Herod.

I thanke you, my knyghts, but loke ye, make no tarieng,
Go arme your self in stele shynyng bright;
And conceyve in your mynds, that I am your kyng,
Gevyng you charge, that with all your myght
In confirmacion of my tytell of ryght,
That ye go and loke for myn advantage,
And sle all the children that come in your sight
Wiche ben within two yeers of age.
Now be ware, that my byddyng ye truly obey,
For non but I shall reigne with equyte;
Make all the children on your swerds to dey,
I charge you, spare not oon for mercy nor pyte.
Am not I lord and kyng of the cuntre?
The crowne of all Jerusalem longith to me of right;
Who so ever sey nay of high or lowe degre,
I charge you, sle all suche that come in your syght.

Miles j.

My lord, be ye sure, accordyng to your will,
Like as ye charge us be streigt commaundement.

All the children of Israell doubtles we shall kylle
Within to yeers of age, this is our entent.

Miles ij.

My lord of all Jurye, we hold you for chef regent,
By tytell of enheritaunce as your auncestors be forn;
He that seith the contrary, be Mahound, shalbe shent,
And curse the tyme that ever was born.

Herod.

I thanke you, my knyghts, with hooll affection,
And whan ye come a geyn I shall you avaunce;
Therfor quyte you wele in feld and town,
And of all the fondlyngs make a delyveraunce.

[*Here the Knyghts shall departe from Herowd to Israell; and WATKYN shall abyde, seyng thus to Herowd:* —

Now, my lord, I beseche you to here my dalyaunce,
I wole aske you a bone, if I durst a right;
But I were loth ye shuld take ony displesaunce:
Now for Mahounds sake, make me a knyght.
For oon thyng I promyse you, I will manly fight,
And for to avenge your quarrell I dare undertake;
Though I sey my self, I am a man of myght,
And dare live and deye in this quarrell for your sake;
For whan I com amonge them, for fere thei shall quake;
And, though thei sharme and crye, I care not a myght,
But with my sharpe sworde ther ribbes I shall shake
Evyn thurgh the guttes for anger and despight.

Herod.

Be thi trouthe, Watkyn, woldest thu be made a knyght?
Thu hast be my servaunt and messanger many a day,
But thu were never provid in battaile nor in fight,
And therfor to avaunce the so sodenly I ne may:
But oon thyng to the I shall say,
Be cause I fynde the true in thyn entent,
Forth with my knyghts thu shalt take the way,
And quyte the wele, and thu shall it not repent.

Watkyn.

Now a largeys, my lord, I am ryght wele apaid,
If I do not wele, ley my hed upon a stokke;
I shall go shew your knyghts how ye have seid,
And arme my self manly and go forth on the flokke,
And if I fynde a young child I shall choppe it on a blokke,
Though the moder be angry the child shalbe slayn:
But yitt I dredde no thyng more than a woman with a rokke,
For if I se ony suche, be my feith, I come a geyn.

Herowd.

What, shall a woman with a rokke drive the away?
Fye on the, traitor, now I tremble for tene,
I have trusted the long, and many a daye;
A hold man and an hardy I went thu haddist ben.

Watkyn.

So am I, my lord, and that shalbe seen,
That I am a hold man and best dare a hyde,
And ther come an hundred women I wole not fleen,
But fro morrowe tyll nyght with them I dare chide.
And therfor, my lord, ye may trust unto me;
For all the children of Israell your knyghts and I shall kylle,
I will not spare on, hutt dede thei shall be,
If the fader and moder will let me have my wille.

Herowd.

Thu lurdeyn, take hed what I sey the tyll,
And high the to my knyghts as fast as thu can:
Sey, I warne them in ony wyse ther blood that thei spille,
A bought in every cuntre, and lette for no man.

Watkyn.

Nay, nay, my lord, we wyll let for no man,
Though ther come a thousand on a rought;
For your knyghts and I will kylle them all, if we can:
But for the wyves that is all my dought,
And if I se ony walkyng a bought,
I will take good hede tyll the be goon,

And assone as I aspye that she is oute,
By my feith, into the hous I will go anon.
 And this I promyse you, that I shall never slepe,
But evermore wayte to fynde the children alone;
And if the moder come in, under the bench I will crepe,
And lye stille ther tyll she be goon,
Than manly I shall come out and hir children sloon,
And whan I have don I shall renne fast away:
It she founde hir child dede, and toke me ther alone,
Be my feith, I am sure we shuld make a fray.

Herowd.

 Nay, harlott, abyde stylle with my knyghts I warne the,
Tyll the children be slayn all the hooll rought;
And whan thu comyst home agayn I shall avaunce the,
If thu quyte thee like a man whill thu art ought,
And if thu pley the coward, I put the owt of dought,
Of me thu shalt neyther have fe nor advauntage,
Therfor I charge you the contre be well sought,
And whan thu comyst home shalt have thi wage.

Watkyn.

 Yis, ser, be my trouthe, ye shall wele knowe
Whill I am oute how I shall aquyte me,
For I propose to spare neither high nor lowe;
If ther be no man wole smyte me:
The most I fere the wyves will hete me,
Yitt shall I take good hert to me and loke wele abought.
And loke that your knyghts be not ferre fro me,
For if I be alone I may sonè gete a flought.

Herod.

 I say, hye the hens, that thu were goon,
And unto my knyghts loke ye take the way,
And sey, I charge them that my commaundement be don
In all hast possible without more delay;
And if ther be ony that will sey you nay,
Redde him of his lyff out of hand anon;
And if thu quyte the weell unto my pay,

I shall make the a knyght aventryous whan thu comyst
home.

Watkyn.

Syr knyghts, I must go forth with you,
Thus my lord commaunded me for to don;
And if I quyte me weell whill I am amonge you,
I shalbe made a knyght aventrys whan I come home:
For oon thyng I promyse you, I will fight anon,
If my hert faile not whan I shalbe gynne;
The most I fere is to come amonge women,
For thei fight like devells with ther rokke whan thei spynne.

Miles j.

Watkyn, I love the, for thu art even a man;
If thu quyte the weell in this grett viage,
I shall speke to my lord for the that I can,
That thu shalt no more be neither grome nor page.

Miles ij.

I wyll speke for the that thu shall have better wage,
If thu quyte the manly amonge the wyves;
For thei be as fers as a lyon in a cage,
Whan thei are wroken ought to reve men of ther lives.

[*Here the Knyghts and Watkyn walke abought the place tyll Mary and Joseph be conveid in to Egipt.*]

Angelus.

O Joseph, ryse up, and loke thu tary nought;
Take Mary with the, and in to Egipt flee;
For Jesu thy sone pursuyd is and sought
By kyng Herowd, the wiche of grete inyquyte
Commaunded hath thurgh Bedlem cite,
In his cruell and furyous rage,
To sle all the children that be in that cuntre,
That may be founde within to yeers of age:
Ther shall be shewe in that region
Diverse myracles of his high regalye,
In all ther temples the mawments shall falle down,
To shew a tokyn towards the partie,

This child hath lordship, as prophets do speake,
And at his comyng thurgh his myghty hond,
In despyght of all idolatrye,
Every oon shall falle whan he comyth in to the lond.

Joseph.

O good lord, of thi gracious ordenaunce,
Like as thu list for our journey provide,
In this viage with humble attendaunce
As God disposeth and list to be our gyde,
Therfor upon them bothe mekely I shall abide,
Praying to that Lord to thynk upon us three,
Us to preserve wheder we go or ryde
Towards Egipte from all advercitie.

Mary.

Now, husband, in all hart I pray you, go we hens,
For dredd of Herowd that cruell knyght:
Gentyll spouse, now do your diligens,
And bryng your asse, I pray you, a non ryght,
And from hens let us passe with all our myght.
Thankyng that Lord so for us doth provide,
That we may go from Herowd that cursed wyght,
Wiche will us devour if that we abide.

Joseph.

Mary, you to do plesaunce without ony lett
I shall brynge forth your asse without more delay;
Fulsone, Mary, theron ye shalbe sett,
And this litell child that in your wombe lay,
Take hym in your armys, Mary, I you pray,
And of your swete mylke let him sowke nowe,
Mawger Herowd and his grett fray:
And as your spouse, Mary, I shall go with you.
This ferdell of gere I ley upon my bakke:
Now I am redy to go from this cuntre,
All my smale instruments is putt in my pakke.

[*Et exeunt.*]

Now go we hens, Mary, it will no better be,
For drede of Herowd, a paas I wyll high me.
Lo, now is our geer trussid both more and lesse:
Mary, for to plese you with all humylite
I shall go be fore, and lede forth your asse.

[*Here Mary and Joseph shall go out of the place, and the godds shall fall: and than shall come in the women of Israell with young children in ther armys, and than the knyghts shall go to them sayng as foluth:* —

Miles j.

Herke, ye wyffys, we be come your houshold to visite;
Though ye be never so wroth nor wood,
With sharpe swerds that redely will byte,
All your children within to yeers age in our cruell mood
Thurghe out all Bethleem to kylle and shed ther young
blood,
As we be bound be the commaundement of the kyng:
Who that seith nay we shall make a flood
To renne in the stretis by ther blood shedyng.

Miles ij.

Therfor unto us ye make a delyveraunce
Of your young children, and that anone,
Or ells, be Mahounde, we shall geve a myschaunce,
Our sharpe swerds thurgh your bodies shall goon.

Watkyn.

Therfor be ware, for we will not leve oon
In all this cuntre that shall us escape,
I shall rather slee them everychoon,
And make them to lye and mowe like an ape.

Mulier j.

Fye on you, traitors of cruell tormentrye,
Wiche with your swerds of mortall violens, —

Mulier ij.

Our young children, that can no socoure but crie,
Wyll slee and devoure in ther innocens.

Mulier iij.

Ye false traitors unto God, ye do grett offens
To sle and morder young children that in the cradell slumber.

Mulier iiij.

But we women shall make a geyns you resistens
After our power, your malice to encomber.

Watkyn.

Peas, you folyshe quenys, wha shuld you defende
Ageyns us armyd men in this apparaile?
We be bold men, and the kyng us ded sende
Hedyr in to this cuntre to hold with you battaile.

Mulier j.

Fye upon the coward, of the I will not faile
To dubbe the knyght with my rokke rounde;
Women be ferse when thei list to assaile
Suche proude boyes to caste to the grounde.

Mulier ij.

Avaunt, ye skowtys, I defye you everychone,
For I wole bete you all my self alone.

[*Watkyn hic occidet per se.*]

Mulier j.

Alas, alasse, good cossynnes, this is a sorowfull peyn,
To se our dere children that be so yong
With these caytyves thus sodeynly to be slayn:
A vengeaunce I aske on them all for this grett wrong.

Mulier ij.

And a very myscheff must come them a monge,
Wherso ever thei be come or goon;
For thei have killed my yong sone John.

Mulier iij.

Gosippis, a shamefull deth I aske upon Herowde our kyng,
That thus rygorously our children hath slayn.

Mulier iiij.

I pray God bryng hym to an ille endyng,
And in helle pytte to dwelle ever in peyn.

Watkyn.

What, ye harlotts? I have aspied certeyn,
That ye be tratorys to my lord the kyng,
And therfore I am sure, ye shall have an ille endyng.

Mulier j.

If ye abide, Watkyn, you and I shall game
With my distaff that is so rounde.

Mulier ij.

And if I seas thanne have I shame,
Tyll thu be fellid down to the grounde.

Mulier iij.

And I may gete the within my hounde,
With this staffe I shall make thee lame.

Watkyn.

Yee, I come no more ther, be seynt Mahound;
For if I do, methynketh I shall be made tame.

Mulier j.

Abyde, Watkyn, I shall make the a knyght.

Watkyn.

Thu make me a knyght? that were on the newe;
But for shame, my trouthe I you plight,
I shud bete you bak and side tyll it were blewe;
But, be my God Mahounde, that is so true,
My hert be gynne to fayle, and waxeth feynt,
Or ells, be Mahounds blood, ye shuld it rue,
But ye shall lose your goods as traitors atteynt.

Mulier. j.

What, thu jahell, canst not have do?
Thu and thi cumpany shall not depart,
Tyll of our distavys ye have take part. —
Therfor ley on, gossippes, with a mery hart,
And lett them not from us goo.

[*Here thei shall bete Watkyn; and the Knyghts shall come to rescue hym, and than thei go to Herowds hous sayng,* —

Miles j.

Honorable prynce of grett apparayle,
Thurgh Jerusalem and Jude, your wyll we have wrought,
Full suerly harneysed in arms of plate and maile,
The children of Israell unto deth we have brought.

Miles ij.

Syr, to werke your commaundement we lettid nought,
In the strets of the children to make a flood;
We sparid neither for care nor thought,
Thurgh Bethlem to shedde all the young blood.

Watkyn.

In feyth, my lord, all the children be dede,
And alle the men out of the cuntre be goon;
Ther be but women, and thei crie in every stede,
A vengeaunce take kyng Herode, for he hath our children slean!
And bidde, a mischeff take him both evyn and morn!
For kylling of ther children on you thei crie oute;
And thus goth your name all the cuntre abought.

Herodes.

Oute, I am madde, my wyttes be nei goon,
I am wo for the workyng of this werke wylde;
For as wele I have slayn my frends as my foon,
Wherfor I fere, deth hath me begyled;
Notwithstondyng syn thei be all defyled,
And on the young blood of Bethlem wrought wo and wrake,
Yitt I am in no certeyn of that yong child;
Now for woo myn herte gynneth to quake.
Alas, I am so sorowful and sett in of sadnes,
I chille and chevere for this orrible chaunce;
I co̅mmaunde you all, as ye wole stond in my grace,
Aft this yong kyng to mak good enqueraunce,
And he that bryngeth me tydyngs I shall hym avaunce.
Now unto my chamber I purpose me this tyde,
And I charge you, to my precept geve attendaunce,
In ony place wher ye goo or ryde.

What, out, out allas! I wene I shall dey this day;
My hert tremblith and quakith for feer,
My robys I rende a to; for I am in a fray,
That my hert will brest asunder evyn heer. —
My lord Mahound, I pray the with hert enteer,
Take my soule in to thy holy hande,
For I fele by my hert, I shall dey evyn heer.
For my leggs falter, I may no lenger stande.

[Here dieth Herowde, and ***SYMEON*** *shall sey as foluyth: —*

Now, God, that art both lok and keye
Of all goodnesse and goostly governaunce,
So geve us grace thi lawys to obeye,
That we unto the do no displeasaunce;
Lett thi grace of mercifull habondaunce
Upon me shyne, that callid am Symeon,
So that I may without any variaunce
Teche thi people thi lawis everychon.
From the sterrid hevyn, lord, thu list come down
In to the closett of a pure virgyn,
Our kynde to take for mannys salvation,
Thi grett mercy thu lowe lyst enclyne,
Lyke as prophetys by grace that is divyne
Have prophecied of the, sythe longe afforn;
It is fulfilled, I knowe be ther doctryne,
And of a chast maide, I wote wele, thu art born.
Now, good Lord, hertly I the pray,
Here my requeste, grounded upon right:
Most blissed Lord, lett me never dey
Tyll that I of the may have a sight;
Thu art so glorious, so blissed, and so bright,
That thi presence to me shuld be gret solas;
I shall not reste, but pray bothe day and nyght
Tyll I may behold, o Lord, thi swete face.

[Here shall ***OUR LADY*** *come forth holdyng Jesu in hir armys, and sey this language foluyng to Joseph: —*

Joseph, my spouse, tyme it is, we goo
Unto the temple to make an offrynge
Of our swete sone; the law commandith so,
And ij yonge dowys with us for to bryng
In to a prests hands, without tarieng,
I shall presente for an observaunce,
Our babe so blissed wiche is but yonge
With me to go, I pray you, make purviaunce.

Joseph.

Most blissed spouse, me list not to feyne,
Fayn wold I plese you with hooll affeccion;
Behold now, wyff, here are dowys tweyne,
Of wiche ye shull make an oblacion,
With our child of full grett devocion:
Goth forth a forn, hertly I you pray,
And I shall folue, void of presumpcion,
With true entent as an old man may.

[*Here Maria and Joseph go towards the temple with Jesu and ij dowes, and* OUR LADY *seith unto Symeon,* —

Heyll, holy Symeon, full of grett vertu;
To make an offryng I gan my self perveye
Of my sovereyne sone that callid is Jesu,
With ij yonge dowes, the lawe to obeye,
Toward this temple, grace list me conveye,
Of Godds sone to make a presentacion;
Wherfore, Symeon, hertly I you pray,
In to your hands take myn oblacion.

[*Here shall* SYMEON *receyve of Maria, Jesu, and ij dowis, and holde Jesu in his armys, expownyng* Nunc dimittis *etc. seyng thus,* —

Welcome, lord, excellent of power;
And welcome, Maria, with your sone sovereyne:
Your oblacion of hooll herte and enteer
I receyve, with these dowys tweyne;
Welcome, babe, for joye what may I seyn?
Atwen myn armys now shall I thee embrace:

My prayer, Lord, was not made in veyn,
For now I se thy celestiall face.

[Here declare Nunc dimittis.]

O blissed Lord, aft thi language,
In parfight peas now lett thy servaunt reste;
For why, myn eyen have seyn thi visage,
And eke thyn helthe thurgh my meke request:
Of the derk dungeon let the gats brest
Before the face of thyn people alle;
Thu hast brought triacle and bawme of the best
With sovereyne suger geyn all bitter galle:
I mene thi self, Lord, gracious and benigne,
That woldest come down from thyn high glorye
Poyson to repelle, thi mercy doth now shyne
To chainge thyngs that are transitory,
Thu art the light and the hevynly skye
To the relevyng of folk most cruell,
Thu hast brought gladnesse to our oratorye,
And enlumyned thy people of Israell.

[Here shall ANNA, PROPHETISSA *sey thus to Virgynes:* —

Ye pure virgynes, in that ye may or can,
With tapers of wex loke ye come forth here,
And worship this child very God and man,
Offrid in this temple be his moder dere.

[Here virgynes as many as a man wyll shall holde tapers in ther hands; and the first seyth, —

Virgo j.

As ye commaunde we shall do our dever
That lorde to plese echon for our partye,
He makyth for us so comfortable chere
That we must nede your babe magnifie.

Symeon.

Now, Mary, I shall tell you how I am purposed;
To worship your lord I wil go percession,
For I see Anna with virgynes disposed
Mekly as now to your sonys laudacion.

Maria.

Blissed Symeon, with hertly affection
As ye have seyd I concent therto.

Joseph.

In worship of our child with grett devossion
Abought the tempill in order let us go.

Symeon.

Ye virgynes alle, with feythfull entent
Dispose your silf a songe for to synge,
To worship this childe that is here present,
Whiche to mankende gladnes list bryng,
In tokyn our herts, wiche joye doth spryng,
Betwyn myn armys this babe shalbe born,
Now, ye virgynis, to this Lord praysing,
Syngyth *Nunc dimittis* of whiche I spak afforn.

[*Here shall Symeon bere Jesu in his armys goyng a percession rounde aboute the tempill, and al this wyle Vrgynis singe* Nunc dimittis; *and whan that is don* SYMEON *seyth*, —

O Jesu, chef cause of our welfare,
In yone tapirs ther be thinges iij,
Wax week and lyght, whiche I shall declare
To the apporprid by moralite:
Lorde, wax betokyneth thyn humanyte,
And week betokyneth thy soule most swete,
Yone lyght I lyken to the godhede of the,
Brighter than Phebus for al his fervent hete,
Pes and mercy han set in the here swete
To slake the sharpnes, o Lorde, of rigour,
Very God and man grace togedir mete,
In the tabirnacle of thy modrys bower:
Now shalt thu exile wo and al langour,
And of mankende tappese infernall stryf,
Record of prophets thou shalt be redemptour,
And singuler repast of everlastyng lyf.

My sprete joyeth thu art so amyable,
I am not wery to loke on thi face,
Our trowe entent let it be acceptable,
To the honor of the shewys in this place;
For thy friends a dwellyng thu shalt purchase,
Brighter than berall outher clere crystall,
Thee to worship as chef welle of grace;
On both my knees now down knele I shall.

Maria.

Now, Symeon, take me my childe that is so bright,
Chef lodesterre of my felicyte;
And all that longyth to the lawe of right
I shall obeye, as it lyth in me.

Symeon.

This, Lord, I take you knelyng on my kne,
Whiche shall to blisse folk ageyn restore,
And so be callid sonne of tranquylyte,
To geve them drynke that hem thyrstyd sore.

[*Here MARIA receyveth hir sone thus seyng,* —

Now is myn offrynge to an ende conveyed;
Wherfore, Symeon, hens I wolde hende.

Symeon.

The lawes, Mary, fulwell ye han obbeyed
In this tempill with hert and mende.
Now ferwell, Lord, comfort to all mankende:
Ferwell, Maria, and Joseph on you waytyng.

Joseph.

Celestiall socour our sone mot you sende.
And for his high mercy geve you his blissyng.

[*Here Maria and Joseph goyng from the tempill seyng:* —

Maria.

Husbond, I thank you of your gentilnes.
That thu han shewed onto me this day,
With our child most gracious of godenes:
Let us go hens, hertly I you pray.

Joseph.

Go forthe afforn, my owne wyf, I sey,
And I shall come aftir stil upon this ground,
Ye shal me fynde plesant at every assaye;
To cheryshe you, wyf, gretly am I bonde.

Symeon.

Nowe may I be glad in myn inwarde mynde;
For I have seyn Jesu with my bodely eye,
Wiche on a cross shall bey al menkende,
Slayn by Jews at the mount of Calvery,
And throw evyns grace here I will provysye
Of blissid Mary how she shall suffre peyn,
Whan hir swete sone shall on a rood deye;
A sharpe swarde of sorow shall cleve hir hert atweyn.
Anna prophetissa, hertly I pray you nowe,
Doth your devir and your diligent labour,
And take these virgynis everychon with you,
And teche hem to plese God of most honour.

Anna, Prophetissa.

Lyke as ye say, I will do this hour:
Ye chast virgynis, with all humilite
Worshipe we Jesu that shalbe our savyour;
Alle at ones come on, and folowe me.

Anna, Prophetissa.

Shewe ye sume plesur as ye can,
In the worship of Jesu, our Lady, and seynt Anne.

Poëta.

Honorable soverignes, thus we conclude
Our matter, that we have shewid here in your presens:
And though our eloquens be but rude,
We beseeche you all of your paciens,

To pardon us of our offens;
For aft the sympyll cunnyng that we can,
This matter we have shewid to your audiens,
In the worship of our Lady and hir moder seynt Anne.
 Nowe of this pore processe we make an ende,
Thankyng you all of your good attendaunce;
And the next yeer, as we be perposid in our mynde,
The disputacion of the doctors to shew in your presens.
Wherfor now, ye vyrgynes, or we go hens,
With all your cumpany you goodly avaunce:
Also ye menstralles doth your diligens,
A fore our depertyng geve us a daunce.

FINIS.

GOD'S PROMISES.

A Tragedy or enterlude manyfestyng the chefe promyses of God unto man by all ages in the olde lawe, from the fall of Adam to the inçarnaçyon of the lorde Jesus Christ. Compyled by Johan Bale, Anno Domini MDXXXVIII.

It is uncertain where this play was first printed, but most probably in the Low Countries, or in Switzerland.

GOD'S PROMISES.

Baleus, Prolocutor.

If profyght maye growe, most Christen audyence,
By knowlege of thynges whych are but transytorye,
And here for a tyme, of moch more congruence,
Advantage myght sprynge, by the serche of causes heavenlye,
As those matters are, that the Gospell specyfye;
Without whose knowledge no man to the truthe can fall,
Nor ever atteyne to the lyfe perpetuall.
For he that knoweth not the lyvynge God eternall,
The father, the sonne, and also the holye Ghost,
And what Christ suffered for redempcyon of us all,
What he commaunded, and taught in every coost,
And what he forbode, that man must nedes be lost,
And cleane secluded, from the faythfull chosen sorte,
In the heavens above, to hys most hygh dysconforte.
Yow therfor, good fryndes, I lovyngely exhort
To waye soche matters, as wyll be uttered here,
Of whom ye may loke to have no tryfeling sporte
In fantasyes fayned, nor soche lyke gaudysh gere,
But the thyngs that shall your inwarde stomake chear,

To rejoyce in God for your justyfycacyon,
And alone in Christ to hope for your salvacyon.
Yea, first ye shall have the eternal generacyon
Of Christ, like as Johan in hys first chaptre wryght,
And consequentlye of man the first creacyon,
The abuse and fall, through hys first oversyght,
And the rayse agayne through God's hygh grace and myght:
By promyses first, whych shall be declared all,
Then by hys owne sonne, the worker pryncypall.
After that Adam bywayleth here hys fall,
God wyll shewe mercye to every generacyon,
And to hys kyngedome, of hys great goodnesse call
Hys elected spouse, or faythfull congregacyon,
As here shall apere by open protestacyon,
Whych from Christe's birthe shall to hys death conclude:
They come that therof wyll shewe the certytude.

ACTUS PRIMUS.

Pater cœlestis.

In the begynnynge, before the heavens were create,
In me and of me was my sonne sempyternall
With the holy Ghost, in one degre or estate
Of the hygh Godhed, to me the father coequall,
And thys my sonne was with me one God essencyall,
Without separacyon at any tyme from me.
True God he is, of equall dignyte.
Sens the begynnynge, my sonne has ever be,
Joined wyth hys Father in one essencyall beynge.
All thynges were create by hym in yche degre,
In heaven and earthe, and have their dyverse workynge:
Wythout hys power, was never made anye thynge,

That was wrought; but through hys ordynaunce,
Each have hys strength and whole contynuance.
In hym is the lyfe and the *just* recoveraunce
For Adam and hys, which nought but deathe deserved.
And thys lyfe to men is an hygh perseveraunce,
Or a lyght of faythe, wherby they shall be saved.
And thys lyght shall shyne amonge the people darkened
With unfaythfulnesse. Yet shall they not with hym take,
But of wyllfull hart hys lyberall grace forsake.
Whych wyll compell me agaynst man for to make
In my dyspleasure, and sende plages of correccyon,
Most grevouse and sharpe, hys wanton lustes to slake,
By water and fyre, by syeknesse and infeccyon,
Of pestylent sores, molestynge hys compleccyon,
By troublouse warre, by derthe and peynefull scarsenesse,
And after thys lyfe be an extreme heavynesse.
I wyll first begynne with Adam for hys lewdenesse,
Whych for an apple neglected my commaundement.
He shall contynue in laboure for hys rashenesse,
Hys onlye sweate shall provyde hys food and raymennt:
Yea, yet must he have a greatter ponnyshment,
Most terryble deathe shall brynge hym to hys ende
To teache hym how he hys lord God shall offende.

[*Hic præceps in terram cadit Adamus, ac post quartum versum denuo resurgit.*]

Adam primus homo.

Mercyfull Father, thy pytiefull grace extende
To me carefull wretche, whych have mesore abused,
Thy precept breakynge. O Lorde, I mynde to amende,
If thy great goodnesse wolde now have me excused,
Most heavenlye Maker, lete me not be refused,
Nor cast from thy syght for one pore synnefull cryme,
Alas I am frayle, my whole kynde ys but slyme.

Pater cœlestis.

I wott it is so, yet art thu no lesse faultye,
Than thu haddyst bene made of matter moch more worthye.

I gave the reason, and wytte to understande
The good from the evyll, and not to take on hande,
Of a braynelesse mynde, the thynge whych I forbad the.

Adam primus homo.

Soch heavye fortune hath chefelye chaunced me,
For that I was left to myne owne lyberte.

Pater cœlestis.

Then thu art blamelesse, and the faulte thu layest to me.

Adam primus homo.

Naye all I ascribe to my own imbecyllyte.
No faulte in the Lorde, but in my infirmyte,
And want of respect in soche gyftes as thu gavest me.

Pater cœlestis.

For that I put the at thyne owne lyberte,
Thu oughtest my goodnesse to have in more regarde.

Adam primus homo.

Avoyde it I cannot, thu layest it to me so harde.
Lorde, now I perceyve what power is in man,
And strength of hymselfe, whan thy swete grace is absent.
He must nedes but fall, do he the best he can,
And daunger hymselfe, as apereth evydent;
For I synned not to longe as thu wert present;
But whan thu wert gone, I fell to synne by and by,
And the dyspleased. Good lorde I axe the mercy.

Pater cœlestis.

Thu shalt dye for it, with all thy posteryte.

Adam primus homo.

For one faulte, good lorde, avenge not thyself on me,
Who am but a worme, or a fleshelye vanyte.

Pater cœlestis.

I saye thu shalt dye, with thy whole posteryte.

Adam primus homo.

Yet mercy swete lorde, yf anye mercy maye be.

Pater cœlestis.

I am immutable, I maye change no decre;
Thu shalt dye, I saye, without anye remedye.

Adam primus homo.

Yet gracyouse Father, extende to me thy mercye,
And throwe not awaye the worke whych thu hast create
To thyne owne Image, but avert from me thy hate.

Pater cœlestis.

But art thu sorye from bottom of thy hart?

Adam primus homo.

Thy dyspleasure is to me most heavye smart.

Pater cœlestis.

Than wyll I tell the what thu shalt styeke unto,
Lyfe to recover, and my good faver also.

Adam primus homo.

Tell it me, swete Lorde, that I maye therafter go.

Pater cœlestis.

Thys ys my covenant to the and all thy ofspryngc.
For that thu hast bene deceyved by the serpent,
I wyll put hatred betwixt hym for hys doynge,
And the woman kynde. They shall herafter dyssent;
Hys sede with her sede shall never have agrement;
Her sede shall presse downe hys heade unto the grounde,
Slee hys suggestyons, and hys whole power confounde.
Cleave to thys promyse, with all thy inwarde powre,
Fyrmelye enclose it in thy remembraunce fast;
Folde it in thy faythe with full hope day and houre,
And thy salvacyon it will be at the last.
That sede shall clere the of all thy wyckednesse past,
And procure thy peace, with most hygh grace in my syght.
Se thu trust to it, and holde not the matter lyght.

Adam primus homo.

Swete lorde, the promyse that thyself here hath made me,
Of thy mere goodnesse, and not of my deservynge,
In my faythe I trust shall so establyshed be,
By helpe of thy grace, that it shall be remaynynge
So longe as I shall have here contynuynge,
And shewe it I wyll to my posteryte,
That they in lyke case have therby felycyte.

Pater cœlestis.

For a closynge up, take yet one sentence with the.

Adam primus homo.

At thy pleasure, Lorde, all thynges myght ever be.

Pater cœlestis.

For that my promyse maye have the deper effect
In the faythe of the and all thy generacyon,
Take thys sygne with it, as a seale therto connect.
Crepe shall the serpent, for hys abhomynacyon;
The woman shall sorowe in paynefull propagacyon.
Like as thu shalt finde thys true in outwarde workynge,
So thynke the other, though it be an hydden thynge.

Adam primus homo.

Incessaunt praysynge to the most heavenlye lorde
For thys thy socoure, and undeserved kyndnesse
Thu byndest me in hart thy gracyouse gyftes to recorde,
And to beare in mynde, now after my heavynesse,
The brute of thy name, with inwarde joye and gladnesse.
Thu dysdaynest not, as wele apereth thys daye,
To fatche to thy folde thy first shepe goynge astraye.
Most myghtye maker, thu castest not yet awaye
Thy synnefull servaunt, whych hath done most offence.
It is not thy mynde for ever I shuld decaye,
But thu reservest me, of thy benyvolence,
And hast provyded for me a recompence,
By thy appoyntment, like as I have receyved
In thy stronge promyse, here openly pronounced.
Thys goodnesse, dere lorde, of me is undeserved,
I so declynynge from thy first instytucyon,
At so lyght mocyons. To one that thus hath swerved,
What a lorde art thu, to geve soche retrybucyon!
I, damnable wretche, deserved execucyon
Of terryble deathe, without all remedye,
And to be put out of all good memorye.
I am enforced to rejoyce here inwardelye,
An ympe though I be of helle, deathe, and dampnacyon,

Through my owne workynge: for I consydre thy mercye
And pytiefull mynde for my whole generacyon.
It is thu, swete lorde, that workest my salvacyon,
And my recover. Therfor of a congruence,
From hens thu must have my hart and obedyence.
  Though I be mortall, by reason of my offence,
And shall dye the deathe, like as God hath appoynted:
Of thys am I sure, through hys hygh influence,
At a serten daye agayne to be revyved.
From grounde of my hart thys shall not be removed,
I have it in faythe and therfor I will synge
Thys Antheme to hym that my salvacyon shall brynge.

[*Tunc sonora voce, provolutis genibus, Antiphonam incipit,* O sapientia, *quam prosequetur chorus cum organis, eo interim exeunte: vel sub eodem tono poterit sic Anglice cantari.*]

O eternal sapyence, that procedest from the mouthe of the hyghest, reachynge fourth with a great power from the begynnynge to the ende, with heavenlye swetnesse dysposynge all creatures, come now and enstruct us the true waye of thy godlye prudence.

Finit Actus primus.

ACTUS SECUNDUS.

Pater cœlestis.

I have bene moved to stryke man dyverselye,
Sens I lefte Adam in thys same earthly mansyon;
For whye? he hath done to me dyspleasures manye,
And wyll not amende hys lyfe in anye condycyon:
No respect hath he to my worde nor monycyon,
But doth what hym lust, wythout dyscrete advysement,
And wyll in no wyse take myne advertysement.

Cain hath slayne Abel, hys brother, an innocent,
Whose bloude from the earthe doth call to me for vengeaunce:
My children with mennis so carnallye consent,
That their vayne workynge is unto me moche grevaunce:
Mankynde is but fleshe in hys whole dallyaunce.
All vyce encreaseth in hym contynuallye,
Nothynge he regardeth to walk unto my glorye.
My hart abhorreth hys wylfull myserye,
Hys cankred malyce, hys cursed covetousenesse,
Hys lustes lecherouse, hys vengeable tyrannye,
Unmercyfull mourther, and other ungodlynesse.
I will destroye hym for hys outragyousnesse,
And not hym onlye, but all that on earthe do stere,
For it repenteth me that ever I made them here.

Justus Noah.

Most gentyll maker, with hys frayleness sumwhat beare,
Man is thy creature, thyselfe cannot saye naye.
Though thu punysh hym, to put hym sumwhat in feare,
Hys faulte to acknowledge, yet seke not hys decaye.
Thu mayest reclayme hym, though he goeth now astraye,
And brynge hym agayne, of thy abundaunt grace,
To the fold of faythe, he acknowlegynge hys trespace.

Pater cœlestis.

Thu knowest I have geven to him convenyent space,
With lawfull warnynges, yet he amendeth in no place.
The naturall lawes, which I wrote in hys harte,
He hath outraced, all goodnesse puttynge a parte:
Of helthe the covenaunt, whych I to Adam made,
He regardeth not, but walketh a damnable trade.

Justus Noah.

All thys is true, lorde, I cannot thy words reprove,
Lete hys weaknesse yet thy mercyfull goodnesse move.

Pater cœlestis.

No weaknesse is it, but wylfull workynge all,
That reigneth in man through mynde dyabolycall.
He shall have therfor lyke as he hath deserved.

Justus Noah.

Lose hym not yet, lorde, though he hath depelye swerved.
I knowe thy mercye is farre above hys rudenesse,
Beyenge infynyte, as all other thynges are in the.
Hys folye therfor now pardone of thy goodnesse,
And measure it not beyonde thy godlye pytie.
Esteme not hys faulte farder than helpe may be,
But graunt hym thy grace, as he offendeth so depelye,
The to remembre, and abhorre hys myserye.
Of all goodnesse, lorde, remembre thy great mercye
To Adam and Eve, breakynge thy first commaundement.
Them thu relevedest with thy swete promyse heavenlye,
Synnefull though they were, and their lyves neglygent.
I knowe that mercye with the is permanent,
And will be ever, so longe as the worlde endure:
Than close not thy hande from man, whych is thy creature.
Beynge thy subject, he is undreneth thy cure,
Correct hym thu mayest, and so brynge hym to grace.
All lyeth in thy handes, to leave or to allure,
Bytter deathe to geve, or graunte most suffren solace.
Utterlye from man averte not then thy face,
But lete hym saver thy swete benyvolence,
Sumwhat, though he fele thy hande for hys offence.

Pater cœlestis.

My true servaunt Noah, thy ryghtousnesse doth move me
Sumwhat to reserve for mannys posteryte.
Though I drowne the worlde, yet wyll I save the lyves
Of the and thy wyfe, thy three sonnes and their wyves,
And of ych kynde two, to mayntenyne yow herafter.

Justus Noah.

Blessed be thy name, most myghtye mercyfull maker,
With the to dyspute, it were unconvenyent.

Pater cœlestis.

Whye doest thu saye so? be bolde to speke thy intent.

Justus Noah.

Shall the other dye without any remedye?

Pater cœlestis.

I wyll drowne them all, for their wylful wycked folye,
That man herafter therby maye knowe my powre,
And feare to offende my goodnesse daye and houre.

Justus Noah.

As thy pleasure is, so myght it alwayes be,
For my helthe thu art, and sowle's felycyte.

Pater cœlestis.

After that thys floude have had hys ragynge passage,
Thys shall be to the my covenaunt everlastynge.
The sees and waters so farre never more shall rage,
As all fleshe to drowne, I wyll so tempre their workynge;
Thys sygne wyll I adde also, to confirme the thynge.
In the cloudes above, as a seale or token clere,
For savegarde of man, my raynebowe shall apere.
Take thu thys covenaunt for an ernest confirmacyon
Of my former promyse to Adam's generacyon.

Justus Noah.

I wyll, blessed lorde, with my whole hart and mynde.

Pater cœlestis.

Farewele then, just Noah, here leave I the behynde.

Justus Noah.

Most myghtye maker, ere I from hens depart,
I must geve the prayse from the bottom of my hart.
Whom may we thanke, lorde, for our helthe and salvacyon
But thy great mercye and goodnesse undeserved?
Thy promyse in faythe, is our justyfycacyon,
As it was Adam's, whan hys hart therin rested,
And as it was theirs, whych therein also trusted.
Thys faythe was grounded in Adam's memorye,
And clerelye declared in Abel's innocencye.
Faythe in that promyse, olde Adam ded justyfye,
In that promyse faythe, made Eva to prophecye.
Faythe in that promyse, proved Abel innocent,
In that promyse faythe, made Seth full obedyent.

That faythe taught Enos, on God's name first to call,
And made Mathusalah the oldest man of all.
That fayth brought Enoch to so hygh exercyse,
That God toke hym up with hym into paradyse.
Of that faythe the want, made Cain to hate the good,
And all hys ofspryngc to peryshe in the flood.
Faythe in that promyse, preserved both me and myne:
So will it all them whych folowe the same lyne.
Not onlye thys gyfte thu hast geven me, swete lorde,
But with it also thyne everlastynge covenaunt,
Of trust for ever, thy raynebowe bearynge recorde,
Nevermore to drowne the worlde by floude inconstaunt,
Alae I can not to the geve prayse condygne,
Yet wyll I synge here with harte meke and benygne.

[*Magna tunc voce Antiphonam incipit*, (O oriens splendor,) *&c. in genua cadens; quam chorus prosequetur cum organis ut supra, vel Anglice sub eodem tono*]

O most orient clerenesse, and lyght shynynge of the sempiternall bryghtnesse! O clere sunne of justyce and heavenlye ryghtousnesse! come hyther and illumyne the prisoner, syttynge now in the darke prison and shaddowe of eternall deathe.

Finit Actus secundus.

ACTUS TERTIUS.

Pater cœlestis.

Myne hygh displeasure must nedes returne to man,
Consyderynge the synne that he doth daye by daye;
For neyther kyndenesse, nor extreme handelynge can.
Make hym to knowe me by any faythfull waye,
But styll in myschefe he walketh to hys decaye.

If he do not sone hys wyckednesse consydre,
He is like, doubtlesse, to perysh all togydre.
In my syght, he is more venym than the spyder,
Through soch abuses as he hath exercysed,
From the tyme of Noah, to this same season hyder.
An uncomelye acte without shame Cham commysed,
When he of hys father the secrete partes reveled.
In lyke case Nemrod against me wrought abusyon,
As he raysed up the castell of confusyon.
Ninus hath also, and all by the devyl's illusyon,
Through ymage makynge, up raysed idolatrye,
Me to dyshonoure. And now in the conclusyon
The vyle Sodomytes lyve so unnaturallye,
That their synne vengeaunce axeth contynuallye,
For my covenaunte's seke, I wyll not drowne with water,
Yet shall I vysyte their synnes with other matter.

Abraham fidelis.

Yet, mercyfull lorde, thy gracyousnesse remembre
To Adam and Noah, both in thy worde and promes:
And lose not the sowles of men in so great nombre,
But save thyne owne worke, of thy most dyscrete goodness.
I wote thy mercyes are plentyfull and endles.
Never can they dye, nor fayle, thyself enduryngc,
Thys hath faythe fixed fast in my understandynge.

Pater cœlestis.

Abraham my servaunt, for thy most faythfull meanynge,
Both thu and thy stocke shall have my plentouse blessynge.
Where the unfaythfull, undre my curse evermore,
For their vayne workynge, shall rewe their wyckednesse sore.

Abraham fidelis.

Tell me, blessed lorde, where wyll thy great malyce lyght.
My hope is, all fleshe shall not perysh in thy syght.

Pater cœlestis.

No trulye Abraham, thu chauncest upon the right.
The thynge I shall do, I wyll not hyde from the,
Whom I have blessyd for thy true fydelyte:

For I knowe thou wilt cause both thy chyldren and servauntes,
In my wayes to walke, and trust unto my covenauntes,
That I may perfourme with the my earnest promes.

Abraham fidelis.

All that wyll I do, by assystence of thy goodnes.

Pater cœlestis.

From Sodom and Gomor, the abhomynacyons call
For my great vengeaunce, whych wyll upon them fall.
Wylde fyre and brymstone shall lyght upon them all.

Abraham fidelis.

Pytiefull maker, though they have kyndled thy furye,
Cast not awaye yet the *j*ust sort with the ungodlye.
Paraventure there maye be fiftye ryghteouse persones
Within those cyties, wylt thu lose them all at ones,
And not spare the place, for those fyftye ryghteouse sake?
Be it farre from the soch rygoure to undertake.
I hope there is not in the so cruell hardenesse,
As to cast awaye the just men with the rechelesse,
And so to destroye the good with the ungodlye:
In the *j*udge of all, be never soch a furye.

Pater cœlestis.

At Sodom, if I may fynde just persones fiftye,
The place wyll I spare for their sakes verelye.

Abraham fidelis.

I take upon me, to speake here in thy presence,
More then become me, lorde pardon my neglygence:
I am but ashes, and were lothe the to offende.

Pater cœlestis.

Saye fourth, good Abraham, for yll dost thu non intende.

Abraham fidelis.

Happlye there maye be fyve lesse in the same nombre;
For their sakes I trust thu wylt not the rest accombre.

Pater cœlestis.

If I amonge them myght fynde but fyve and fortye,
Them wolde I not lose for that *j*ust companye.

Abraham fidelis.

What if the cytie maye fortye ryghteouse make?

Pater cœlestis.

Then wyll I pardone it for those same fortye's sake?

Abraham fidelis.

Be not angrye, lorde, though I speake undyscretelye.

Pater cœlestis.

Utter thy whole mynde, and spare me not hardelye.

Abraham fidelis.

Perauventure there maye be thirty founde amonge them.

Pater cœlestis.

Maye I fynde thirty, I wyll nothynge do unto them.

Abraham fidelis.

I take upon me to moche, lorde, in thy syght.

Pater cœlestis.

No, no, good Abraham, for I knowe thy faythe is right.

Abraham fidelis.

No lesse, I suppose, than twenty, can it have.

Pater cœlestis.

Coulde I fynde twenty, that cytie wolde I save.

Abraham fidelis.

Ones yet wyll I speake my mynde, and than no more.

Pater cœlestis.

Spare not to utter so moche as thu hast in store.

Abraham fidelis.

And what if there myght be ten good creatures founde?

Pater cœlestis.

The rest for their sakes myght so be safe and sounde,
And not destroyed for their abhomynacyon.

Abraham fidelis.

O mercyfull maker, moche is thy tolleracyon
And sufferaunce of synne. I se it now in dede,
Witsave yet of faver out of those cyties to leade
Those that be faythfull, though their flocke be but small.

Pater cœlestis.

Loth and hys howsholde, I wyll delyver all,
For ryghteousnesse sake, whych is of me and not them.

Abraham fidelis.

Great are thy graces in the generacyon of Sem.

Pater cœlestis.

Well Abraham, well, for thy true faythfulnes,
Now wyll I geve the my covenaunt, or third promes.
Loke thu beleve it, as thu covetyst ryghtuousnesse.

Abraham fidelis.

Lorde so regarde me, as I receyve it with gladnesse.

Pater cœlestis.

Of manye peoples the father I wyll make the,
All generacyons in thy sede shall be blessyd:
As the starres of heaven, so shall thy kyndred be;
And by the same sede the worlde shall be redressed.
In cyrcumcysyon shall thys thynge be expressed,
As in a sure seale, to prove my promyse true,
Prynt thys in thy faythe, and it shall thy sowle renue.

Abraham fidelis.

I wyll not one *jote*, lorde, from thy wyll dyssent,
But to thy pleasure be alwayes obedyent,
Thy lawes to fullfyll, and most precyouse commaundement.

Pater cœlestis.

Farwele Abraham, for heare in place I leave the.

Abraham fidelis.

Thankes wyll I rendre, lyke as it shall behove me.
Everlastynge prayse to thy most gloryouse name,
Whych savedyst Adam through faythe in thy sweet promes
Of the womannys sede, and now confyrmest the same
In the sede of me. Fosoth great is thy goodnes.
I can not perceyve, but that thy mercye is endles,
To soch as feare the, in every generacyon,
For it endureth without abrevyacyon.
Thys have I prynted in depe consyderacyon,
No worldly matter can race it out of mynde.

For ones it wyll be the fynall restauracyon
Of Adam and Eve, with other that hath synde;
Yea, the sure helthe and rayse of all mankynde.
Helpe have the faythfull therof, though they be infect,
They condempnacyon where as it is reject.
Mercyfull maker, my crabbed voyce dyrect,
That it maye breake out in some swete prayse to the;
And suffre me not thy due lawdes to neglect,
But lete me shewe forth thy commendacyons fre.
Stoppe not my wynde pypes, but geve them lyberte,
To sounde to thy name, whych is most gracyouse,
And in it rejoyce with hart melodyouse.

[*Tunc alta voce canit Antiphonam*, O rex gentium, *choro eandem prosequente cum organis, ut prius, vel Anglice hoc modo:* —

O most myghtye governour of thy people, and in hart most desyred, the harde rocke and true corner stone, that of two maketh one, unynge the Jews with the Gentyles in one churche, come now and releve mankynde whom thu hast fourmed of the vyle earthe.

Finit Actus tertius.

ACTUS QUARTUS.

Pater cœlestis.

Styll so increaseth the wyckednesse of man,
That I am moved with plages hym to confounde.
Hys weakenesse to ayde, I do the best I can,
Yet he regardeth me no more than doth an hounde.
My worde and promyse in hys faythe taketh no grounde;
He wyll so longe walke in hys owne lustes at large,
That nought he shall fynde hys folye to dyscharge.

Sens Abraham's tyme, whych was my true elect,
Ismael have I founde both wycked, fearce, and cruell:
And Esau in mynde with hatefull murther infect.
The sonnes of Jacob to lustes unnatural fell,
And into Egypte ded they their brother sell.
Laban to ydolles gave faythfull reverence,
Dina was corrupt through Sichem's vyolence.

Ruben abused hys father's concubyne,
Judas gate chyldren of hys own doughter in lawe:
Yea, her in my syght went after a wycked lyne.
Hys sede Onan spylte, his brother's name to withdrawe.
Achan lyved here without all godlye awe.
And now the chyldren of Israel abuse my powre
In so vyle maner, that they move me everye howre.

Moses sanctus.

Pacyfye thy wrathe, swete lorde, I the desyre,
As thu art gentyll, benygne, and pacyent,
Lose not that people in fearcenesse of thine yre
For whom thu hast shewed soche tokens evydent,
Convertynge thys rodde into a lyvelye serpent,
And the same serpent into thys rodde agayne,
Thy wonderfull power declarynge very playne.

For their sakes also puttest Pharao to payne
By ten dyverse plages, as I shall here declare.
By bloude, frogges, and lyce; by flyes, death, botche, and blayne;
By hayle, by grassoppers, by darknesse, and by care;
By a soden plage, all their first gotten ware,
Thu slewest, in one nyght, for hys fearce cruelnesse.
From that thy people witholde not now thy goodnesse.

Pater cœlestis.

I certyfye the, my chosen servaunt Moses,
That people of myne is full of unthankefulnes.

Moses sanctus.

Dere lorde, I knowe it, alas! yet waye their weakenesse,
And beare with their faultes, of thy great bounteousnesse.
In a flamynge bushe havynge to them respect,

Thu appoyntedst me their passage to direct,
And through the reade see thy ryght hande ded us lede
Where Pharoe's boost the floude overwhelmed in dede.
Thu wentest beforn them in a shynynge cloude all daye,
And in the darke nyght in fyre thu shewedest their waye.
Thu sentest them manna from heaven to be their food.
Out of the harde stone thu gavest them water good.
Thu appoyntedst them a lande of mylke and honye.
Let them not perysh for want of thy great mercye.

Pater cœlestis.

Content they are not with foule nor yet with fayre,
But murmour and grudge as people in dyspayre.
As I sent manna they had it in dysdayne,
Thus of their welfare thay manye tymes complayne.
Over Amalech I gave them the vyctorye.

Moses sanctus.

Most gloryouse maker, all that is to thy glorye.
Thu sentest them also a lawe from heaven above,
And dalye shewedest them manye tokens of great love.
The brazen serpent thu gavest them for their healynge,
And Balaam's curse thu turnedest into a blessynge.
I hope thu wilt not dysdayne to help them styll.

Pater cœlestis.

I gave them preceptes, which they will not fulfyll,
Nor yet knowledge me for their God and good lorde,
So do their vyle dedes with their wyked hartes accorde
Whyls thu hast talked with me famylyarlye
In Synai's mountayne, the space but of dayes fortye,
These sightes all they have forgotten clerely,
And are turned to shamefull ydolatrye.
For their God, they have sett up a golden calfe.

Moses sanctus.

Let me saye sumwhat, swete Father, in their behalfe.

Pater cœlestis.

I wyll first conclude, and then saye on thy mynde.
For that I have founde that people so unkynde,

Not one of them shall enjoye the promyse of me,
For enterynge the lande, but Caleb and Josue.

Moses sanctus.

Thy eternall wyll evermore fulfylled be.
For dysobeydence thu slewest the sonnes of Aaron,
The earthe swellowed in both Dathan and Ahiron.
The adders ded stynge other wycked persones els,
In wonderfull nombre. Thus hast thu ponnyshed rebels.

Pater cœlestis.

Never wyll I spare the cursed inyquyte
Of ydolatrye, for no cause, thu mayst trust me.

Moses sanctus.

Forgeve them yet, Lorde, for thys tyme, if it may be.

Pater cœlestis.

Thynkest thu that I wyll so sone chaunge my deere?
No, no, frynde Moses, so lyght thu shalt not fynde me,
I wyll ponnysh them all; Israel shall it se.

Moses sanctus.

I wote, thy people hath wrought abhomynacyon,
Worshyppynge false goddes, to thy honour's derogacyon,
Yet mercyfullye thu mayest upon them loke;
And if thu wylt not, thrust me out of thy boke.

Pater cœlestis.

Those great blasphemers shall out of my boke cleane,
But thu shalt not so, for I knowe what thu doest meane.
Conduct my people, myne angell shall assyst the,
That synne at a day wyll not uncorrected be.
And for the true zele that thu to my people hast,
I adde thys covenaunt unto my promyses past.
Rayse them up I wyll a prophete from amonge them,
Not onlyke to the, to speke my wordes unto them.
Whoso heareth not that he shall speake in my name,
I wyll revenge it to hys perpetual shame.
The passover lambe wyll be a token just
Of thys stronge covenaunt. Thys have I clerely dyscuste,
In my appontyement thys houre for youre delyveraunce.

Moses sanctus.

Never shall thys thynge depart from my remembraunce.
Laude be for ever to the most mercyfull lorde,
Whych never withdrawest from man thy heavenlye comfort,
But from age to age thy benefytes doth recorde
What thy goodnesse is, and hath bene to hys sort.
As we fynde thy grace, so ought we to report.
And doubtlesse it is to us most bounteouse,
Yea, for all our synnes most rype and plenteouse.
Abraham our father founde the benyvolouse,
So ded good Isaac in hys dystresse amonge.
To Jacob thu wert a gyde most gracyouse.
Joseph thu savedest from daungerouse deadlye wronge.
Melchisedech and Job felt thy great goodnesse stronge,
So ded good Sara, Rebecca, and fayre Rachel,
With Sephora my wyfe, the doughter of Raguel.
To prayse the, swete lorde, my faythe doth me compell,
For thy covenaunte's sake wherin rest our salvacyon,
The sede of promyse, all other sedes excell,
For therin remayneth our full justyfycacyon.
From Adam to Noah, in Abraham's generacyon,
That sede procureth God's myghty grace and powre;
For the same sede's sake, I wyll synge now thys howre.

[*Clara tunc voce Antiphonam incipit*, O Emanuel, *quam chorus (ut prius) prosequetur cum organis, vel Anglice canat*, —

O hygh kynge Emanuel, and our lege lorde! the longe expectacyon of Gentyles, and the myghtye saver of their multytude, the healthe and consolacyon of synners, come now for to save us, as our Lorde and our Redeemer.

Finit Actus quartus.

ACTUS QUINTUS.

Pater cœlestis.

For all the faver I have shewed Israel,
Delyverynge her from Pharaoe's tyrannye,
And gevynge the lande, *fluentem lac et mel*,
Yet wyll she not leave her olde ydolatrye,
Nor know me for God. I abhorre her myserye.
Vexed her I have with battayles and decayes,
Styll must I plage her, I se no other wayes.

David rex pius.

Remembre yet, lorde, thy worthye servaunt Moses,
Walkynge in thy syght, without rebuke of the.
Both Aaron, Jetro, Eleazar, and Phinees,
Evermore feared to offende thy mageste,
Moch thu acceptedst thy servant Josue.
Caleb and Othoniel sought the with all their hart,
Aioth and Sangar for thy folke ded their part.
Gedeon and Thola thy enemyes put to smart,
Jayr and Jephte gave prayses to thy name.
These, to leave ydolles, thy people ded coart.
Samson the stongest, for hys part ded the same.
Samuel and Nathan thy messages ded proclame.
What though fearce Pharao wrought myschef in thy syght,
He was a pagane, laye not that in our lyght.
I wote the Benjamytes abused the wayes of ryght,
So ded Helye's sonnes, and the sonnes of Samuel.
Saul in hys offyce was slouthful daye and night,
Wycked was Semei, so was Achitophel.
Measure not by them the faultes of Israel,
Whom thu hast loved of longe tyme so inteyrlye,
But of thy great grace remyt her wycked folye.

Pater cœlestis.

I cannot abyde the vyce of ydolatrye,
Though I shuld suffer all other vyllanye.
Whan Josue was dead, that sort from me ded fall
To the worshyppynge of Asteroth and Baal,
Full uncleane ydolles, and monsters bestyall.

David rex pius.

For it they have had thy righteouse ponnyshment,
And for as moch as they did wyckedly consent
To the Palestynes and Chananytes ungodlye
Idolaters, takynge to them in matrymonye,
Thu threwest them undre the kynge of Mesopotamye,
After thu subduedest them for their idolatrye.
Eyghtene years to Eglon, the kynge of Moabytes,
And xx. years to Jabin, the kynge of Chananytes,
Oppressed they were vii. years of the Mydyanytes,
And xviii. years vexed of the cruell Ammonytes.
In three great battayles, of three score thousand and fyve,
Of thys thy people, not one was left alyve.
Have mercye now, lorde, and call them to repentaunce.

Pater cœlestis.

So longe as they synne, so longe shall they have grevaunce.
David my servaunt, sumwhat must I say to the,
For that thu latelye hast wrought soch vanyte.

David rex pius.

Spare not, blessed lorde, but saye thy pleasure to me.

Pater cœlestis.

Of late dayes thu hast mysused Bersabe,
The wyfe of Urye, and slayne hym in the fyelde.

David rex pius.

Mercye, lorde, mercye, for doubtlesse I am defyelde.

Pater cœlestis.

I constytute the a kynge over Israel,
And the preserved from Saul, whych was thy enemye.
Yea, in my faver, so moch thu dedyest excell,
That of thy enemyes I gave the vyctorye.

Palestynes and Syryanes to the came trybutarye.
Why hast thu then wrought soch folye in my syght,
Despysynge my worde, against all godlye ryght?

David rex pius.

I have synned, lord, I beseech the, pardon me.

Pater cælestis.

Thu shalt not dye, David, for thys inyquyte,
For thy repentaunce; but thy sonne by Bersabe
Shall dye, for as moch as my name is blasphemed
Among my enemyes, and thu the worse estemed.
From thy howse for thys the swerde shall not depart.

David rex pius.

I am sorye, lorde, from the bottom of my hart.

Pater cælestis.

To further anger thu doest me yet compell.

David rex pius.

For what matter, lorde? I beseech thy goodnesse tell.

Pater cælestis.

Why dedest thu numbre the people of Israel?
Supposest in thy mind therin thu hast done well?

David rex pius.

I cannot saye naye, but I have done undyscretelye
To forget thy grace for a humayne pollycye.

Pater cælestis.

Thu shalt of these three chose whych plage thou wilt have,
For that synnefull acte, that I thy sowle maye save.
A scarcenesse VII. years, or else III. monthes exyle,
Eyther for III. dayes the pestylence most vyle,
For one thu must have, there is no remedye.

David rex pius.

Lorde, at thy pleasure, for thu art full of mercye.

Pater cælestis.

Of a pestylence, then III. score thousand and ten
In III. dayes shall dye of thy most puysant men.

David rex pius.

O lorde, it is I whych have offended thy grace,
Spare them and not me, for I have done the trespace.

Pater cœlestis.

Though thy synnes be great, thy inwarde harte's contrycyon
Doth move my stomake in wonderfull condycion.
I fynde the a man accordynge to my hart;
Wherefor thys promyse I make the, ere I depart.
A frute there shall come forth yssuynge from thy bodye,
Whom I wyll advaunce upon thy seate for ever.
Hys trone shall become a seate of heavenlye glorye,
Hys worthy scepture from ryght wyll not dyssever,
Hys happye kingedome, of fayth shall perysh never.
Of heaven and of earthe he was autor pryncypall,
And wyll contynue, though they do perysh all.
Thys sygne shalt thu have for a token specyall,
That thu mayst beleve my wordes unfaynedlye,
Where thu hast mynded, for my memoryall,
To buylde a temple, thu shalt not fynysh it trulye;
But Salomon thy sonne shall do that accyon worthye,
In token that Christ must fynysh every thynge
That I have begunne, to my prayse everlastynge.

David rex pius.

Immortall glorye to the, most heavenlye kynge,
For that thu hast geven contynuall vyctorye
To me thy servaunt, ever sens my anoyntynge,
And also before, by manye conquestes worthye.
A beare and lyon I slewe through thy strength onlye.
I slew Golias, which was VI. cubites longe.
Agaynst thy enemyes thu madest me ever stronge.
My fleshlye fraylenesse made me do deadlye wronge,
And cleane to forget thy lawes of ryghteousnesse.
And though thu vysytedst my synnefulnesse amonge,
With pestylent plages, and other unquyetnesse;
Yet never tokest thu from me the plenteousnesse

Of thy godly sprete, which thu in me dedest plant.
I havynge remorce, thy grace coulde never want.
  For in conclusyon, thy everlastynge covenaunt
Thu gavest unto me for all my wycked synne;
And hast promysed here by protestacyon constant,
That one of my sede shall soch hygh fortune wynne,
As never ded man sens thys worlde ded begynne.
By hys power he shall put Sathan from hys holde,
In rejoyce whereof to synge wyll I be bolde.

[*Canora voce tunc incipit Antiphonam,* O Adonai, *quam (ut prius) prosequetur chorus cum organis, vel sic Anglice:* —

O lorde God Adonai, and gyde of the faythfull howse of Israel, whych sumtyme aperedst in the flamyng bushe to Moses, and to hym dedst geve a lawe in mounte Syna, come now for to redeme us in the strengthe of thy ryght hande.

Finit Actus quintus.

ACTUS SEXTUS.

Pater cœlestis.

  I brought up chyldren from their first infancye,
Whych now despyseth my godlye instruccyons.
An oxe knoweth hys lorde, an asse hys master's dewtye,
But Israel wyll not know me, nor my condycyons.
Oh frowarde people, geven all to superstycyons,
Unnaturall chyldren, expert in blasphemyes,
Provoketh me to hate, by their ydolatryes.
  Take hede to my wordes, ye tyrauntes of Sodoma,
In vayne ye offer your sacryfyce to me.
Dyscontent I am with yow heastes of Gomorra,
And have no pleasure whan I your offeryngcs se,
I abhorre your fastes and your solempnyte.

For your tradycyons my wayes ye set apart,
Your workes are in vayne, I hate them from the hart.

Esaias propheta.

Thy cytie, swete lorde, is now become unfaythfull,
And her condycyons are turned up so downe.
Her lyfe is unchast, her actes be very hurtefull,
Her murther and theft hath darkened her renowne.
Covetouse rewardes doth so their conscyence drowne,
That the fatherlesse they wyll not help to ryght,
The poore wydowe's cause come not afore their syght.
Thy peceable pathes seke they neyther daye nor nyght;
But walke wycked wayes after their fantasye.
Convert their hartes, lorde, and geve them thy true lyght,
That they maye perceyve their customable folye:
Leave them not helplesse in so depe myserye,
But call them from it of thy most specyall grace,
By thy true prophetes, to their sowle's helthe and solace.

Pater cœlestis.

First they had fathers, than had they patryarkes,
Than dukes, than judges to their gydes and monarkes:
Now have they stowte kynges, yet are they wycked styll,
And wyll in no wyse my pleasaunt lawes fulfyll.
Alwayes they applye to ydolles worshyppynge,
From the vyle begger to the anoynted kynge.

Esaias propheta.

For that cause thu hast in two devyded them,
In Samaria the one, the other in Hierusalem.
The kynge of Juda in Hierusalem ded dwell,
And in Samaria the kynge of Israel.
Ten of the twelve trybes bycame Samarytanes,
And the other two were Hierosolymytanes.
In both these cuntreyes, accordynge to their doynges,
Thu permyttedest them to have most cruell kynges.
The first of Juda was wycked kynge Roboam,
Of Israel the first was that cruell Hieroboam;

Abia than folowed, and in the other Nadab,
Than Basa, then Hela, then Zambri, Joram and Achab.
Then Ochosias, then Athalia, then Joas;
On the other part was Jonathan and Achas.
To rehearce them all that have done wretchydlye
In the syght of the, it were longe verelye.

Pater cœlestis.

For the wycked synne of fylthye ydolatrye,
Whych the ten trybes ded in the lande of Samarye,
In space of one daye fyfty thousand men I slewe,
Thre of their cyties also I overthrewe,
And left the people in soche captyvyte,
That in all the worlde they wyst not whyther to fle.
The other ii. trybes, whan they from me went back
To ydolatrye, I left in the hande of Sesack,
The kynge of Egipt, whych toke awaye their treasure,
Convayed their cattel, and slewe them without measure.
In tyme of Achas, an hondred thousande and twentye
Were slayne at one tyme for their ydolatrye.
Two hondred thousande from thens were captyve led,
Their goodes dyspersed, and they with penurye fed.
Seldom they fayle it, but eyther the Egipcyanes
Have them in bondage, or els the Assyreanes:
And alone they maye thanke their ydolatrye.

Esaias propheta.

Wele, yet blessed lorde, releve them with thy mercye.
Though they have been yll by other prynces dayes,
Yet good Ezechias hath taught them godlye wayes.
Whan the prynce is good, the people are the better;
And as he is nought, their vyces are the greatter.
Heavenlye lorde, therfor send them the consolacyon,
Whych thu hast covenaunted with every generacyon.
Open thu the heavens, and lete the lambe come hither,
Whych wyll delyver thy people all togyther.
Ye planetes and cloudes, cast downe your dewes and rayne,
That the earth maye beare out helthful saver playne.

Pater cœlestis.

Maye the wyfe forget the chylde of her owne bodye?

Esaias propheta.

Naye, that she can not in anye wyse verelye.

Pater cœlestis.

No more can I them whych wyll do my commandementes,
But must preserve them from all inconvenyentes.

Esaias propheta.

Blessed art thu, lorde, in all thy actes and judgementes.

Pater cœlestis.

Wele, Esaias, for thys thy fydelyte,
A covenaunt of helthe thu shalt have also of me.
For Syon's sake now I wyll not holde my peace,
And for Hierusalem, to speake wyll I not cease
Tyll that ryghteouse lorde become as a sunne beame bryght,
And their just saver as a lampe extende hys lyght.
A rodde shall shut fourth from the olde stocke of Jesse,
And a bryght blossome from that rote wyll aryse,
Upon whom alwayes the sprete of the lorde shall be,
The sprete of wysdome, the sprete of heavenly practyse,
And the sprete that wyll all godlynesse devyse.
Take thys for a sygne, a mayde of Israel
Shall conceyve and beare that lord Emanuel.

Esaias propheta.

Thy prayses condygne no mortal tunge can tell,
Most worthye maker and kynge of heavenlye glorye,
For all capacytees thy goodnesse doth excell,
Thy plenteouse graces no brayne can cumpas trulye,
No wyt can conceyve the greatnesse of thy mercye,
Declared of late in David thy true servaunt,
And now confirmed in thys thy latter covenaunt.
Of goodnesse thu madest Salomon of wyt most pregnaunt,
Asa and Josaphat, with good kynge Ezechias,
In thy syght to do that was to the ryght pleasaunt.
To quench ydolatrye thu raysedest up Helias,
Jehu, Heliseus, Michas, and Abdias,

And Naaman Syrus thu pourgedst of a leprye.
The workes wonderfull who can but magnyfye?
  Aryse, Hierusalem, and take faythe by and bye,
For the verye lyght that shall save the is commynge.
The Sonne of the lord apere wyll evydentlye,
Whan he shall resort, se that no *joye* be wantynge.
He is thy saver, and thy lyfe everlastynge,
Thy release from synne, and thy whole ryghteousnesse.
Help me in thys songe to knowledge his great goodnesse.

[*Concinna tunc voce Antiphonam inchoat,* O radix Jesse *quam chorus prosequeter cum organis, vel Anglice hoc modo canet:* —

O frutefull rote of Jesse, that shall be set as a synge amonge people, agaynst the worldly rulers shall fearcely open their mouthes. Whom the Gentyles worshypp as their heavenlye lorde, come now for to delyver us, and delaye the tyme no longar.

Finit Actus sextus.

ACTUS SEPTIMUS.

Pater cœlestis.

  I have with fearcenesse mankynde oft tymes corrected,
And agayne I have allured hym by swete promes.
I have sent sore plages, when he hath me neglected,
And then by and by, most confortable swetnes.
To wynne hym to grace, bothe mercye and ryghteousnes
I have exercysed, yet wyll he not amende.
Shall I now lose hym, or shall I hym defende?
  In hys most myschefe, most hygh grace will I sende
To overcome hym by favoure, if it may be.

With hys abusyons no longer wyll I contende
But now accomplysh my first wyll and decre.
My worde beynge flesh, from hens shall set hym fre,
Hym teachynge a waye of perfyght ryghteousnesse,
That he shall not nede to perysh in his weaknesse.

Johannes baptista.

Manasses is past, whych turned from the hys harte,
Achas and Amon have now no more ado,
Jechonias with others, whych ded themselves avarte
Fro the to ydolles, may now no farther go.
The two false judges, and Bel's wycked prestes also,
Phassur and Semeias, with Nabuchodonosore,
Antiochus and Triphon, shall the dysplease no more.

Thre score yeares and ten, thy people into Babylon
Were captyve and thrall for ydolles worshyppynge.
Hierusalem was lost, and left voyde of domynyon,
Brent was their temple, so was their other buyldynge,
Ther hygh prestes were slayne, ther treasure came to nothyng;
The strength and bewtye of thyne owne heretage,
Thus dedest thu leave then in myserable bondage.

Oft had they warnynges, sumtyme by Ezechiel
And other prophetes, as Esaye and Hieremye,
Sumtyme by Daniel, sumtyme by Ose and Johel,
Ay Amos and Abdias, by Jonas and by Sophonye,
By Nahum and Micheas, by Agge and by Zacharye,
By Malachias, and also by Abacuch,
By Olda the wydowe, and by the prophete Baruch.

Remembre Josias, whych toke the abhomynacyon
From the people, then restorynge thy lawes agayne.
Of Rechab consydre the faythfull generacyon,
Whom to wyne drynkynge no fryndshyppe myght constrayne.
Remembre Abdemelech, the frynde of truthe certayne,
Zorobabel the prynce, whych ded repare the temple,
And Jesus Josedech, of vertu the exemple.

Consydre Nehemias, and Esdras the good scrybe,
Mercyfull Tobias, and constaunt Mardocheus;

Judith and quene Hester, of the same godly trybe,
Devoute Mathias, and Judas Machabeus.
Have mynde of Eleazar, and then Joannes Hircanus,
Waye the earnest faythe of thys godlye companye,
Though the other cleane fall from thy memorye.

Pater cœlestis.

I wyll Johan, I wyll, for as I sayd afore,
Rygour and hardenesse I have now set apart,
Myndynge from hens fourth to wynne man evermore
By wonderfull kyndenesse to breake hys stubberne hart,
And change it from synne. For Christ shall suffre smart,
In mannys frayle nature for hys inyquyte,
Thys to make open, my massenger shalt thu be.

Johannes baptista.

As thy pleasure is, so blessed lorde appoynte me,
For my helthe thu art, and my sowle's felycyte.

Pater cœlestis.

Longe ere I made the, I the predestynate,
Before thu wert borne I the endued with grace.
In thy mother's wombe wert thu sanctyfycate
By my godlye gyft, and so confirmed in place,
A prophete, to shewe a waye before the face
Of my most dere sonne, whych wyll come: then untyll
Applye the apace thyne offyce to fulfyll.
Preache to the people, rebukynge their neglygence,
Doppe them in water, they knowledgynge their offence;
And saye unto them, The kyngedome of God doth cum.

Johannes baptista.

Unmete, lorde, I am, *Quia puer ego sum.*
An other than that, alac, I have no scyence
Fyt for that offyce, neyther yet cleane eloquence.

Pater cœlestis.

Thu shalt not saye so, for I have geven the grace,
Eloquence and age, to speake in desart place.
Thu must do therefor as I shall the advyse,
My appoynted pleasure fourth utter in any wyse;

My stronge myghtye wordes put I into thy mouthe,
Spare not, but speake them to east, west, north and southe.

[*Hic extendens Dominus manum, labia Joannis digito target, ac ori imponet auream linguam.*]

Go now thy waye fourth, I shall the never fayle,
The sprete of Helias have I geven the alredye.
Persuade the people, that they their synnes bywayle;
And if they repent their customable folye,
Longe shall it not be ere they have remedye.
Open thu their hartes; tell them their helth is commynge
As a voyce in desart; se thu declare the thynge.
I promyse the sure, thu shalt washe hym amonge them
In Jordane, a floude not farre from Hierusalem.

Johannes baptista.

Shewe me yet, good lorde, whereby shall I knowe that man,
In the multytude whych wyll resort to Jordan.

Pater cœlestis.

In thy mother's wombe of hym haddest thu cognycyon.

Johannes baptista.

Yea, that was in sprete. I wolde now knowe hys person.

Pater cœlestis.

Have thu no feare, Johan, hym shalt thu knowe full well,
And one specyall token afore wyll I the tell.
Super quem videris spiritum descendentem et manentem
Super eum, hic est qui baptizat spiritu sancto.
Amonge all other whom thu shalt baptyse there,
Upon whom thu seyst the Holy Ghost descende
In shappe of a dove, restynge upon hys shuldere,
Holde hym for the same, that shall the worlde amende
By baptysm of sprete, and also to man extende
Most specyall grace. For he must repare hys fall,
Restorynge agayne the justyce orygynall.
Take now thy journaye, and do as I the advyse;
First preache repentaunce, and than the people baptyse.

Johannes baptista.

Hygh honour, worshypp, and glorye be unto the,
My God eternall, and patrone of all puryte.
Repent, good people, for synnes that now are past,
The kyngdome of heaven is at hande very nye.
The promysed lyght to yow approcheth fast,
Have faythe, and applye now to recyve him boldelye.
I am not the lyght, but to beare testymonye
Of hym am sent, that all men maye beleve,
That hys bloude he wyll for their redemptyon geve.
He is soch a lyght as all men doth illumyne,
That ever were here, or shall be after thys.
All the worlde he made by hys myghtye power devyne,
And yet that rude worlde wyll not knowe what he is.
Hys owne he enterynge, is not regarded of hys.
They that receyve hym, are God's true chyldren playne,
In sprete regenerate, and all grace shall attayne.
Manye do recken, that I Johan Baptyst am he,
Deceyved are they, and that wyll apere in space.
Though he come after, yet he was longe afore me.
We are weake vessels, he is the welle of grace,
Of hys great goodnesse all that we have we purchase.
By hym are we like to have a better increes
Than ever we had by the lawe of Moses.
In Moses harde lawe we had not els but darkenes,
Fygure and shaddowe; all was not els but nyght,
Ponnyshment for synne, much rygour, payne and roughnes.
An hygh change is there, where all is turned to lyght,
Grace and remyssyon anon wyll shyne full bryght.
Never man lyved that ever se God afore,
Whych now in our kynde mannys ruyne wyll restore.
Helpe me to geve thankes to that lorde evermore,
Whych am unto Christ a cryar's voyce in the desart,
To prepare the pathes and hygh wayes hym before,
For hys delyght is on the poore symple hart.

That innocent lambe from soch wyll never depart,
As wyll faythfullye receyve hym with good mynde.
Lete our voyce then sounde in some swete musycall kynde.

[*Resona tunc voce Antiphonam incipit*, O clavis David, *quam prosequctur chorus cum organis, ut prius, vel in Anglico sermone sic:* —

O perfyght keye of David, and hygh scepture of the kyndred of Jacob, whych openest and no man speareth, thu speakest and no man openeth; come and delyver thy servaunt mankynde, bound in prison, sytting in the darknesse of synne and bytter dampnacyon.

Baleus, Prolocutor.

The matters are soch that we have uttered here
As ought not to slyde from your memoryall;
For they have opened soch confortable gere,
As is to the helthe of this kynde universall,
Graces of the lorde and promyses lyberall,
Whych he hath geven to man for every age,
To knytt hym to Christ, and so clere hym of bondage,
As saynt Paule doth write unto the Corinthes playne,
Our fore fathers were undre the cloud of darkenes,
And unto Christe's days ded in the shaddowe remayne;
Yet were they not left, for of hym they had promes,
All they receyved one spirytuall fedynge doubtles.
They dronke of the rocke whych them to lyfe refreshed,
For one savynge helthe, in Christ, all they confessed.
In the woman's sede was Adam first justyfyed,
So was faythfull Noah, so was just Abraham;
The faythe in that sede in Moses fourth multyplyed,
Lykewyse in David and Esaye that after cam,
And in Johan Baptyst, whych shewed the very lam.
Though they se afarre, yet all they had one justyce,
One masse, as they call it, and in Christ one sacryfyce.

A man can not here to God do better servyce,
Than on thys to grounde hys faythe and understandynge.
For all the worlde's synne alone Christ payed the pryce,
In hys onlye deathe was mannys lyfe alwayes restynge,
And not in wyll workes, nor yet in mennys deservynge,
The lyght of our faythe make thys thynge evydent.
And not the practyse of other experiment.
Where is now fre wyll, whom the hypocrytes comment?
Whereby they report they maye at their owne pleasure
Do good of themselves, though grace and fayth be absent,
And have good intentes their madnesse with to measure.
The wyll of the fleshe is proved here small treasure,
And so is mannys will, for the grace of God doth all.
More of thys matter conclude hereafter we shall.

Thus endeth thys Tragedy or enterlude, manyfestynge the chefe promyses of God unto Man by all ages in the olde lawe, from the fall of Adam, to the incarnacyon of the lorde Jesus Christ. Compyled by Johan Bayle. Anno Domini 1538.

GLOSSARY.

GLOSSARY.

A.

A, aye, ever. A is sometimes used instead of I as personal pronoun.
Accombre, 235, to overwhelm, to destroy.
Acold, 65, so called.
Aghe, 175, awe, dread.
Aght, 125, 146, the imp. of awe.
Aleond, 75, by land.
Amelle, 95, among.
Apertely, 24, } evidently.
Appeartely, 34, }
Are, 132, before.
Arere, 48, to raise.
A revant, 192, back again.
Asse, 97, to ask with authority, to command.
Athog, 86, as though.
Augent, 77, august.
Avowtree, 186, adultery.
Awe, 95, to owe, the old present tense of ought.
Awre, 121, } ever-aught.
Awro, 112, }
Awter, 53, 54, altar.

B.

Bale, 17, 149, grief, misery.
Balk, 110, a ridge of land.
Baylle, 102, 106, grief, misery.
Bayne, 17, to belong to, to be of kin to.
Bayne, 8, 78, prepared, ready.
Bedene, 117, immediately.
Begownne, 42, committed.
Beheight, 16, 20, promised.
Behest, 15, covenant; 132, to promise, to command.
Behet, 15, } to promise.
Behite, 14, }
Belamy, 169, 171, 173, bel-ami?
Belighte, 16, to believe.
Belke, 186, to belch.
Belyve, 7, 102, quickly.
Bemys, 42, beams, rays.
Bendys, 185, bands or ribbons.
Benste, 110, 121, benedicite.
Bent, 113, the open field.
Bere, 123, a noise.
Beshew, 29, read beshrew, to curse.
Be-telle, 139, to deceive, to mislead.
Beteyche, 62, to commit.
Beth, 42, be.
Beyn, 155, a bean.
Beyr, 169, a noise.
Bidene, 176, see bedene.
Biggid, 180, builded.
Blawdyr, 48, scandal.
Ble, 148, 151, face, countenance.

Blekyt, 183, blacked.
Bleinde, 149, to shed.
Blente, 31, blinded.
Blonder, 109, sorrow.
Blowre, 103, a pimple, a pustule.
Blure, brought on, 182, bleared the eye, deceived.
Blyn, 3, 7, 17, / Blynne, 151, 162, } to cease, to desist.
Bodword, 98, 173, a message.
Bon, 145, bound.
Bone, 101, 106, a boon.
Boote, 24, profit, gain.
Borghe, 158, a surety.
Bot, but, except; bot if, unless.
Boune, 13, 25, prepared, ready.
Bow, hete the, 44, beat the bush.
Bowke, 185, bulk, stomach.
Bowne, 4, 5, 96, prepared, ready.
Bowrde, 120, a joke.
Boyn, 147, 152, a boon.
Boytt, 149, a compensation; more commonly help or succour.
Brade, 153, a start, a sudden turn or assault; 164, to start.
Brand, 137, a sword.
Brefes, 179, 182, letters.
Brest, 141, 142, to burst.
Brodelle, 165, a blackguard.
Bronde, 74, 201, a sword.
Brymly, 176, fiercely.
Bryth, 42, bright.
Bun, 111, 136, bound.
Burde, 6, a board.
Bynke, 190, a bench.
Byth, 42, but.

C.

Carl, 99, a churl, a bondman.
Carp, 100, to relate, to talk.
Catyfes, 175, 176, caitiffs.
Catyfnes, 147, 188, captivity, wretchedness.
Cele, 129, 141, / Ceylle, 127, } happiness.
Charys, 119, turns, jobs.
Chefe, 122, to succeed.
Chepe, 114, merchandise.
Chevithe, 154, to make a bargain.
Chyte, 131, to chide.
Clekyt, 183, hatched.
Clok, 111, to clock, the noise a hen makes when she has ceased to lay, and is desirous of sitting upon her eggs.
Clowte, 54, a mark, a blow.
Cokwold, 43, 45, a cuckold.
Conseil, 72, concealment.
Cop, 133, a cup.
Courte-rollar, 182, the writer or keeper of the rolls of a court of law.
Couthe, 95, 112, could.
Cowle, 8, colewort, cabbage.
Crak, 125, to boast.
Croyne, 125, 133, to crone, to utter a low murmuring sound.
Crisp, 185, fine linen or cobwed lawn.
Crumpe, 178, the cramp.
Cuker, 184, part of a woman's head dress.

D.

Dalle, 135, 179, the hand.
Dalyawnce, 50, dalliance, conjugal conversation.
Darfe, 175, hard, cruel.
Dayntethe, 162, a dainty thing.
Dede, 137, 149, death; 103, 107, dead.
Deeme, 37, to redeem.
Deene, 7, see bedene.
Defyne, 26, to defy.
Deiryne, 26, dear.
Delf, 95, to dig.
Delfe, 156, a grave.
Deme, 188, to doom, to judge.
Dere, 157, 176, hurt, damage.
Derfe, 190, hard, cruel.

Dern, **181**, concealed, secret.
Devyr, **45**, duty.
Diggs, **9**, ducks.
Dight, **5**, **13**, **27**. to prepare, to dress.
Dold, **109**, stupid, confused.
Dole, **22**, a part.
Doket, **185**, a shred or piece.
Dowse, **117**, a slut.
Doylle, **103**, **148**, dolor, grief.
Dray, **119**, to draw.
Dre, **148**, **152**, to endure.
Dresse, **64**, to address.
Dug, **185**, to cut?
Dustards **137**, dastards?
Dwere, **41**, a door.
Dyght, **78**, **137**, prepared.
Dyke, **93**, to make ditches.
Dyng, **107**, **168**, to cast down.
Dytars, **181**, inditers, accusers.

E.

E, aye.
Ee, **116**, **176**, the eye.
Eeyne, **110**, **165**, the plural of eye.
Effe, **143**, again.
Eich, each.
Elyke, **96**, alike.
Emelle, **94**, **99**, among.
Enderes, **89**, the last.
Enewe, **126**, **186**, enough.
Everichan, **10**, **107**, every one.
Eyvin, **62**, even, equal, fellow.

F.

Fa, **136**, faith.
Faed, **149**, faded.
Fang, **106**, **133**, to take.
Fard, **133**, afraid.
Farde with fantasye, **16**, full of deceit.
Farly, **162**, strange.
Farne, **128**, **129**, past part. of fare.
Fassion, **74**, falchion.
Fature, **100**, **166**, **168**, a lazy, idle fellow.
Fawcun, **74**, a falcon.
Fax, **183**, the hair of the head.
Faye, **13**, **48**, faith.
Fayne, **60**, **63**, glad, desirous.
Feare, a mate, a comrade; in fere, **27**, in company, together.
Feature, **26**, **34**, a deceiver.
Fee, **95**, cattle.
Feetly, **50**, fitly.
Feigne, **21**, glad, desirous.
Fell, **21**, skin, hide.
Felle, **94**, **148**, many.
Felter, **185**, to entangle.
Ferd, **41**, **42**, fared.
Ferde, **175**, **178**, fear.
Ferdell, **208**, a bundle.
Fere, a mate, a comrade; in fere, **79**, **81**, in company, together.
Fere, **98**, to put in fear.
Ferray, of, **182**, on a foray.
Fetyld, **180**, prepared, made ready for use.
Feyne, **214**, to be glad.
Flekyt, **183**, mended.
Flemyd, **193**, driven out, put to flight.
Flume, **163**, a river.
Flyt, **103**, **104**, to fly, to flee from.
Flytars, **179**, **186**, scolders,
Foche, **100**, to fetch.
Fon, **155**, to be foolish.
Fon, **184**, found.
Fone, **3**, foe.
Fonge, **4**, see fang.
Food, **151**, offspring.
Foore, **115**, **191**, the imp. of fare.
Fordo, **78**, **95**, to destroy.
Forebyer, **16**, Redeemer.
Forfete, **42**, to forfeit, to transgress.
Forgang, **110**, to forego.
Forn, **55**, before.
Forrakyd, **117**, overdone with walking.
Forspokyn, **131**, bewitched.

Fortaxed, 109, wrongly taxed.
Forthy, 34, 101, therefore, for this cause.
Forthynk, 113, 127, to repent, to grieve.
Foryeten, 7, forgotten.
Fott, 127, to fetch, to take.
Founde, 17, } to try, to attempt.
Fownde, 138, 158, } to try, to attempt.
Fowre, 103, 112, the imp. of fare.
Foya, 147, the plural of foe.
Foyne, 118, 142, a heap, an abundance.
Frankishfare, 6, nonsense.
Frast, 98, 178, to inquire, to tempt.
Fryg, 185, a freik, a man.
Fryth, frith; be fryth, 68, by sea.
Fun, 94, 111, found.
Fyld, field; be fyld, 68, by land.

G.

Gadlyng, 156, 168, an idle fellow.
Gang, 122, 133, to go.
Gar, 131, 132, to cause, to make.
Garray, 106, 129, array, troops.
Gart, the imp. of gar.
Gate, way; alle gate, 154, alway.
Gawde, 94, 102, tricks.
Gaytt, 153, see gate.
Gent, 50, gentle.
Gere, 168, 178, gear.
Gett, 184, fashion.
Geyn, 139, given.
Glase, 119, gloss, appearance.
Glede, 83, a fire.
Gowles, 31, gulls.
Gramercy, 42, 46, 48, many thanks.
Gramory, 183, Latin learning.
Gramyd, 55, angered, afflicted.
Grathly, 163, suddenly, swiftly.
Grayd, 168, past part. of graythe to prepare.
Greesly, 34, grisly, horrible.
Greete, 20, grit, gravel, earth.
Grete, 152, 178, to weep.
Grewys, 186, grieves.
Grill, 4, to anger, to pain.
Grise, 177, to shudder, to tremble.
Grofen, 104, past part. of grufe to grow.
Gruch, 156, to repine.
Grysely, 25, 179, grisly, horrible.
Gyn, 52, to begin.
Gyrd, 131, to strike off.
Gyse, 42, 43, guise, way, fashion.

H.

Haghe, 105, an interjection of astonishment.
Hak, 125, 133, to hack, to sing badly.
Hamyd, 109, hemmed in, surrounded.
Hap, 124, to wrap up, to cover.
Har, 84, 165, to harry, to plague.
Hardely, 103, 139, certainly.
Harie, 79, trouble.
Harnes, 115, 122, brains.
Haro, 177, } the ancient Norman *Hue and Cry*.
Haroo, 124, } the ancient Norman *Hue and Cry*.
Harro, 165, } the ancient Norman *Hue and Cry*.
Harsto, 165, hearest thou.
Hatters, 128, spiders.
Hawvelle and jawvelle, 186, havers and jabbering, idle talk.
He, 6, 130, high.
Heale, 9, health.
Height, 27; see beheight.
Heings, 28.
Hek, 119, a door.
Hem, him, them.
Hend, 12, courteous, kind.
Hent, 86, 98, to take; hente 21, taken, caught.
Hete, 152, 153, to promise.
Hethyng, 182, scorn, derision.
Hetyng, 135, a promise.
Heynde, 97, 132, courteous, kind; 107, applied to inanimate objects, commodious.

Heytt, 105, promised.
High, 209, to hie, to hasten.
Hight, 16, 137, called.
Hir, her.
Hodys, 51, hoods.
Hoket, 182, 185, scorn.
Hole, 98, to fetch, to take.
Honde, 42, 54, the hand.
Hone, 106, to delay.
Hose, 125, hoarse.
Houle, 17, to know.
Hurlyd, 185, staring, bristled,
Hyde, 10, 180, } to hie, to
Hye, 7, 8, 78, } hasten.
Hyge, 42, 55, high.
Hyght, 125, promised.
Hynd, 68, 69, courteous, kind.
Hyne, 115, 180, a servant.
Hyne, 26, to hie, to hasten.
Hyne, 192, hence.
Hytt the pynne, 55, to knock the right nail on the head, to guess right.

I.

Ich, I.
Ich, 126, 141, each.
Ilk, 117, 141, each.
Ilke, 15, 170, same.
Ilkon, 195, each.
Ill-a-hale, 156, ill luck to you, ill luck on it.
Inclysse, 29, in clysse, in glory?
Intraste, 167, entrace?
Iwys, 150, 155, certainly.

J.

Jabell, 211, a gossip.
Jape, 184, deceit.
Jape, 116, a deceiver.
Jesen, 81, 85, a lyingin childbed.
Jowke, 185, a dissembler.

K.

Kelle, 185, a caul, part of a woman's head dress.
Ken, 19, 21, the knee.
Ken, 94, 95, 98, to know.
Kerne, 84, an idle person, a vagabond.
Keysar, 80, Cæsar or emperor.
Knave, 128, a boy; knavechild, 120, man-child.
Knowlych, 55, to acknowledge.
Kohet, 182, cocked, coquetish.
Kun thank, 94, to thank.
Ky, 44, to kyte, to look.
Kyd, 147, 170, past part. of kythe.
Kynke, 179, to draw the breath audibly, to laugh aloud.
Kynnys, 45, kind, manner.
Kyppys, 128, skips.
Kythe, 146, to show, to make evident.

L.

Laghe, 175, law.
Lakan, 117, 149, a play thing, a toy.
Lake, 114, 125, to play.
Lare, 99, lore, learning.
Lathe, 166, loathsome.
Lawdys, 114, the laudes or lauds, the concluding part of the Matins service.
Lay, 55, song, affair, thing.
Lay, 201, law.
Leare, 25, to learn, to teach.
Ledden, 9, language.
Lede, a people, a nation; in lede, 165, 165, among the people.
Ledyr, 115, lazy.
Lee, 51, pleasure.
Leech, 54, to cure, to preserve.
Leeven, 16, 17, to believe; also to leave.
Lefe, 110, to believe.
Legge, 171, to alledge, to cite.
Lele, 127, loyal, faithful.
Lente, 17, tarrying.
Lere, 118, 172, to learn, to teach.

Let, 17, to cease.
Letherly, 114, lowly, meanly.
Lever, 126, 179, } the comparitive of leyf, leave
Levyr, 45, }
Levyn, 132, lightning.
Lewd, 134, 142. unlettered, one of the leod or common people.
Lewtye, 12, lawty, fidelity.
Ley be, 62, lay by, cease.
Leyche, 62, a physician.
Leyd, in, 151; see lede.
Leygis, 64, leagues.
Ley-land, 112, unploughed land.
Leyn, 99, 116, to lend, to grant.
Leynd, 97, 102, to tarry, to remain.
Libarde, 8, a leopard.
Ligged, 16, lurked.
Loe, 10, to think.
Lollar, 182, one of the sect of the Lollards.
Looe, 65, a lowe, a mount.
Loppys, 103, lops, fleas.
Lorden, see lurdan.
Lore, 7, learning, direction.
Loryd, 101, learned.
Lose, 194, praise.
Losell, 101, } a dissolute lazy fellow.
Lossell, 26, 28 }
Losyngere, 86, a liar.
Loten, 112, see sowre.
Lowd and still, 4, at all times.
Lowte, 27, } to bow, to bend.
Lowtl, 52, }
Luddokkys, 185,
Lufly, 134, lovely.
Lurdan, 101, 164, } a dissolute lazy fellow.
Lurdeyn, 205, }
Lyere, 149, flesh.
Lymbo, 164, 168. Limbus is the name given by the Church of Rome to the place in which it is supposed the righteous were confined before our Saviour's death.
Lyme, 25, a limb, an assistant.
Lyst, 94, lust, pleasure.

M.

Ma, 156, my.
Maculacion, 53, a spot, a stain.
Make to make, 7, mate to mate, like to like.
Maken, 9, to mate, to associate.
Maroo, 124, an associate.
Mase, 97, 164, the 3rd person singular of may to make.
Masyd, 170, amazed, bewildered.
Maugre, 203, in spite of, notwithstanding.
Maweless, 28, unsubstantial, false.
Mawgre, 208, in spite of, notwithstanding.
Mawmentry, 139, idolatry.
Maye, 25, 34, a maid.
Maylle easse, 126, mal-aise, illness.
Mayne, 20, 23, main, might.
Meanye, 7, 13, see meneye.
Measse, 98, a mess, the measles, leprosy, scurvy.
Mede, 84, 153, reward, desert.
Medille-erd, 178, the middle habitation between heaven and hell, the world.
Mete, 194, to move,
Mekylle, 99, 104, much.
Melle, 27, 49, to meddle, to contend.
Melle, 97, 156, to tell, to speak.
Mener, 134, handsome.
Meneye, 104, 120, 157, } a noun of multi-
Menyee, 130, 150, }
tude, having in general a relative signification according to its connexion. Thus the meneye of a king is his court and retinue; of a general, his army; of our Saviour, his disciples. Anglo Saxon maniu, mœnigeo, or mœnigu, the word used by Ælfric

for the congregation of the Children of Israel.

Meng, 152, to mingle.

Ment, 76, 77, 100, meant, minded.

Meselle, 104, measled, afflicted with leprosy or scurvy.

Meve, 60, to move, to moot, to argue.

Meyne, 115, 192, the bass part in singing.

Mickle, 22, 28, much.

Missaes, 156, what is mis-said, lies, &c.

Mom 99, to mumble.

Mon, 104, 107, 108, must.

Mote, 25, 30, to moot, to argue.

Mow, 140, to make mouths, grimaces.

Moytt, 151, 170, to moot, to argue.

Muf, 99, to move.

Mychers, 137, 179, cheaters.

Myn, 14, 17, 150, to have in mind, to remember.

Myn, 100, less.

Myssase, 180, to mis-say, to lie, to contradict.

Myster, 190, need.

Mystyz, 54, mysterious, unknown.

N.

Napand, 195, gasping.

Nate, 159, to have occasion for.

Nately, 115, neatly.

Nawre, 121, the negative of awre.

Ne, nor.

Neemly, 118, nimbly.

Negons, 195, negh ones? Neighbours.

Neowell, 75, a Christmas carol.

Nere hande, 109, 191, almost, very near.

Nesh, 128, tender.

Neven, 98, 115, to name, to speak.

Nigremy, 54, necromancy.

Nonys, 127, nonce, purpose.

Nores, 126, } a nurse.
Noryse, 141. }

Note, 11, 125, } business, occupation.
Noyte, 98, 170, }

Notht, 41, nought.

Noye, 5, 7, annoyance, hurt.

Nurry, 26, a nursling, a child.

Nyfyls, 185, trifles.

O.

Oder, 195, other.

Okerars, 185, usurers.

Onys, 45, once.

Or, ere, before.

Outehorne, 195, an outlaw.

Owth, 49, 55, ought, any thing.

P.

Parde, 46, 110, par Dieu, by God.

Parrage, 71, parentage, extraction.

Pay, 82, liking, satisfaction.

Pay, 106, to please.

Payer, 24, to impair, to lessen.

Perde, 125, 151, see parde.

Peryng, 77, appearing.

Pety enime, 45, a mean adversary, a slanderer.

Pight, 149, to complain.

Pighte, 22, 55, fixed.

Pleyny, 45, 189, to complain.

Po, 110, a peacock.

Postee, 18, 19, power.

Profles, 25, proofs.

Prow, 44, 169, profit.

Pyrie, 66, a sudden wind.

Pystylle, 111, an epistle.

Q.

Quantyse, 95, 158, cunning.

Quere, 67, choir.

Qweasse, 126, to wheeze, to breath with difficulty.

Qwedyr, 46, to quiver, to shake.

R.

Race, 51, train?

Rad, 114, 150, afraid.

Radly, 107, quickly.
Rafte, 28, reft, taken away.
Ragman, roll of, 182, any authentic catalogue or list drawn up *secundum regimen.*
Rake, 139, range, liberty.
Rakyd, 117, forrakyd.
Ramyd, 109, thrust, cast down.
Rape, 55, to hasten.
Rathly, 151, ready,
Reach, 34, to reck, to care.
Read, 19, 28, } advice, counsel.
Red, 6, 84, }
Red, 18, 33, to advise, to counsel.
Refe, 109, 167, to bereave, to rob.
Rek, 119, 193, to reck, to care.
Reme, 80, 87, realm.
Renderars of reffys, 179, those who undertake to restore stolen goods for a reward.
Rerd, 178, a voice, a noise.
Rew, 157, to compassionate.
Reylle, 118, to ramble about.
Ro, 146, rest.
Rode, 147, } the cross.
Roode, 33, 114, }
Rok, 122, a distaff.
Rollar; see courte-rollar.
Rome, 6, to roam.
Rowners, 185, whisperers.
Rude, 152, 159; see rode.
Ruled out of raye, 30, deprived of reason.
Runkers, 185, double tongued.
Rused, 153, praised.
Ryth, 42, right.

S.

Sagh, 151, to say.
Sairjour, 26, saviour.
Sakles, 146, blameless, innocent.
Sam, 151, 142, together.
Sawe, 24, 93, a saying, a report.
Sawgeoure, 182, a soldier.
Sawter, 167, 184, the psalter.
Saynt, 115, say it.
Schape, 53, 55, to escape.
Schapp, 82, shape, make.
See, 21, 30, a seat, a throne.
Seekerly, 17, certainly.
Seith, 51, since.
Sekyr, 42, sure, certain.
Selcowth, 96, seldom, extraordinary.
Sely, 109, 110, simple.
Sen, 143, 145, since.
Serys, 48, 49, sirs.
Seth, 22, since.
Seven, to set all in, 135, to put all in order.
Sew, 107, to follow.
Sey, 87, to assay, to attempt.
Seyd, 49, 97, seed; 49, said.
Seyr, 171, various.
Sharme, 204, to sham.
Shekyls, 111, ague, trembling.
Shente, 25, 57, ruined, destroyed.
Sheynd, 106, 132, to ruin, to destroy.
Shone, 110, the plural of shoe.
Shrew, 25, 113, a cursed fellow.
Shrewe, 48, 119, to curse.
Shroges, 125, rough uninclosed ground more or less covered with brushwood.
Sith, 8, 14, since.
Skant, 78, scant, scarcely.
Skape, 99, 119, to escape.
Skawde, 130, a scold.
Skawte, 193.
Skraw, 134, a scroll.
Slea, 34, to slay.
Slewthe, 186, sloth.
Slich, 4, } slime
Slicke, 5, }
Sloghe, 122
Slokyn, 133, to slake, to quench.
Slose, 133, sloth.
Slyke, 98, such like.
Slyth, 112, to slit, to tear.
Snek, 119, the latch of a door.

Sofferent, 59, sovereign.
Sonde, 42, 54, 62, a message, a messenger.
Soore, 61, exceedingly.
Sote, 200, } true.
Soth, 12, 17, } true.
Sothren, 116, boiled, eaten away.
Sounde, 17, a voice, a word.
Sowe, 98, 102, to ensue, to follow.
Sowre loten, 112, sour leaven is derived from leaving the piece of dough to ferment; loten signifies the same, and is the part. of lœtan, to leave.
Soyn, 95, 97, soon.
Sparte, 183, spare it.
Speareth, 256, asketh, enquireth.
Spere, 70, spirit.
Spill, 4, 15, } to destroy.
Spylle, 94, 95, } to destroy.
Springe, 24, 29, to flourish, to succeed.
Spyr, 181, to ask, to enquire.
Spytus, 110, 176, spiteful.
Stad, 162, } staid, placed.
Sted, 111, 148, } staid, placed.
Steake, 11, to fasten with sticks.
Stede, 123, 131, a place.
Stevyn, 132, a voice.
Stoure, 165, a trouble, a perilous situation.
Stower, 13, a steer.
Stowke, 183, twelve sheaves of corn piled up.
Stownde, 178, an acute pain.
Sufferntis, 60, sovereigns.
Suspowse, 127, suspicion.
Swedylle, 124, 130, to swathe, to bind.
Swelt, 127, to die.
Swepys, 153, whips.
Swevyn, 122, a dream.
Swilk, 184, 187, such.
Swongen, 153, past part. of swinge to beat.
Swych, 43, such.
Swynk, 115, 119, to toil.
Swythe, 107, swift, quick.
Sybbe, 49, 55, a relation by blood, a kinsman, a kinswoman.
Syn, 112, 127, since, afterwards.
Syse, 55, assize, judgement.
Syth, 41, time.
Sythen, 95, 98, since, afterwards.

T.

Tane, 120, taken.
Taxed, see fortaxed.
Taylle, 170, an account.
Teene, to take, 19, to take heed to.
Tene, 13, 132, grief.
Tent, 43, 94, attention, heed.
Tent, 178, 183, to take heed to.
Teyche, see beteyche.
Teyn, 188, grief.
Teyn, 137, 171, to affllict, to provoke.
Thar, 186, 189, to need.
Tharmes, 122, guts.
The, thee, they.
Thew, 182, service.
Tho, 187, those.
Thole, 119, 149, to suffer.
Thoner, 104, thunder.
Thraw, 147, 154, a short space of time.
Threpe, 114, to trip.
Thurt, 169, 190, the imp. of thar.
Thyrlyd, 151, pierced through.
To and til are used indiscrimately with reference both to time and place.
Tollare, 182, a speaker.
Tolle, 46, to tell.
Tome, 128, 178, empty.
Ton, 54, toes.
Topeas, 6, topmast.
Trantes, 166, tricks.
Trayn, 161, an artifice, a contrivance.

Trete, on, 179, in an entreating manner.
Tristur, 181, the place allotted to a person in hunting.
Trowse, 117, } to tie up the breeches.
Truse, 63, }
Truage, 75, toll, custom.
Trus, 185, 192, to pack, to go.
Twayne, 17, } to divide.
Twyn, 144, 164, }
Twyfyls, 185, two-folds.
Twyk, 143, to twitch, to pull suddenly.
Tyne 147, 180, to lose.
Tyte, 107, 131, quick, swift; as tyte, 156, as quick as possible.
Tythyng, 63, 73, tidings.
Tytter, 103, a tittle, the least distance.

U.

Umthynke, 171, to deliberate.
Unethes, 182, } scarcely.
Unothes, 153, }
Unfeayne, 35, unfeigned.
Unys, 104, probably a mistake in the original copyist for nuys, ewes.
Ure, 110, to experience.

V.

Verament, 36, verily, truly.
Voket, 175, an advocate.
Vowgard, 194,
Vroken, 207, revenged.

W.

Walk-mylne, 185, a fulling mill.
Wall, weale and wytt, 19, power, felicity and wisdom.
Wan, 96, imp. of win, to go.
War, 117, worse.
Warloo, 152, 155, } a warlock, a wizard.
Warlow, 101. }
War-oute, 192, a term used in driving.
Warry, 14, 109, to curse.
Warte, 183, wear it, spend it.
Wate, 130, wote, knew.
Wate, 190, wet.
Wax, on thy, 183, of thy growth.
Wayt 111, 116, to know.
Wede, 83, 135, raiment.
Wedurs, 65, 110, clouds.
Weete, 6, the tide.
Welkin, 15, the sky.
Welland, 105, boiling.
Welner, 122, well nigh.
Wema, 143, an exclamation demanding attention.
Wend, 10, 50, to go.
Wene, 5, 7, to think.
Went, 205, weened, thought.
Wenyand, 123, an illusion to the belief that actions undertaken in the wane of the moon would be unsuccessful.
Werd, 51, the world.
Were, 36, 178, confusion, war.
Were, 140, 175, doubt, uncertainty.
Were, 98, to defend.
Weyn, 113, 134, to ween, to think.
Weyn, 96, doubt.
Weynde, 95, 100, to go.
Whik, 128, quick, living.
Witt, 35, to know.
Witterly, 19, 24, verily, truly.
Wode, 83, 86, mad.
Won, 94, 98, to dwell.
Wonden, 159, wrapped in a winding sheet.
Wonys, 127, dwelling places.
Wonys, 86, once.
Woode, 121, 209, mad.
Wraggers, 179, wranglers.
Wrake, 102, 189, revenge.
Wranke, 52, a trick? wrong?
Wrast, 98, wrest.
Wrears, 179, perverters.

Wreke, 167, } wreak, revenge.
Wreyche, 87, }
Wright, 169, a carpeiter.
Wroken, 13, } past part.
Wrokyn, 131, 181, } of wrake to reveige.
Wt, with.
Wyn, 162, joy, pleasure.
Wynde, 25, 64, to go.
Wys, 33, to know.
Wyse, 45, 51, way.
Wytt, 25, 102, to kiow.

Y.

Yare, 134, apt, ready.
Yate, 167, 168, a gate.
Ych, 231, each
Yede, 105, 121, the imp. of go or gaig.
Yister, 122, yesterday.
Yl-a-haylle, 102, ill luck to you, ill luck on it.
Ylk, 138, same.
Yode, 105, 114, the imp. of go or gang.
Yt, that.

ERRATA.

P. 37, l. 11, from bottom, for *Witt*, read *With*.
" 63, " 23, for *oo*, read *goo*.
" 70, " 5, from bottom, for *incarnate*, read *incarnate*.
" 78, " 16, for *do*, read *fordo*.
" 112, " 17, for *tylle*, read *stylle*.
" 138, " 17, for *hy*, read *by*.
" 169, " 21, for *knew*, read *knew*.

Lightning Source UK Ltd.
Milton Keynes UK
UKOW01f1055250118
316811UK00009B/412/P